Kids Talking

Kids Talking

Learning Relationships and Culture with Children

John Meyer

ROWMAN & LITTLEFIELD PUBLISHERS, INC.
Lanham • Boulder • New York • Toronto • Oxford

ROWMAN & LITTLEFIELD PUBLISHERS, INC.

Published in the United States of America
by Rowman & Littlefield Publishers, Inc.
A Member of the Rowman & Littlefield Publishing Group
4501 Forbes Boulevard, Suite 200, Lanham, Maryland 20706
www.rowmanlittlefield.com

PO Box 317
Oxford
OX2 9RU, UK

British Library Cataloguing in Publication Information Available

Library of Congress Cataloging-in-Publication Data

Meyer, John, 1964–
  Kids talking : learning relationships and culture with children / John
Meyer.
    p. cm.
Includes bibliographical references and index.
  ISBN 0-7425-2705-0 (cloth : alk. paper) — ISBN 0-7425-2706-9 (pbk. :
alk. paper)
  1. Interpersonal communication in children. 2. Interpersonal
relations in children. I. Title.
  BF723.C57M49 2003
  302.3'46'083—dc21

                                                    2003011859

Printed in the United States of America

♾™ The paper used in this publication meets the minimum requirements of
American National Standard for Information Sciences—Permanence of Paper
for Printed Library Materials, ANSI/NISO Z39.48-1992.

To the children, teachers, and staff members at the center for child development, with thanks for their help in building a happy life.

Contents

1 Introduction 1

2 Repeated Interaction Patterns: Revealing Culture
   in Recurring Routines 19

3 Managing Changing Relationships 29

4 Are We Friends? Children's Statements,
   Proximity, and Touch 51

5 Revealing Culture: Invoking the Rules 67

6 Discipline Dogma 77

7 Power and the Use of Control 89

8 Uncertain Relationships: Power Differences
   and Seeking Adult Support 117

9 Children Expressing and Controlling Feelings:
   Tragedy or Comedy? 133

10 Initiating Roles and Play: Growing Relationships
    along the Way 151

11 Children's Strategies for Expressing and
    Receiving Affection 163

12 Children in Conflict 175

13 Adults in Conflict: Research Pitfalls 195

14 The Emotional Impact of Working with Children   213

15 Findings and Implications: Child Interactions
    and Child-Care Cultures   225

References   245

Index   251

About the Author   259

1

Introduction

Origins always draw scientists and scholars seeking explanations. Exploring communication has proven to be no different. While applying qualitative and ethnographic approaches to studying human communication in organizations and relationships, "going back to the beginning" was always a temptation when doing research. So much of adult communication seemed to be determined by how we learned to communicate with people around us when we were children. I had several enlightening and exhilarating experiences communicating with children that I considered to be not much more than babies (they were four years old at the time), and I realized that communication among recently verbal children is fraught with communication strategies. After such fun interactions occurred when I was volunteering for a local community organization, I decided to take a "professional approach" and find out how children manage relationships with peers and teachers at their youngest verbal ages. For many, their first organization entered, besides family and perhaps church, was a child-care center. Thus, I became a volunteer at a child-development center, interacting with the children in their classrooms and on the playground, observing their communication with one another and with me while also trying to be of some assistance to the center's staff. My primary role was to be a researcher, observing the communication patterns present; but I was also a communicator, becoming part of the organization's culture.

Along with seeking to understand preschool children's relationship management strategies, I sought to uncover the nuances of children's symbol use in one of their first organizations outside of their family. I first found that there were not many nuances. Children communicated and managed their relationships with their hearts (and their agendas) on their sleeves. It was generally not hard to figure out, on first appearance, what a child was trying

1

to get someone to do or what he or she was feeling. Of course, as time went on, things appeared more complicated, but the fact remained that children communicated openly and honestly, especially about relationships, while adults masked similar communication behind more subtle messages. The sum of all these messages, though, creates the context for communication, in whatever setting we may find ourselves. Whether open and honest, or disguised and strategic, the types and themes of messages exchanged formed the organization's culture, and suggested to children how they should fit in.

I approached communication from the perspective that, through a process of one message following another, people create their social reality. As messages are attempted and responded to, certain fragments of meaning are agreed upon and shared. These shared symbols then provide the framework for mutual perceptions of reality. Such creation of symbols through interaction, or symbolic interactionism, is one foundational perspective for studying communication (Mead 1934). Social reality as created through communication implies that each message is potentially important as a foundation of that reality. Any social organization, to continue to exist, requires members to make sense of that organization through communication within it. This sense-making process produced extra drama for children, as they were still forming their own personalities based on surrounding communication. While creativity and flexibility in symbol-use are necessary for communication, organization participants also develop patterns that must be followed for others to respond and understand (Giddens 1979). From early in life, humans are primed to notice repeated patterns, needed for learning symbols and themes. As children develop an understanding of patterns, some can be invoked as symbols to represent an act or idea, and young children incorporate patterns into their own communication. They move from nonverbal to verbal symbols, and from simple to more complex symbols (Cazden 1972). As children learn the rules of language, they also learn social rules and adapt to varying social roles (Cicourel 1974). By noticing recurring patterns of communication, children learn the expectations of others. A child-development center provides them with an organization on which to base their perception of social expectations, or a "generalized other" (Mead 1934). According to symbolic interactionism, even the simplest and most "obvious" messages could impact the child's own self-image as well as contribute to the center's social reality, or culture. I sought to understand and detail the world of symbols impacting on and invoked by children in the setting of a child-development center.

The major questions that guided my research as I began spending time with children were: How do children initiate and improve relationships with their peers? How do they manage relationships that have grown undesirable? And, how do children and adults adapt to one another to build and manage relationships? While many seemingly obvious communication strategies may be employed, the potential for creativity even for young children remained enormous. I sought to discover, "in their own words" and actions, what children did to adapt to their social world, influence it, and make it their own. I had in mind a variety of interested parties as I gathered data: parents, teachers, and child-development workers, along with anyone interested in child interactions. Of course, scholars, like myself, interested in the origins and development of communication strategies would chime in as well. So many adults, though once children themselves, seem to have trouble communicating with them. At times, I must include myself in this group. All who care about children, however, should want to feel more comfortable communicating with them. How can we better understand and communicate with very young children, and seek to influence them or "mold them" into becoming effective communicators? This we must do for the sake of their happier relationships and happier lives. Such a goal was one key motivator as I undertook this research. Children's communication proved to be a rich and mysterious world to explore.

Given the novelty of even the simplest verbal and nonverbal symbol use for children, I sought to observe them and write about their communication from a fresh perspective. "Well," the reader may certainly ask, "who hasn't?" But my goal was to preserve, as meticulously as I could, communication events in a child-development center. I tried to take the perspective of a newcomer, "washed up on the shores" of a particular child-development center culture, trying to understand how and why children and adults there exchanged messages the way they did. Of course, I must acknowledge my background that helped me understand the communication there. Through recording daily observations in a journal, I accumulated quite a set of communication events. Most of these I simply observed transpiring, but I became a part of the center culture too, and so participated in many events and recorded my reactions. Then it became necessary to don my "scholar's hat"; I had to try to make sense of all these events somehow and put some order to them. I faced the dilemma of how to communicate findings from the masses of data in the journals. A narrative approach seemed to be the fresh perspective sought. Other studies have formed hypotheses and tested them, presenting data in tables and in descriptions of confirmed hypotheses. I wanted to present my results in a more reader-friendly format, and I became convinced the effort would be worth it. My goal was to try to understand the communication world of children in a child-development center, and to communicate that world in as vivid and readable a fashion as possible. The reader may judge the success of the result, but as the author I can say I was more fulfilled by telling my stories this way than I would have been by using more traditional means.

BACKGROUND SCHOLARSHIP

Before plunging in to tell my stories, I should sketch in a general way what we already know about communication in relationships, children's development and communication, organizational cultures, and research already done in

child-care centers. At the root of all these areas of knowledge stand relationships; they are central to any human life, and people communicate to form and
manage them. They fulfill our basic social needs for inclusion, affection, and
control. All children need experience in relationships to experience social
growth and become communicatively healthy. Being in relationships with
other children and adults serves key developmental functions (Hartup 1989).

Interpersonal relationships are rule-governed communication systems,
which develop as people interact with one another (Cahn 1987). People are
motivated to establish and stay in relationships with one another for ego support, self-affirmation, stimulation, and security (Cahn 1987). As long as relationship members perceive understanding and support from the other party,
they will tend to stay in and invest more energy in a relationship. If another
person enhances the perception of one's own desired identity, that relationship is likely to grow. On the other hand, if that other person calls into question one's desired identity, one experiences increased uncertainty and
reduced support from that person, and the relationship is likely to change
(Cupach and Metts 1994). We thus seek greater intimacy with another in a
relationship, but hesitate to reveal too much about ourselves for fear of em-
barrassment and because of uncertainty about how the other party will react.

Several models of relationship development have been proposed. A key to
this process, according to Berger and Bradac (1982), is reducing uncertainty
about the other party. If a child finds himself or herself in close proximity to another child, interest in understanding and predicting the behavior of the other
increases. The same is true for the child in relation to nearby adults. A child will
act in certain ways and see if the other acts in expected or comforting ways. As
uncertainty is reduced through verbal or nonverbal communication, a relationship is formed and enhanced. Interaction proceeds, which can lead to a closer
relationship or a more distant or ending relationship, depending upon many
factors, including tensions over how much autonomy, predictability, and openness are desired by each party (Baxter 1988). To explore the process, I sought
to discover key strategies enacted to enhance or dissolve relationships among
four- and five-year-old children in a child-care organization's culture. Nonverbal strategies, like enacted proximity, facial expressions, and laughter, as well
as verbal strategies, like questions and responding statements, are crucial for
young children as they learn to use very basic communication skills.

Knapp and Vangelisti (1992) set forth a basic set of stages of growing and dis-
solving relationships, involving levels of growing closeness and, alternatively,
distance. Interacting with growing confidence, children reduce uncertainty
about one another and reduce the social distance between them. Even at ages
four and five, managing relationships involves keeping track of complicated,
interrelated variables. Four key interactional tensions to manage in a relationship are: independence versus dependence, affection versus instrumentality,
judgment versus acceptance, and expressiveness versus protectiveness (Rawl-

ins 1992). First, how much will the other party influence the child's actions? Will commands be accepted, will imitations of behavior be in order, or will a simple tolerant playing near one another be enough? How much one child may trust or rely on another will be a key question. Second, what motives sparked a relationship? Most young children develop relationships for convenience— another happens to be nearby and available to play with, and the other will accept suggestions and commands, or the other child provides access to a desired toy or treat. The instrumentality of children's relationships, however, can be transcended to reach a level of ongoing affection, or a more genuine friendship to adult eyes. How often or how much a relationship extends beyond a child's needs or desires of the moment will always be in question. Third, for young children, how to balance showing acceptance of the other with pronouncing judgments or criticisms will require effort. While helpful, friendly comments and consideration facilitate trust and support, the needs of the moment and blunt emotional reactions elicit judgmental commands and statements. However, friends expect each to protect the other's feelings. Strategic choices children learn to make to manage these variables affect their relationships, and hence their overall communication ability and self-concept.

Children as young as three have been found to adapt their speech to varied listeners (Ochs and Schieffelin 1983). Young children often use short, simple sentences to describe an act, and see what response comes from another. Repeating another's phrase, rather than being mere imitation, may indicate shared meaning. A shared social reality is constructed through verbal as well as nonverbal interaction (Cicourel 1974). By age five, children make subtle distinctions among types of words and phrases used, and adjust their symbol use to fit social roles, both in serious and "play" interactions (Anderson 1986). As children invoke mutually understood and approved symbols through words and actions, they unite for a time, managing inherent tensions and contradictions to enact relationships.

Sharing a sense of humor appreciation, for instance, facilitates relationship development for children (Graham 1995). Young children have been found to commonly invoke humor for prosocial purposes (Socha and Kelly 1994). Use of humor, or the ability to "entertain" another, reduces social distance and enhances children's ability to initiate good relationships (Wanzer, Booth-Butterfield and Booth-Butterfield 1996). I sought to observe and document multiple strategies, including humor, that children used in a child-care center.

In *Relational Transitions*, Richard Conville (1991) details the ever-progressing and ever-changing nature of relationships. In trying to balance their own needs with the other's, the parties in a relationship move through four phases. First, a state of *security* prevails, with both parties stressing similarities between them and feeling comfortable with the relationship at a given level. Inevitably, however, some kind of change will occur, leading to some *disintegration* of the relationship; this involves increasing uncertainty and the questioning of a relationship. As a result, both parties start to stress their differences and experience a phase of *alienation*, in which their old roles no longer function and the relationship passes a kind of turning point. In the fourth phase, *resynthesis*, both parties have adjusted to the changes in roles and start to stress similarities once again, and the relationship stabilizes again, though it is different from what it was before. Rather than repeating, relationships evolve—whether toward more intimacy and closeness or toward more separation and distance. Certain patterns may be repeated, but the relationship itself is constantly developing. Children, as they leave the family environment to communicate in other contexts, must grow more sophisticated in managing such relational transitions. This kind of relationship model can serve as a useful backdrop for understanding children's— and later adults'—exploration and managing of relationships.

A major challenge in forming relationships is adapting one's own symbol use to that of the other person. In extended relationships, people match an openness-closedness cycling in communication to that of their partner (Vanlear 1991). Thus, parties gradually grow "closer" symbolically by consistent use of open communication with one another. Intimacy, or the sharing of inmost thoughts and desires with another person, becomes a goal of relationships. Yet the selfish part of us that *wants* must be balanced by an altruism that gives some to the other person (Carr 1988). Instrumental "getting" from a relationship needs mitigating by affectionate "giving" to the other. Children must overcome this paradox, and as they are naturally egocentric this is difficult at first. There must be a degree of mutual self-satisfaction of both parties for the relationship to continue. Children have been found to develop relational skills such as comforting others as they improve their ability to meet others' needs through communication (Burleson 1982; 1994). Yet, when we rely on someone else to satisfy our needs, conflict is inherent in the situation (Carr 1988). Children are learning how much to give, how much to take, and what to expect from relationships.

CHILDREN AND COMMUNICATION DEVELOPMENT

Studies show that by the age of five, most children have gained the vast majority of their basic knowledge of grammar and syntax, as well as awareness of the rules of interaction that govern nonverbal behavior (Allen and Brown 1976). Preschool children show dramatic developments in the abilities to tell stories, take turns in interaction, and use expanded vocabulary (McLaughlin 1998). Vocabulary and intelligence, of course, keep growing, but by age five most children are able to verbally communicate quite clearly, and thus can use a variety of strategies for initiating and managing relationships. The focus of their communication has reached a level of egocentrism, and thus is primarily self-focused, yet their development has moved away from autism, or a total inward focus, toward a middle ground between that and socially directed communication and the logic of reason. Selman (1980) showed ages five and six as the time children move from an undifferentiated and egocentric level of perspective-taking to a differentiated and subjective level, suggesting that perceptions of others come into their awareness and start being refined. As children age, their mental and communicative development follow the orthogenetic principle: standard or random thoughts give way to more hierarchical, categorized thought processes, which allow the conception of others and the adaptation of communication strategies to various others (Delia and O'Keefe 1979). Context is also crucially important—a child might be verbally sophisticated in some settings, while uncomfortable with more than one word in others (Allen and Brown 1976). By the age of five, then, children have begun to learn to assume different roles and to enact the roles that society has "assigned" to them. Emotional development is crucial to tailoring communication to others in relationships, as well. Children learn to understand and label their own emotions, and then learn that others feel emotions, too, and may feel differently than they do (Denham 1998). Emotions to some degree enhance more strategic and differentiated communication. Too much emotion, of course, limits communication effectiveness (Sypher and Sypher 1988). Even preschoolers have learned—to a limited degree—how not to express all emotions felt (Saarni and Weber 1999), though four- and five-year-olds are more likely to show negative true feelings than are older children (Philippot, Feldman, and McGee 1992). More popular children have often been found to be better able to understand others' emotional states, and keep their own emotional expression more controlled.

Interaction with peers allows children to develop social competency, which requires awareness of others' viewpoints (Foot, Chapman, and Smith 1995). Children placed so that they spend time together and develop reciprocal, mutual interactions will likely develop closer relationships. For young children, perceived similarities join doing activities together as major determinants of friendship and, hence, relationship development (Rubin and Ross 1982). Children who have a sense of "the other" and the need for reciprocity in interaction are more socially competent and apt to develop stronger and more rewarding relationships (Haslett and Samter 1997). Even as young as two years of age, children have been found to be fairly sophisticated at using social manipulation to get their needs met (Rubin and Ross 1982). However, as they grow, popular children are found to demonstrate concern for others (Burleson and Waltman 1987), engage in cooperative play, and effectively participate in "patterned social interaction" (Rubin and Ross 1982, 45). Key social skills that children develop in order to avoid loneliness and depression include the abilities to seek similarities with others, follow specific norms in small groups, and adapt to the needs of a partner in a friendship dyad (Parker 1986; Parker and Asher 1993). Important rules children must master to form effective relationships include balancing compliance and autonomy, developing self-control of emotions in conflicts, and recognizing obligations in mutual activity (Bigelow, Tesson, and Lewko 1996). Those unable to participate due to uncontrolled aggression or lack of cognitive or linguistic skills tend to be isolates in the classroom or other peer groups.

Children at age five have a noted tendency to focus on one friend at a time, in the sense that their friend is the child they happen to be playing with at the moment (Selman 1980). Still, how they treat that one child and manage that relationship matter, since they are practicing relational management for the future. While the current, shared participation is most important for children's friendships at that age, they are also learning to reduce ego-involvement in activities to allow for sharing, compromise, and more equal exchanges, allowing for the perspective of the other (Rawlins 1992). More popular children are found to be better at understanding others' verbal messages in addition to "reading" others' emotional expressions effectively (Parker 1986). The extensive pretending and games that children engage in are ways to test their current friends and try out relationship management strategies. Most are fairly straightforward, like a simple command or request to play together, or a simple nonverbal mutual activity. Researchers have noted gender differences in initiating interaction even in very young children; girls tend to use polite, mature strategies, while boys tend to command, approach aggressively, or simply try to join in an ongoing activity (Foot, Chapman, and Smith 1995).

Friendship at the preschool age has been characterized as egocentric and fleeting, primarily exhibited through joint activity and physical closeness, and not viewed by the children as a stable relationship (Mannarino 1995). Repeated experiences with the same child, of course, are necessary, yet young children will "be your friend" for openly extrinsic motivations like having someone to play with or getting to play with a desired toy. Social skills are developing—and noticed even by preschool peers. Well-liked children clearly have greater communication skills. Coherent discourse has been found to be fundamental to such popularity (Hazen and Black 1989). As children grow, they are able to use more and more abstract mental constructs to adapt persuasive messages to others (Delia, Kline, and Burleson 1979). Extensive research has shown that central to developing effective relationships, friendships, and popularity for children is an ability to account for, adjust to, and be kind to the other party in the interaction (Sypher and Applegate 1984). More socially accepted or sought-after children are more likely to behave cooperatively and provide support and help to peers. Popular preschool children use more positive, reinforcing behaviors, and are sociable and responsive to the needs of others; unpopular children, on the other hand, are more aggressive, disagreeable, and less likely to give reasons or suggest alternatives for their actions (Foot, Chapman, and Smith 1995). Children who are more often rejected or rebuffed by their peers tend to be with-drawn and less socially mature (Howes, Hamilton, and Matheson 1994). Chances for interaction and sharing activity in common with others are clearly needed for children to develop relational skills. A child-care center could be an ideal venue for such development.

FROM HOME TO CHILD CARE

Communication as part of day-care center life and communication at home both play a part in promoting social maturity, as children have been found to bring interaction patterns from home to child care, modify those patterns based on interactions with peers, and then return to modify parent-child in-teractions at home (Howes 1987). Thus, the quality of care found at both venues helps to predict personal maturity and social skills in children (Lamb, Hwang, Broger, and Booksten 1988). The two organizations, family and child care, form a summative and, we hope, collaborative relationship to in-fluence a child's communication.

The family is the most crucial source of a child's social skills and communi-cation patterns. Family communication has been shown to relate to many later-developing social behaviors. A child learns basic communication compe-tencies, including verbal strategies and self-control, as well as develops a ba-sic self-concept, through communication with family members (Stafford and Bayer 1993). Especially important for children is the initial personal "attach-ment" developed with a significant other as an infant. At birth, most sensation comes through touch, and the lack of tactile stimulation through cuddling, ca-ressing, or hugging has been fatal for otherwise well-cared-for babies (Vargas 1986). A child seeks a comfortable, close attachment with (most often) his or her mother, and recurring or constant deprivation of such attachment leads to alternative attachment styles as the child gets older; a more secure style may be replaced by an avoidant, ambivalent, or disorganized style (Solomon and George 1999). Children may learn in their family that caregivers are to be trusted, and thus they feel secure, or they may learn that caregivers are unreli-able in some way, and thus feel anxious or detached in developing relation-ships. Most children develop elements of both security and anxiety or detach-ment from their family experiences. Many researchers have found communication within the family to be central to a child's initial development of communication styles; child-care centers and schools thus may only build on what skills exist when children walk through their doors. "If the norms of family, peer group, and school are roughly similar, the child will have his com-munication reinforced at every turn. If the family and peer group norms con-flict with those of the school, however, there is very little chance that the edu-cation system will prevail, either in or out of the classroom," according to Allen and Brown (1976, 31). At any child-care center, events at home and parental communication styles are a topic of conversation among staff members, as children's communication so clearly reflects what happens at home. When communication expectations at home and school differ, the child inevitably has problems fitting in well at the child-care center. The child's relationships with his or her parents are quite crucial to his or her communication with others; parents of unpopular five-year-olds have been found to be more controlling, directive, and intrusive in their interactions (Foot, Chapman, and Smith 1995). Thus, rejection of children in parental communication will often lead to peer rejection of those same children (Haslett and Samter 1997).

The day-care center is often the child's first regular experience of an organization other than his or her own family, and integrating the two can occur smoothly, roughly, or never at all (Bradbard, Endsley, and Mize 1992). The impact and prominence of child-care centers are growing. Children growing up in recent years, with 50 percent divorce rates and more women working outside of the home, must be cared for somewhere. In 1995, one of four American children was growing up in a single-parent home, 96 percent of which were headed by women (Zigler and Gilman 1996). The three most common types of care were: by a paid caregiver in the home, at a family day-care in a home, or at a child-care center. There has been extensive study of the worth of care at home versus care at a day-care center, and the results have been decidedly mixed (Caruso 1989; Clarke and Alison 1986; Van-Crombrugge and Vandemeulebroecke 1991). Intellectual and psychological development are found to be stimulated in both places, with family care winning out in terms of emotional development and health. The latter factors, however, can be enhanced by a clean child-care environment with loving, supportive teachers. Good, quality child-care centers have been found to positively nurture children, use small group activities, and have adult-to-child ratios of one to three for infants, one to four for toddlers, and one to five for preschoolers. A more common ratio for the latter, however, has been one adult per eight preschoolers (Zigler and Gilman 1996). Child-care staff members who have low morale, low pay, and high turnover more likely will show a lack of warmth, low stimulation of communication and learning, and potential child neglect during daily care. The most important and beneficial factor, beyond safety and feeding, is consistent and loving nurturing and communication from trusted adults. Clearly, the form of communication experienced is the key to good childhood social development, whether at home or in a child-care center.

Improving children's communication gives them more power to influence their world (Wood 1976) and increases their motivation to interact with others. Consistent communication from caring adults is crucial for training and empowering children; but interaction with other children is important, as well. At ages three and four, prior experience with peer interaction has led to higher levels of sociability and social skill observed (Foot, Chapman, and Smith 1995).

We know that complementary and reciprocal social play generally emerges between children between the ages of one and two, and pretend social play often begins at age two. Early interaction with peers at child-care centers or in other venues has been found to be crucial for children's development of key communication skills for functioning in groups, including leadership, decision making or problem solving, conflict management, and rapport building (Keyton 1994). Even young children organize their society through communication (Goodwin 1990), and those with more communication skills will be more involved in and satisfied with the emerging communication-created social order. Recommended models stress three child abilities to be promoted by child-care staff members: building mutual respect, enacting fairness or justice, and generating several alternatives in communication situations (Carlson and Larson 1991). Children who can be diplomatic rather than aggressive are viewed as more popular. Thus, interaction with peers allows children to practice and refine communication skills needed for functioning in any social group.

CHILD-CARE CULTURES

Child-care centers develop an organizational culture, as does any organization. Culture has turned out to be a "foundational term through which the orderliness and patterning of much of our life experience is explained" (Smircich 1983, 341). Communication is essential for this explanation, as it "creates and constitutes the taken-for-granted reality of the world" (Pacanowsky and O'Donnell-Trujillo 1982, 121). Through recurring rituals or patterns of communication, participants gain a sense of regularity and shared reality. As parts of communication become routine, persons in organizations play given roles as culture is enacted like a drama (Pacanowsky and O'Donnell-Trujillo 1983). Understanding this ongoing drama enhances understanding of cultural members' values and sense of self. As humans create culture through interaction, the culture influences how individuals communicate as they follow its established patterns and rules. Shared meanings emerge through interaction, and organizational cultures may then be viewed as systems of shared meaning. Gradually, as children grow older, key parts of their identity stem from the groups or organizations within which they interact (Cheney 1991). Thus, as children assimilate into a child-care center and its culture, their identification with that organization may become integral to their own self-concept.

In studies of child-care cultures, great impact on children's styles and strategies of communication has been shown (Anderson 1989; Haskins 1985). As founders and leaders of child-care organizations, adults determine key elements of their continuing organizational culture (Schein 1985). Adults, as those in power, initiate and reinforce child-care center cultures and enact power differences recurrently through communication there

(Mumby 1993). Leavitt and Power (1989) observed adults in a child-care center deny the legitimacy of children's emotions, for example, while helping children re-construe those emotions. Adults would fail to recognize or respond to certain emotional expressions, and would focus on performance or behavior by the children rather than understanding or naming the children's feelings. An overall narrative, or "myth" as Leavitt and Power (1989) named the concept, served as the source of the child-care center's vision and preferred communication strategies. Other studies have shown that the adults certainly set the tone of any child-care center's culture. Adult agreement on goals and methods of working with children made for a more unified and supportive communication climate in child-development centers studied (Palmerus and Hagglund 1991). The presence of more adults per child *increased* the amount of child-centered activities, while a large class of children under the care of only one or two adults required adults to spend more time keeping basic order rather than interacting extensively with children.

Children, too, develop pivotal communication patterns and "oral traditions" that guide their interactions and play (Nervius 1989). Adults might "plant the seed" for such patterns, but children may seize on a play story or myth and enact and reenact it in various ways. This story then serves as a template on which future play of the same type can be based; for instance, a mother and father going to work may serve as the basis for playing "house," or a superhero capturing a villain for "chase" games outside. These patterns develop through children's communication, and through them children learn their own social roles by understanding those of others. Children take on the attitude of the other, then arouse communicative action by the other that complements their own attitude, and together they produce a joint activity that brings them together in a mutually and subtly negotiated interaction sequence (Denzin 1977; Mead 1934). Recent research has found ten key relationship management strategies used by young children in child-care centers: making statements about friendship, managing proximity, touching, listening, expressing feelings, engaging in conflict, joking or teasing, playing or taking roles with one another, controlling others, and invoking rules (Meyer and Driskill 1997). All of these strategies had a wide application for the children in the child-development center where I volunteered, and thus recur in the present work as chapter titles or subheadings.

PREVIOUS STUDIES OF CHILDREN

Other books have sought to detail the challenge of studying social relations among children. Graue and Walsh (1998) provide stories about the dilemmas of doing research in the child-development center setting. Children create meaning by participating with others in culturally organized, routine practices, and becoming privy to those practices as an adult was necessarily problematic.

Graue and Walsh (1998) note that "thick description" through extensive field notes and reflections allows researchers to systematically understand children's cultures, and suggest presenting results in narrative forms, much as this book does. Bigelow, Tesson, and Lewko (1996) gathered extensive survey data from children of varied ages, providing details of the rules children follow in forming relationships across a variety of contexts. Holmes (1998) focused on gender differences between researchers and children and their effects on communication, finding herself distressed by the lack of affection or caring communication, especially between genders. She found that a cold and distant culture results from a stress on power differences between children and adults. In any child-care setting, one can find an inherent conflict between providing a warm, caring environment for all children and needing to avoid touching and hugging, especially with school-aged children, for fear of misinterpretation or charges of abuse. Greig and Taylor (1999) detail social research with children, starting from "square one" with Piaget's (1971) developmental theory (preschool children have generally passed the "sensori-motor" stage by age three and are in the "pre-operational" stage until about age seven), and stressing the importance for children of special, multiple, positive early attachments, and moving through a variety of instruments one may use to test children. Greig and Taylor (1999) include few narratives, but all the books noted here include some and point to the necessity of observing children to understand their communication. Other forms of data gathering, whether tests, sociometric models, or content analysis, draw their construction or origination from narratives based on observation of children's communication.

I have chosen to present the communication patterns and relationships I observed and participated in as narratives, because narratives are often the key to our understanding of communication events (Conville 1997; 1991) and enhance our memory of them (Black and Bern 1981). Narratives serve as a key form of reasoning for humans, and thus may be deployed as a powerful teaching tool (Fisher 1987). An immediate sense of the active communication experienced in a relationship emerges from narratives (Bochner and Ellis 1992; Crawford 1996). I decided to tell my stories to supplement childhood communication research in a somewhat unique way. Other researchers have participated with children in child-development centers as I have (notably Corsaro 1985). Such valuable research tested hypotheses and extended the research outlined in this chapter. My goal, however, was to further enrich our understanding of actual messages and strategies used by the children to manage their relationships in a child-care culture, moving beyond data rooted in social science, controllable experiments, and formulas to events evoking dramatic, tragic, and comic elements (Browning 1992). I noted, in reviewing early research, that the stories the researchers would tell about spending time conducting research and communicating with children were the most fascinating part of their writings for me. Their unique organizational narratives contained universal elements that could enhance our understanding of all communication. I decided to make that narrative style the centerpiece of my own presentation of research results.

NOTES ON RESEARCH METHODS

I pursued this research in "naturalistic" fashion, seeking to enter the children's world and understand their communication within it. As Denzin (1977, 29) noted, such research involves a "studied commitment to actively enter the worlds of native people and to render those worlds understandable from the standpoint of a theory that is grounded in the behaviors, languages, definitions, attitudes, and feelings of those studied." Thus, I sought, as a "child-care detective," to tell stories hoping to "evoke a richer, deeper sense of the experience of observing and interpreting organizational lives" (Goodall 1994, xii). I wanted to report in detail my findings, but also to capture the sense of mystery and excitement found when entering into interactions with children and those who work with them in "their" places. Though children are all around us, and we were once like them, their culture is different from adult culture; as enacted through their communication, it is a mystery worthy of study (Fine and Sandstrom 1988). Others have attempted to capture the social worlds of children. Most have explored the interaction of older children, as Fine (1987) did when interacting and becoming friends with Little League baseball players. He noted clashes between the planned, ordered, ideal baseball world of the adults and the spontaneous, changing, situational social roles the boys took as they communicated with one another, developing their own peer culture. Katriel (1991) presented a compelling snapshot of Israeli life from a childhood culture perspective. Children enacted detailed, repeated, and mutually understood patterns, often unthinkingly, that created and reinforced a sense of solidarity and togetherness among them, preparing them for adult life in Israel. Younger children's development of language has also been studied through ethnography, with the finding that children learn language through using it, rather than being formally taught. Interacting with other children leads more directly to learning symbol use than a controlling method of formal instruction ever could (Cazden 1972). As children learn the rules of language, they also learn about social structure, and four- and five-year-olds are just beginning to move from specific, nonverbal cues to more general, abstract verbal symbols (Cicourel 1974). As children understand more words and grammatical patterns, they also understand social groupings and rankings. The interactional goals of newly verbal children shape the actual words and grammatical forms they use (Ervin-Tripp and Mitchell-Kernan 1977). Thus, ethnographic methods reveal children's social worlds to us in overarching views of child society as well as in specific instances of language development. My purpose here is to address patterns of relational and cultural development. How do children manage relationships? What symbols do they use to develop and build a child-care center culture? I have sought here to uncover those patterns and discern their meaning.

Qualitative methods have been most useful for studying a communication culture, a culture woven by members in the course of their communication (Pacanowsky and O'Donnell-Trujillo 1982; Pilotta, Widman, and Jasko 1988). Study of the symbols invoked in group interactions as a culture is created requires rich troves of data. A qualitative investigator "goes into the field" to examine the taken-for-granted but important ideas and practices that constitute and reconstitute organizational cultures (Schwartzman 1993).

My study focuses on one child-development center on the campus of a medium-sized southern university that serves seventy children, ages infant through nine. For four years (not including vacations and breaks from school when the center was closed), I observed and participated in interactions among three-year-olds, four-year-olds, five-year-olds, staff members, and occasionally older school-aged children. The child participants included similar numbers of both genders and came from a variety of ethnic and cultural backgrounds. The center was led by a woman who had been director for five years when I began spending time there. Each classroom had a lead teacher who had a college degree, and multiple aides who worked varied hours on varied days; most of these were college students. Many were studying child development or elementary education. Almost all were female—during my time there, only one male teacher aide worked in the three classrooms I typically encountered, and semester staff meetings might see two or three males, total, working at the center among about thirty women.

The center sat between open intramural fields and a small house used for family counseling next to a residential neighborhood on one side and a row of fraternity houses on the other. A driveway curved up to the front doors, while side and rear doors led to three playgrounds, separated by short chain-link fences. Tall pine trees were found throughout the playgrounds, along with other, smaller trees and areas of grass. Swing sets, slides, and other climbers dotted each playground. Inside, bright, airy classrooms with large, festive bulletin boards and cubbies for children's things housed each twelve- to twenty-member class of children. Younger children's classrooms were smaller in space as well as numbers, with the four-year-olds' classroom being the largest, with twenty children. Pictures and posters lined the walls, but windows were many and large, so that even the children could easily look out. One glass wall in each classroom concealed an observation booth for use by college students and faculty for coursework and research. In the classrooms, small shelves and tables delineated ever-changing areas of play and work and "circle time," during which the children would gather on the floor for instruction, games, and stories. Lunch and morning and afternoon snacks were eaten at the classroom tables, and naps were taken on fold-up mats on the classroom floor. The center opened at 7:30 A.M. and closed at 5:30 P.M. each weekday.

About one-fifth to one-fourth of the children in each classroom were African American, and one or two children in each were from the international student community. Teachers and teacher aides fell into similar proportions of ethnic representation, with several lead teachers being African American. (In the two classrooms where I observed over three years, one lead teacher was African American, while two were not.) The net result was that center classrooms were ethnically diverse places, reflecting the campus community they served. Doubtless, some differences in children's communicative styles were based on ethnic and cultural backgrounds, but I chose not to focus on this issue, since I was also relatively unconcerned with the kind of family or socioeconomic backgrounds the children came from. The relevant communication, for my research, was how symbols in messages served to create and influence relationships and the organizational culture at the center. Clearly, historical, social, and racial backgrounds could play a large part in how children and staff members communicated, as Heath (1983) so compellingly explored in the Carolinas during school integration times. In the mid-1990s at the child-development center, such differences seemed less noticeable, or blended with all the other differences inherent in the children's family backgrounds. Race issues did emerge at times, yet race did not seem to be a major consideration for the children in their interactions, and rarely seemed to be for the adult staff members. I wanted to see what would emerge from the variety of individual communication strategies used by children with varying backgrounds and communication skills.

For the sake of avoiding extensive note taking while interacting in the classroom and outside, I wrote in a journal at the end of each day, as well as during some brief breaks (as did Ceglowski 2000). I sought to preserve direct quotes when possible, and managed to record at least two or three verbatim communication incidents per day. Other instances were described in the journal, and reconstructed as "typical narratives" after several such events or descriptions had been categorized. All narratives included here are taken directly or closely paraphrased from journal entries. Names and some particulars have been changed to protect identities. I was at the center for at least three hours at least two days per week, but often wound up staying longer or returning for briefer periods. I was there mostly in the mornings, but would return for short periods of time on some afternoons. I primarily participated in what was considered the four-year-olds' classroom, though some older "threes" and younger "fives" were also present. I would regularly visit with the three-year-olds in their classroom next door as well, and outside the two classes often shared a playground.

After recording interactions and observations in a journal, I would seek themes and categories, grouped by similarity using constant comparison (Lincoln and Guba 1985; Miles and Huberman 1984). Some of the theme categories I used paralleled relationship management categories from an earlier, similar study (Meyer and Driskill 1997). These relational themes, or strategies, became the basis for many chapters in this book. I sought to have symbols emerge from observations and experiences of communication with the children at the center, rather than approaching the research with specific preconceptions and hypotheses to test. The children and staff, members of the culture, generated the basis of this knowledge themselves (Werner and Schoepfle 1987); I thought of myself as a chronicler or translator, enhancing our understanding of one child-care center in particular while shedding light on how preschool children communicate in general.

WRESTLING WITH MY ROLE

I could not, of course, become fully involved in the children's culture at the center myself. The age roles of our society dictated that I would be looked on as an adult and expected to do "adult" things (Fine and Sandstrom 1988). I became an authority figure by necessity, though not to the degree of the classroom teachers. It was inevitable, as other researchers have found (Ceglowski 2000), that in choosing to interact with children and teachers I would form relationships with them. Clear potential existed for me to benefit the children as well as the teachers at the center by participating rather than merely observing. In addition to getting closer to social interactions among children, I would have the opportunity to enact and model a variety of "good" or "prosocial" communication behaviors in developing relationships with children. Such adult-child interactive relationships have been shown to be valuable for children (Kuehne 1988). I also became an accepted and valued adult at the center; indeed in many ways I was treated as a staff member, which certainly facilitated learning about the culture. Yet there remained key ways in which I was *not* a staff member and could not behave as one; I still needed to take notes and to analyze and reflect on experiences (Ceglowski 2000), and I always lacked a legitimate organizational role.

At first, the children did not know how much authority I really possessed, and I was not sure either! I was always careful to reinforce teacher requests and basic classroom rules, while avoiding giving commands whenever possible. Generally, both staff and children grew comfortable with my role, with the children realizing that, while I was an adult and would enforce rules, I was also a "fun" person who would play with them, and that they were not *really* "in trouble" unless a regular teacher was told about or saw a violation. The staff knew I would help and could be trusted, but most realized that it was not my place to initiate an activity or dramatically refocus or discipline a child. I tried not to take part in direction or discipline, but expectations, diplomacy, and at times the safety of the children required me to act as an adult authority, even if I did not desire to. The children and the other adults at the center accepted that I was more interested in talking, participating, and playing than in controlling or telling people what to do. In ways, mine was not too different from the roles of some part-time student staff members at the center, and other student observers were often present and interacted with the children; so my unusual role did not stand out as much as it might have in another child-care center.

While I retained some adult authority, I settled on what could be termed a "friend" role to the children—and to adult staff members—for the most part (Fine and Sandstrom 1988). I had learned from earlier volunteering the powerful relationships that could be quickly formed with children (Ceglowski 2000). Even so, I was surprised again by the power and meaning such relationships engaged. I found myself, as I became emotionally involved with the children, having to back off or distance myself from events at times. I would then remind myself to be patient and *react* more, rather than seek to further *enact* relationships (Corsaro 1985; Holmes 1998). But the evolution of my own relationships provided just as much insight, in the telling of my stories, as did details of the children's relationship management strategies. Unlike some other researchers, who are only reluctantly granted access to work with children (Ceglowski 2000), I was welcomed. The center was created for research and student education on child development. While I never found myself in a dramatic disagreement over the actions of a staff member, as Ceglowski (2000) vividly describes, apparently at times one or two staff members disagreed with some action of mine. I did at times question the strategy of staff members in guiding the children, but never openly, as I felt that would have been inappropriate. Some of these events grew into small conflicts that shed even more light on the child-care center's culture, but these were the exceptions, and I developed many positive relationships with staff members as well as children at the center.

TELLING MY STORIES

All of the research summarized above serves to give the reader a sense of my own background as I tried to make sense of and organize the stories told here. But the experiences themselves, and I hope the telling of them, encapsulate and dramatize the knowledge gained in a more compelling way than any hypothesis I could test, tables I could design, or behavior categories I could list. I have divided the stories into chapters based on themes that emerged from observations and journal entries. I know there is no way words could fully capture the rich experiences I had communicating with children at the child-development center; still, I hope the reader finds these stories enjoyable and enlightening.

2

Repeated Interaction Patterns: Revealing Culture in Recurring Routines

During observations at the child-development center, I found that repeated patterns of interaction were important to and highly sought after by the children. This was true in their relationships with one another, but even more so in their relationships with adults. The ability to recognize patterns has been viewed as the most crucial perceptual skill for humans. Knowing and understanding recurrent patterns and their results can mean survival. Once a pattern becomes familiar, effective responses can be discovered and tried. A baby discovers that crying or laughing obtains some desirable responses and learns that its needs are met in conjunction with the repeated presence of a caregiver's face (Solomon and George 1999). Infants apply such basic recognition of comforting patterns to verbal communication as they grow older and become more proficient at it. A familiar pattern of communication clearly comforted preschool children and enhanced their sense of control. Thus, uncertainty reduction would enhance communication and the growth of effective relationships. Cultural patterns, formed through interactions, led to reduced uncertainty and shared meanings. When enough "sharedness" became evident, communicators began experimenting with new symbols for communicating (Berger and Bradac, 1982). While repeated patterns in the child-care center classrooms among the children could seem relentless to an adult, they served as the backdrop, both comfortable and taken for granted, for enacting a further variety of communication strategies. Understanding the taken-for-granted communication patterns was crucial to further exploration of children's communication strategies.

Children's repetition of patterns became evident early on. For instance, if a child discovered that she liked being read to, which led to more time with and attention from me, she would ask me to read to her at least once a day, if not several times a day, for weeks afterward. During my first year at the center, asking to be picked up was a pattern that several children would repeat daily. Later on, getting me to chase them and getting a ride on my back were endlessly repeated rituals. The game of putting them in the "oven" as gingerbread cookies, followed by my chasing them, survived in some form for over a year. "Put me in the oven!" one or two children would tell me on the playground, and that was all that was needed for all parties to understand the ritual game desired. Even within a single day, children would try to repeat a communication pattern or game that they found fun or rewarding. I thought back to my own childhood and remembered that I often sought to repeat an activity that I had found really fun. It never seemed so much fun the second or third time. For four-year-olds, however, the repetition provided enough fun—along with evidence of a good and stable relationship—that they wanted it continued indefinitely.

CLASSROOM PATTERNS

Each lead teacher at the child-development center created a daily pattern of interaction, or what could be called a "classroom culture," involving a set of ways of doing things and ways of communicating. Ms. Stacey's four-year-olds' classroom was a friendly but brisk, businesslike room. Commands were given in a forceful yet gentle way and were obeyed. Ms. Stacey would often joke and tease to take the edge off of her dictates, and she maintained order within a climate of goodwill and support. Some days she seemed harsher, others friendlier, but the children were always given some leeway and choices about all but major activities and key classroom rules. Ms. Tanya, in the three-year-olds' classroom, maintained a similar sense of order and routine, but with a "softer," more approachable style. I felt a sense of support—for both children and other adults in the room—more strongly from Ms. Tanya than from Ms. Stacey. Ms. Stacey talked less and kept to herself more, but she was always very loving toward the children. When Ms. Stephanie took over as the new lead teacher for the four-year-olds, her style was more laissez-faire, and the children were given so much latitude that the classroom seemed more chaotic than before. She gradually toughened her stance, however, until she achieved a balance of loving control much like Ms. Tanya's.

Each day's overall pattern was comfortably consistent and predictable for the children. The activities occurred in the same order each day, with, of course, allowances for special activities and situations. In the early morning, the children played at the tables and in the play areas quite freely and creatively. Ms. Stacey moved around the classroom shelves and in and out of the classroom, getting ready for the day's circle time. The two assistant teachers sat in various places in the classroom, observing and interacting with the children.

Ms. Stacey would approach some children and gently but firmly make positive suggestions, like "Keep the blocks on the floor" and "That stays in the home living area." Then the lights were flashed, and "clean-up time" was announced or sung. During what seemed to be controlled chaos, all the classroom areas did get cleaned up, some by the children. The children sat on carpet squares set out by one of the teachers, and Ms. Stacey would say, "It's my turn to talk. You need to listen." The children generally did get quite attentive. Then, after learning something about the week's topic for that day, pairs of children were sent to wash their hands at the classroom's two sinks and sit at the cleaned-off tables set for snack. The same ritual was used to send the children to lunch, often after they heard a story sitting on the floor. After snack, the children cleaned up their places, threw their remnants in the trash, and returned to sit at the tables or on the floor, in preparation for going outside. After lunch, the children knew to wash up, get their mats out of their cubbies, and prepare for naptime. Much talking and playing around accompanied this process, and teachers would repeat, "Get on your mat," or "Lay down," several times, but eventually the quiet of naptime would settle over the center. The children expected each activity as it came up, and seemed to value the routine.

INDIVIDUAL REPEATED PATTERNS

Children at four and five years of age are so full of energy. They were busy with many activities here and there in the classroom, building with blocks or playing roles in the "home living" area, doing puzzles and reading books, drawing or painting at the art table. With so much to do and so much new for them, it was no surprise that their relationships changed and developed quickly. The children seldom seemed to do any one thing for more than twenty minutes. Only during the relatively brief circle times and snack and lunch times did they sit quietly as a group. Yet, as they developed relationships with other children and with me, I came to learn how important repeated patterns were to the children, and how many repeated patterns of communication gave order to the surface chaos of their daily activity.

Some children would begin a pattern of greeting others on arrival. A child might show he valued our relationship and continue to develop it by saying, "Hi, Mr. John," or "Mr. John!" and rushing over to tell me something when I arrived. Some would do this immediately when I arrived; others would wait until my presence with the class that day was more established. Children followed a similar ritual with peers they interacted with frequently, as well as with teachers, especially the lead teacher. Over time, a few added running over to get a hug to their greeting ritual with me. I certainly grew to feel like much more than an observer as I found myself repeating, and looking forward to, these developing relational patterns.

Other repeated patterns were sought by children to strengthen relationships. One strong ritual began during my second year observing at the center as I prepared to leave while the children were laying down for their naps. Some of the teachers would rub some children's backs for a few minutes as naptime began. I did this one day for one girl who asked me to. Sure enough, what one wanted, several others wanted, so I then rubbed three other children's backs. Within a few days I was always in demand to rub some of the children's backs before I left. "Rub my back!" I would hear, or more politely, "Mr. John, would you rub my back?" I was moved by their desire for this ritual of closeness, and found it impossible to refuse. This delayed my typical departure time from the center by about a half hour, causing me some concern at first. However, as I saw the importance of back rubs to the children I found I did not begrudge the time, and the repeated closeness ritual of rubbing backs came to appeal to me, too. One day a four-year-old asked me, "Mr. John, will you rub my back at naptime?" when only half the morning had yet gone by. Back rubs were a clear symbol to the children of a closer relationship, and they were reassured by them.

One variation on this ritual occurred when I joked with Derek as naptime began, saying, "Shall I fold you up [in your blanket] and make a Derek sandwich?" He grinned and nodded, so I folded his blanket over him, to his delight. For many days after that, as I was leaving the center at naptime, he would ask me, "Mr. John, will you make me a sandwich?" I could see how these repeated patterns not only provided affection and closeness for the children, but reinforced and strengthened our relationship by making our mutual behavior predictable.

If a game one child played looked like fun, of course, other children would want to join in, and they would seek to repeat the game for days or even weeks afterward. Once, some plastic baseball bats and balls were available on the playground, and Nick wanted me to throw a ball for him to hit. He had such fun that he wanted me to do it again later that day, and again the next day. Several other children also came over wanting a turn at batting the ball. They would try to hit it several times and then grow tired and move away, but Nick seemed never to tire of the game. He could continue as long as we were outside, and wanted to play for several weeks, as long as those baseball toys were on the playground. He always wanted *me* to pitch to him, as well, if he could get me to.

Once a pattern of interaction had started, especially with an adult, the children wanted it to continue. The predictability of such repeated interactions seemed to reassure them that the relationship was sound. Also, one child's interaction with me, indicating a closer relationship, prompted several other children to want that kind of interaction. One morning, I helped Jacob climb to the top of a climbing pole and slide down. Sure enough, a whole group of children came over, wanting similar help. Involving the children by name was a sure bet to create a repeatedly desired interaction. One morning I was reading a story to four boys, and one character said "Greetings."

"What's 'greetings'?" asked Jim.

"'Greetings' is like saying 'hello,'" I said. "Greetings, Jim. That's like saying 'Hello, Jim.'" Seeing his friends looking on with interest, I said, "Greetings, Travis. That's like saying 'Hello, Travis.'" Next to Travis was Chris, who looked at me expectantly, smiling. I said, "Greetings, Chris." He smiled and nodded.

"What about me?" said Brent after a pause.

"Greetings, Brent," I said, finishing out the progression and giving all present a chance to participate in the repeated pattern. They all definitely wanted a turn in a new, patterned interaction, which seemed to communicate inclusion and closeness in our relationship.

BASIC CHILD-ADULT BONDING: REPEATED CHASE GAMES

Other patterns that children wanted to repeat included having me push them in a swing, having me watch them climb on the monkey bars, and getting me to chase them. I noticed a snowball effect as more and more children would join in an activity initiated by myself or other children. One child might ask me to chase her, for instance, and then two more would join in, saying, "Chase *me!*" For several sets of children, getting me to chase them became a simple ritual for building a relationship with me; it was often the first repeated "game" or interaction with me that they felt comfortable asking for or joining in with other children. For many months, the children would pretend to be gingerbread cookies that I was chasing. I had told two children one day that they were gingerbread girls in the oven, cooking for me to eat, and they had run away. "Get back in that oven!" I would yell, and give chase to a laughing child or two. Several other children joined this game, wanting to be gingerbread cookies and get chased, too. After that day, those children and others who were new and observed our pattern for a while would invoke that symbolism repeatedly to initiate chase games. As time went on and individual children copied the pattern and improvised variations on the game, a structure for social interaction formed. Soon, all the children had to say was "Put me in the oven," or "You have to cook me," or even "I'm your cookie" to initiate this chasing game.

As the three-year-olds repeated "Mr. John, put me in the oven" the most, I noted that, in general, the younger the child, the more repetitions of a fun game or pattern were attempted. However, even six- and seven-year-olds who saw me during summers and remembered me would seek to repeat a familiar and fun game. "I know a game," said six-year-old Michael to me one day. "We could be gingerbreads and you could chase us." I enjoyed how he described the game as a new idea, though we had played it every day for three weeks that summer. This version of the chase game lasted among the three-through-five-year-olds for more than a year, through varying interested children. Some children became sophisticated in developing variations of the ritual. Sarah and Michelle came up to me on the playground one day. "Put me in the oven," they each said to me. I moved them over next to a tree, and they said, "Not *that* oven," and suddenly were very picky about which "oven"—or tree—they wanted to be "put into." Then, as they ran off, they both reminded me to "Try to get *me*." I tagged one girl once and said, "Oh boy! Dessert!" She laughed, and another girl playing the gingerbread cookie chase game chimed in, "I wanna be the dessert!"

New children also joined in these recurring games, quickly found them fun, and would then seek to repeat them. Some children found them more fun and relationally meaningful than others, of course, and would more actively try to reinitiate the activity. When Chris was new to the four-year-olds' class, he played the gingerbread cookie chase game one day. A few days later, he saw me again and came over to talk to me, saying, "Hey, remember when we played outside? Remember when we played oven?" I told him I did, and that we could play it again sometime when we were outside. Sure enough, after we went outside it was Chris who came over and said, "Put me in the oven!" just as his "veteran" colleagues had for months.

On another day, a new three-year-old child looked very afraid when I turned to him and included him in the game: "I'll put you in the oven!" I said to him playfully. His eyes grew wide, and he let out an insistent "No-o-o-o!" I respected his fear and left him alone, but after he observed his peers having fun with the game, he joined right in. The game involved several factors the children seemed to value: first, my attention, as I would "cook" them; second, physical contact, as I positioned them by the tree in the "oven" or caught them; and third, the thrill of getting chased by me as they ran away from the "oven." They would laugh excitedly when I said, "Hey! Get back in that oven!" I noted that the children never played this version of chase without me, unless I had been playing with them first. If another child caught them, the children looked much less pleased than when I caught them. Being caught by a peer clearly did not have the relational meaning that they sought. The children developed other play contexts to justify chases among themselves, and would sometimes repeat those also. They could play chase, depending on their mood, for a half hour or more. I would try to humor them and continue playing even after I was tired of it, not wanting to "reject" them by abruptly ending our game, but after a long time I would purposefully be distracted by another child or teacher on the playground, or experience a sense of relief when the children tired of the game and moved to playing something else. Sometimes, I would distract them by bringing up a new topic or game myself. The children were quite determined to play with me and involve me in their activities once they knew I would interact with them.

Another repeated game that evolved in my later months at the child-development center was hide-and-go-seek. As yet another variant of the favored chasing games, this one had the additional excitement potential of hiding with the suspense of being found. It was also a commonly known game that new children could comfortably ask me to play. Four-year-old Eric was new to the class and had observed me playing with and chasing the children outside. Relatively quickly, within two weeks, he was comfortable initiating interaction with me, and he suggested we play hide-and-go-seek. He enjoyed hiding from me, and after I "looked" unsuccessfully for him around the playground, he gleefully showed me where he had hidden.

"Mr. John, here I am; are you looking for me?" Eric would then ask at intervals to get me to chase him. As the weeks went on, he typically would say to me, "Could we play hide-and-go-seek when we get outside?" as a way of initiating interaction with me.

"Yes, we can," I responded one morning. "You *like* hide-and-go-seek, don't you?"

"Yeah, it's my favorite game," said Eric.

Eric had become the initiator of hide-and-go-seek, with various other children joining in daily. Seeing me for Eric meant a time to renew that ritual of playing the game. On days when Eric was not present, after we had all been outside for a while, Chris might suggest, "Can we play hide-and-go-seek?" He and the other children enjoyed playing the game regularly, but it was much more of a "priority ritual" for Eric.

Randy developed the game of chase into a game of putting me in jail. Every day for several weeks, when we would see each other on the playground, he would lead his friends over, grab me by the arms, and say, "Take him to jail. You have to go to jail." I would soon escape, and they would chase me. This ritual was so established that I got tired of that being the only way that Randy would greet me. Indeed, even after Randy finally tired of the game and returned to greeting me with "Hi, Mr. John!" or "Mr. John, watch this!" I noticed that one of his friends, Nasser, would still only approach me to say, "You have to go to jail!" I realized that was the only way he had ever approached me, since he would follow Randy's lead, and had learned no other way to reinitiate our relationship. I would play along with him, and after that ritual he would talk with me about other things, and several times asked me, "Will you come in our class with us?" as the children went inside. But the taking-me-to-jail ritual was clearly Nasser's key for beginning interaction with me, and we never got beyond it, as the semester ended soon after that time.

A PERPETUAL PATTERN: BACK RIDES

Any activity that I did with one child, several others would want to repeat. One day I "flew" Michael around the playground, and then lots of other children wanted me to "fly" them around the playground. Three weeks later, Chris asked for a piggyback ride outside. I gave him one and told him he was my backpack. Other children observed this game, and wanted to play as well. They remembered it for several weeks, and would often start the game by asking to "be your backpack." Even the statements made by me and the children during back rides would sound scripted. Their favorite pattern was for me to look all over the playground for them while they were on my back. "Where are you?" I would keep saying.

The child would often laugh, and eventually say, "Behind your back."

"I don't see anything," I would say, looking around.

"Look at those shoes," they would say. When I put the "backpack" down, I would find the child. He or she would then often run away with my "food" in hand to get me to engage in a chase. While the "backpack" variety of this ritual died out after a few weeks, the children's requests for rides on my back lasted for years after this initial game began.

New children would be introduced to the back ride ritual, as on one day when Michael asked me for a back ride, and I gave him one. Afterward, he told me to kneel down and tried to persuade two of his friends, Jonathan and Nasser, who were new to the classroom, to get a back ride, too. "No way," said Jonathan, and Nasser pretended not to hear Michael. Michael had known me for over a year, but I was still practically a stranger to Jonathan and Nasser. They clearly were not ready for a game indicating a closer or more trusting relationship yet. Michael introduced me to them—"This is Jonathan. This is Nasser"—and I said, "Hi, Jonathan. Hi, Nasser," and we continued to chase each other around the playground. A little while later, Jonathan decided he trusted me enough to ask me for a back ride of his own. Thus, the back ride ritual was passed on.

Some children liked this game so much that they would ask me for several back rides in one day. To prevent that activity from completely taking over my outside time with the children, I limited back rides to one per child per day. "Sure, I'll give you a back ride," I would say. But then, if a child kept on asking, I would say, "You *had* your back ride, remember? You can have another one another day." One day a couple of three-year-old boys kept wanting another back ride, and I tried to make the rule clear to them in a friendly way: "I give every kid *one* back ride. So I gave you *one* back ride. We can do something else now. I still like you; you're still a good buddy; I like giving you back rides. I'll give you another back ride another day." This finally got through to those two boys when I played another game with them. With other children, I would say, "I can't give you another back ride today. But I can do something else with you. How about I chase you?" That would almost always get in response an enthusiastic "Yeah!" and we would chase away. Most children understood the "one back ride" rule even without such a forthright statement, learning this rule as part of the pattern.

It became clear that back rides represented more than just a fun activity to several of the children—for them the rides were a key way to stay in a closer relationship with me. Even parents noticed this. One day after I came out on the playground, Chris came over and leaned against me. "Uncle John, lean down here. . . . I want on your back," he said in his quiet, matter-of-fact way.

"Chris," said a surprised woman's voice nearby. As I looked at her, I realized that she was Chris's mother. "He's not usually so affectionate," she said to me and Ms. Terri, who was standing nearby.

"They all love Mr. John," said Ms. Terri. Besides swelling my own head a little, this incident made me realize that getting back rides could be a way of getting attention and keeping a relationship strong for children normally not "touchy-feely" or affectionate.

A few times I tried to see how the children themselves might perceive their liking for the back ride ritual, and so when Derek asked one day, "Mr. John, I wanna get on your back," I asked him, "Why, Derek?"

"I just want to," said Derek. Other times, with other children, the answer would be, "Because I like it," and that was as abstractly as they could explain their incessant desire for back rides. Patterns of play seemed to give children a desirable script for reinitiating a relationship. Children I had only met two or three times, but had played chase with or given a back ride, would ask for that activity repeated even several weeks later. A few kept asking for back rides when I would see them in the school-aged program, and they were six or seven years old. They wanted to keep that symbol of our relationship, and for older children who had known me for years it was something fairly unique that they did with me. It was certainly a unique ritual at the center; it was rare for other teachers to give back rides.

GETTING CLOSE THROUGH REPEATED PATTERNS

A three-year-old one day got the idea to ask, "Pick me up to the ceiling," and for fun I lifted him up high briefly. Then, for weeks afterward, almost every time I was with the three-year-olds as they got ready for naptime, Travis would say, "Pick me up to the ceiling." It became a well-liked ritual for Travis and his friend Brent, who took his nap nearby. Sometimes, Katie and Ellen would ask me to pick them up, as well. This pattern seemed to be a valued symbol of our good relationship to them, and not repeating the pattern was seen as a dangerous disruption of the relationship. Because repeated patterns of interaction were key for children in relationship development—especially with adults, but with other children, too—it was important to avoid the adult tendency to get bored or impatient with them.

During my observations, repetition of patterns reduced children's uncertainty in interactions, and initiating a familiar pattern then became a way for a child to assert some control over an interaction. A familiar pattern promoted more eye contact, laughter, and a willingness to engage in more complex interactions. Such acts would form a basis for developing further relationships, in which new rituals and routines would spontaneously develop. To effectively facilitate communication among preschool children, some structure or routine needs establishing, and adults should then tolerate, understand, and even appreciate a child's relentless repetition of phrases, questions, or interaction games. Young children expect a repeated, comfortable pattern to become well established before they move on to more complex or alternative communication strategies.

3

Managing Changing Relationships

Most of my observations at the center related to how the children formed, developed, managed, and ended relationships. Four- and five-year-olds took relationship management strategies very seriously, yet they were implemented at a breakneck pace by adult standards. The children's relationships with one another seemed, on the whole, rather fleeting. Friendship and closeness seemed to depend on whim, the children's mood at the time, and the activity each was involved in. Sometimes, the toys that each wanted to play with would influence the closeness of a relationship. Common interests of some sort spurred the development of relationships even at age three or four. The basic personal needs of control, inclusion, and affection (generally in that order) seemed to provoke stronger relationships with whomever was present to meet those needs. The children also experimented with different relationship-building or -ending strategies.

Relationships formed by the children served forthrightly to meet their essential external and interpersonal needs: someone to influence, someone to keep company with, and someone to like them or show approval to them. Even more instrumental needs, like getting to play with another's fun toy, could easily spark a relationship. Children around age five focused most on the instrumental benefits of relationships, but showed signs of learning that friendship could be more permanent (Rawlins 1992). As children interacted with one another, verbal routines or rituals developed, serving as markers of an ongoing relationship (Ervin-Tripp and Mitchell-Kernan 1977). These comforting rituals were added to as the children experimented with a variety of strategies to both "get into relationships" and get what they wanted. Many started to sense that adapting to and being kind to another would fulfill many of those needs over the longer term. Closer relationships would result in the recurring presence of a trusted playmate, and regular, comfortable interaction with a peer. Yet children at ages four and five took a while to learn this, and most of their relationships, along with their strategies for managing them, lasted mere minutes or hours.

As I continued to observe, however, I did notice that most children had one or two friends in the classroom who would be constant over several weeks or months. They also viewed their relationships with their teachers as long-term and important. They were much more likely to tell their teacher that they loved her, for instance, than to say this to a child friend. Many children developed continued affection toward me, which also illustrated how important a relationship with an adult/teacher was for them. Clearly, though, the adults needed to work to sustain such relationships. There had to be continued interaction, demonstrating concern for the child, for that child to reciprocate by initiating interaction to keep the relationship strong. Teachers stressed the need to greet the children in the morning, when they typically entered the classroom at least somewhat quiet and hesitant. Most interaction was initiated by the adults at first in a relationship, until a certain point of comfort and involvement in the relationship on the part of the child was reached. This point was evident when the children would eagerly approach a teacher or other adult to talk or to hug her when they saw her.

CHANGING ALLIANCES

During my first weeks at the center, I watched the shifting alliances that developed between the children as friendships evolved and changed daily. One day, two or three children were playing together and "defending" one another against other children; and the next day they had split into new groupings. They would chase each other around the playground, and some would run *with* one another, while others would run *after* one another. One morning, Andrew and Chris built "motorcycles" out of big blocks out on the playground. They chased away Michael, Greg, and Justin, but they let John come near and interact and play with them. They learned to trust some children not to take blocks away from them or knock their creations down, while other children had not earned their trust. As the children got to know and trust me, they would by turns want to chase me and then to defend me against other children who wanted to chase me. As Yolanda told me one day, "Tell me if any of the kids chase you, and I'll come and fight them." On another day, Teresa and Max were "defending" me against Chris and Greg, sometimes too roughly. Max pushed Greg down on the ground once, when Greg was trying to "get" me. I had to tell Max that was mean and too rough. But the children took their games—and the relational indicators behind them—quite seriously. A few days later I observed Andrew playing on the playground when Chris ran over to him. "Andrew! Andrew!" Chris said breathlessly and urgently. "Will you help us fight William?"

Michael ran up behind Chris and said, "Andrew, will you help us fight Chris?" Andrew was in high demand by two factions, it seemed. Fortunately, these "fights" were playful chases, for the most part, not actual physical punching or hitting, which would have been stopped by an adult. Andrew continued playing where he was, and told them, "I'm building a fire."

"Come on, Andrew!" urged Chris.

"Just a minute," said Andrew, putting him off. "I've got to get this." He added some more sticks to his pile. Andrew did eventually go over to the "fight" where the boys were chasing each other, but I never did find out for sure which side he "fought" on.

Inside, as the children moved from circle time on the floor to washing their hands and sitting at the lunch tables, pairs and threesomes would form. "Let's sit over here," one girl said to another. "Sit by me!" said one boy to another, who did so. Some of these pairings would recur over days and weeks, but many were quite changeable. I observed another pair form outside one day. Mark gave Brian a bead necklace that other children had thrown over the fence, and this gesture led them to play as a pair most of that day. Back inside, they sat together at lunch.

LONG-TERM FRIENDSHIPS

With friendship among four-year-olds primarily related to playing together or sitting together, friendships could change hourly. One morning Brian and Dexter seemed to be playing near each other but separately. If one took a toy the other was building with, the other would yell, but as time went on they learned that they could trust one another. Then, one boy would say something and laugh, and the other boy would do the same. One could not tell if the friendship was temporary and happenstance or long-term just by observing this incident. However, most children did settle on one or two other children with whom they would most often play. Children also developed hierarchies of important relationships, as evident in studies of older children (Parker 1986; Parker and Asher 1993). Even at age four or five an initial social structure would form. It was highly malleable, however, from day to day. I observed Alex and Chris play together regularly for days, but then, over the next couple of weeks, Alex became more interested in playing with Laura and Gina. When those girls were around, Alex was usually playing with them, and Chris wandered around, doing his own thing for the most part. Yet one morning when neither Laura nor Gina was there, Alex and Chris were fast friends again, playing together like nothing had changed. For Alex, nothing had; he had just moved to his second or third choice of playmates. For Chris, it must have been nice to have a steady companion once again! I observed this active hierarchy with several sets of children; a friend would be spurned so that a child could play with more desired others, but then when the new friends were not around, the old friend would regain first-place status.

During my first year at the center, Luke and Justin had become constant friends, especially since they both loved to build with blocks. In many other ways, they were opposites. Luke was quiet with a cooperative disposition, though he could be controlling at times. Justin was usually noisy and active, and often disobedient. They had their disagreements, as I observed one day when outside they began fighting fiercely about something. They were kicking and spitting, and Ms. Stacey had them both sit down for a while. Justin cried and Luke looked very angry. Yet, not long after both were allowed to go play again, they were swinging on the tire swing together. As the children walked to the other playground, Luke ran over to Justin. "Come on, partner," he said, taking Justin's hand. Each would look for the other to sit next to at snack time and lunchtime, as well as during circle time on the floor. Opposites they may have been in many ways, but the friendship lasted.

Shaun and Paul were two other four-year-olds who became friends. They would play together every day, and seemed to enjoy one another's company. What struck me about their relationship once again was how opposite they were in temperament: Paul was tightly wired and had a fierce temper, while Shaun was very quiet and easygoing. Yet they often played happily together, and each seemed to supply something the other needed. Shaun provided calmness and equanimity, while Paul gave assertiveness and energy. They seemed to implicitly trust one another, too; this trust took some time to build. Even though some other children were wary of Paul due to his temper, Shaun could look past it and see Paul as his friend.

TESTING CONTROL WITHIN FRIENDSHIP

Friendships were tested many times involving issues of control. Commands are one of the most noted language forms used by young children (Ochs and Schieffelin 1983). The preschoolers I observed focused so much on the momentary instrumental gain that they would fail to consider the unequal relationship implications of continual commands. The desire for control was clearly central in many children's communication, and as long as another was willing to subordinate him- or herself to a child's mandates, the relationship would work. Often, though, when one party tired of following orders and the other realized things would no longer go his or her way in the interaction, each would head off to somewhere else, and the relationship would end for the present. Or, each would test the other to see how far the other could be pushed verbally. When the children both found a way to account for or accommodate the other, the relationship could be strengthened through such testing.

During my second year at the center, I noticed that Alex and Michael had become friends over the span of two weeks. They both liked to build with blocks or LEGOs, and they often played together. Once, when Alex moved out of the block area, Michael went over and grabbed his arm, saying, "Come back in the block area." Alex went back. At times, Michael would compete with Alex over blocks and puzzles, seeing how much Alex would allow Michael to manipulate him. Alex seemed to like the relationship enough that he would often go along with Michael. But one morning when Michael asked to see a toy that Alex had, Alex got rough, pushing him away.

"I hate you," responded Michael. "I'm not your friend." Then, reinforcing his message, Michael walked away to wash his hands for snack. Alex followed Michael and washed his hands at the sink next to him. As Michael was reaching for a paper towel, Alex pushed him, trying to get one, too.

"Stop it!" asserted Michael. "He's pushing me!" he appealed to a nearby teacher.

"Alex, wait your turn," said a nearby Ms. Gwen. "Michael was in front of you."

Michael walked over to the table and sat down to eat. Alex followed and sat down next to him.

"I'm not your friend," insisted Michael. Yet, as they sat together, they gradually started talking and laughing with one another again. Their friendship resumed, with a stormy test of it passed. One week later, however, I noted that their friendship was less close. Michael was building spiders with Brent out of some construction toys, and Alex wanted to join them. Alex started taking some pieces lying on the table to build with, and Michael said, "No! That's mine!"

"Hey, give that back!" added Brent immediately. Finally, Alex found some pieces to build with that neither boy had claimed, and was trying to say something to Brent when some spit inadvertently came out as he was talking.

"Stop spitting on me!"

"I *didn't* spit on you," Alex quickly tried to explain. "I was trying to talk and some spit came out." He saw Brent move off and head for the teacher.

"I didn't," said Alex more desperately. "I was trying to talk and some spit came out!"

"Ms. Stephanie, Alex spit on me," Brent said to the teacher.

"Alex, move away from that table now. Move away," said Ms. Stephanie forcefully.

Alex moved away, crying hard and protesting. I had the impression that Alex had spat on people in the past, because his explanation was given no credence by the other children or the teacher. Ms. Stephanie took Alex aside and talked to him about needing to *talk* to people, rather than spitting or screaming. After that incident, Alex and Michael did not act as close friends very often.

The strength of relationships could depend on the amount of control each party perceived, as demonstrated one fall morning as the children colored over leaves to make the outlines show up on paper. Ms. Stephanie stapled several such pages together to make each child a little booklet. Since Michael had arrived first, he finished the first one. "Look, I got a leaf book," he said delightedly to me and several other children.

As the other children finished theirs, they would all head over to Michael and say, "See, Michael; I have a leaf book, too!" Michael seemed to be enjoying all of this popularity. He had been playing with Brent that morning, but now, when Brent too came over to show Michael his leaf book, Michael walked away.

"Michael," said Brent. "Wanna look at my book?"

Michael kept walking away.

"Look at my book," insisted Brent.

"No," said Michael, still walking away.

"You said you were my friend," said a disappointed Brent.

"Not anymore," said Michael, who then joined Ivan in the block area. Ivan had recently arrived and immediately sought out Michael as a playmate, and now Michael seemed to think he did not need Brent anymore. But Brent stayed in the block area and played with the other two for a while, and became an accepted part of their group. Michael had become aware that Brent was more desperate for friendship than Michael was, and so Michael could manipulate Brent. Several days later, I passed by Brent on the playground, and he complained that Michael would not be his friend. But after a while, Michael accepted him again. Michael usually had other boys wanting to be his friend, while Brent was much more dependent on Michael. I would observe Michael take advantage of this power in the relationship. He started regularly to say variations of "If you don't build ships with me, I won't be your friend anymore." This threat would generally work with Brent.

One week after the leaf book incident, Michael sat at a table and picked up a LEGO toy that Brent had built and started adding to it. Brent had moved off to see what was going on in the block area. Brent came back over and said to Michael, "What are you doing with that?"

"He's adding things on to it," I interjected after a short silence. I hoped to avoid the argument Brent might make that the LEGO toy was "his," since he had left it and walked away from the area. That meant that other children could play with it if they wanted to, a commonly enforced classroom rule.

"Yeah," agreed Michael. "I'm putting more stuff on for you."

Apparently satisfied, Brent went back over to play in the block area.

After Brent had gone, Michael confided in me. "I'm really *not*," he told me. Michael clearly had followed my lead to deceive Brent and get rid of him. I felt a little guilty for helping with such manipulation, but I also felt some admiration for such sophisticated relationship management from a four-year-old. Some did learn that art quickly.

One Monday I noticed Felicia outside, standing in front of a line of sitting girls. The appearance of a teacher in front of students was borne out; they were indeed playing school. Felicia, Gina, and Brittney played together happily, it seemed, until Lisa arrived. She apparently instigated rebellion, as I saw Felicia go to the other side of the playground and sit sulking for a while. During the outside snack time, Felicia finally came back over at Ms. Teresa's urging and got her snack. She sat on the sidewalk beside Lisa. "I'm not your friend," insisted Lisa.

"Why not?" asked a meek Felicia.

"Because you always have to be the boss," explained Lisa.

"Uh-uh, Gina was the boss," said Felicia.

"I'm not your friend," insisted Lisa.

"No one will be my friend," said Felicia, slowly and morosely. Then she went to get more of the day's snack and sat at the other end of the sidewalk. After a little while, her time served in the "doghouse" seemed to have ended, as I observed her playing with Gina, Brittney, and Lisa again. Felicia had clearly been given a lesson on how not to be so bossy! No one person would be allowed too much control in the four girls' relationships.

Still, control was key to a healthy relationship. Nasser was one four-year-old who took relationship control seriously. He had arrived at the class one morning while his steady friend, Nick, was coloring an airplane for his sister. Nasser wandered around alone for a while, but apparently expected Nick to join him. When Nick continued to color, Nasser suddenly walked over and said, "So you don't wanna play with me. I'll just go somewhere else." This seemed to come out of the blue, since Nasser had just arrived and I had not observed any interaction between the two boys yet that day.

"I have to color an airplane for my sister, if that's all right with you," Nick snapped back at him.

"You don't have to do it; you could do it at home," Nasser said impatiently. He seemed genuinely miffed that Nick had not automatically begun doing something with him when he arrived. Nasser moved off, but later in the day they were playing together once again. Similar interests were not the only sparks for a relationship, it seemed, but relationships also required some ability to think alike, to do something cooperatively, or to share meaning in some way.

Some weeks later, Chris and Nick were in the block area, and Timothy was also in there, giving it the maximum of three children. Nasser approached the area, clearly wanting to play with Nick. "Hey Nick! Commere," said Nasser.

"You always want Nick to play with you," noted Chris. "How about today you let him play with us?"

Nasser did not quite know what to say to this unexpected commentary on their relationship, and he moved away and went over to the quiet corner for a while. When he noticed Timothy leaving the block area, he ran over and got in it and played with Chris and Nick for a while.

Several weeks later, Nasser had developed a closer relationship with Chris. They would often play together, especially outside, but it often turned into wrestling one another or one taking a ball away from the other. Nasser made Chris cry at times, but Chris would return within a few minutes to play with Nasser. Nasser could hit and be aggressive; he would take slights personally and respond with violence. Still, he maintained the loyalty of Nick and Chris, who would regularly play with him.

Girls would test control within their relationships also. In Gina and Michelle's ongoing relationship Gina usually decided what to play and who would play what role. Michelle was often happy to go along with her, but one morning Michelle had had enough. "No, I don't wanna play that," I heard Michelle say in response to one of Gina's suggestions.

"Why—why won't you be my friend?" asked Gina, confused.

"No," said Michelle.

"But I wanna be your friend; why won't you be my friend?" asked Gina.

"Leave me alone!" said Michelle. "Just leave me alone." Michelle was being unusually assertive, and Gina was distressed by this sudden rebellion on the part of her normally cooperative friend. Gina moved away and sat by the wall under the window, quietly miffed, not her usual active, chattering self. Eventually, Gina moved to another area to play, and she and Michelle avoided one another for a while. Most relationships had a balance of control, but Michelle had decided to change that balance, and Gina was not sure how to respond.

Fights and feuds could, at times, remain in effect over several days. Brian had come in one morning, and was wandering about the classroom alone, while Nick and Chris were playing in the block area. Brian joined them in the block area and was soon sitting there crying. Ms. Stephanie asked him what was wrong, and Brian said that Nick had hit him.

"Nick," said Ms. Stephanie.

"We don't *want* him in here," said Nick angrily.

"Nick, come over here," said Ms. Stephanie.

"We don't *want* him in here!" Nick stressed, unusually vocally and violently for him.

"Sit down," said Ms. Stephanie. "Blocks are not for hitting. Blocks hurt." Nick sat in time-out for a while and eventually got distracted, along with Chris and Brian, by the class rainy-day activities of carving a pumpkin and making play-dough. Ms. Tiffany initiated a game of ring-around-the-rosy in the circle area. Chris and Nick happily joined in at first, but when Brian sought to join the circle, and Ms. Stephanie said, "Let Brian have a spot," Chris said, "Then I don't want to play," and sat down in a chair.

"I don't want to play either," said Nick, also sitting down. This protest continued a couple of rounds, with Chris refusing to play when Brian was let into the circle. We then all played once without Nick, Chris, or Brian, who had given up in frustration.

Then Ms. Stephanie invited Brian back, and said, "This time Nick will stay in the circle. I know your mom would like to see you participating." Eventually, tired of sitting alone, even Chris joined the circle and appeared to have some fun.

Later, I heard Brian asking Neil and Chris, "Just one more chance? Please?"

"You do bad things," Nick said, as he and Chris once again moved away. This particular conflict took days to dissolve, making it unusually intense for four-year-olds.

LOVE-HATE RELATIONSHIPS

During the same few months, Brent and Todd developed an interesting relationship. Todd would often try to play with Brent or say something to him, and Brent would take the comments as forms of mean teasing. Brent's usual response was to hit or "strangle" Todd. This would make Todd cry at times, but at other times it seemed like Todd was provoking Brent purposefully. Even after one or the other would cry, Todd would again be near to or playing with Brent. Todd seemed to be the one who kept returning for more interaction—either he felt like he had some power over Brent and was enjoying it, or he wanted some attention and was trying to be his friend. Probably, elements of both motivations were involved.

Gradually, as Brent began to hit and "strangle" other children as well as Todd to get his way, he lost their trust. When Timothy brought some toy trucks to school, for instance, he would not share them with Brent, but offered to share them with Tyler and Michael when they arrived. Brent seemed to become more of a loner who sought attention or affection in undesirable ways. Thus, his continued pestering of Todd made more sense. He would irritate Todd, but then Todd would tolerate him and play with him at intervals. Todd found he had more influence with Brent than any other child, and thus Brent became his "best friend." I got the impression Brent found Todd more of a nuisance than a friend, but still Brent welcomed the attention, so that he too would have a friend.

FRIENDSHIP AS COMMODITY

For preschool children, friendship was viewed as a limited and valuable commodity. A friendship was formed when children were willing to play together and trust each other. That relationship was viewed by most children as fragile and endangered by the intrusion of another person, especially when the intruder was shown friendly attention. Such attention would create questions like, "Are you my friend?" or "Are you his friend?"

Nick, Lance, and Chris were playing in the home living area for quite a while one morning. They were preparing an extensive meal using the toy food, pans, plates, and cups. They had the table well and neatly laid out. Chris, as he often did, was pretending to be a dog. The three boys played together an unusually long time that morning, but I noticed that at intervals Chris would drift off over to the block area, where Michelle and Rachel were playing together, building a zoo. At one point, when Chris was with the girls, Nick asked: "Chris, are you our friend?" Chris nodded briefly.

"Are you our friend?" Nick asked again, checking to make sure. Chris nodded more forcefully.

"Well, if you're our friend you need to play with us," Nick explained.

"I'm playing in here right now," Chris said quietly. He was usually quite soft-spoken, so he was in character. He clearly did not want to reject Nick, but was quite involved with the girls in the block area, surrounded by painstakingly constructed stacks of blocks.

"For a little while?" asked Nick, helping him manage the situation without rejecting anyone.

Chris nodded briefly.

"Are you my friend?" asked Nick, still seeking reassurance.

"Yeah," said Chris, nodding.

"And Travis?" asked Nick, though he was not present that day.

"Yeah," said Chris, nodding. "And I'm her friend, and her . . ." and he pointed at Michelle and Rachel with him in the block area.

"I'm their friend, too; I have *lots* of friends," said Nick, moving back into the home living area with Lance. Chris resumed play with the girls in the block area. This was an unusually extensive relationship check, and clearly the norm of playing with your friends was being renegotiated, as both boys realized that one could be friends with a person one was not with at the moment, and one could have multiple friends. With the norms renegotiated, they happily resumed play separately. Even outside, these cliques maintained themselves, with Nick and Lance playing together and Michelle and Rachel playing together, and Chris alternating between them.

Chris and Nick's conversation was a noteworthy accomplishment of abstract thinking, since normally four- and five-year-olds would be quite concretely possessive of relationships. Once they perceived one, they did not want it disrupted. Jacob and Robert were in the block area building a spaceship together one morning. "Come help me straighten out my side," asked Jacob.

"I can't," said Robert, busy in his own rectangle he had made of blocks.

"Yes you *can*, Robert," insisted Jacob, irritated.

"I straightened up my own side," said Robert. They continued to play together with the blocks for a while. Then Nick came over and showed them bracelets he had built with plastic toys around his arms.

Robert, looking alarmed, said, "Jacob's playing with *me!*"

"Look at my super-muscles," said Nick to Jacob.

Jacob finally looked at Nick and grinned, but then went over to get more blocks.

"Jacob's playing with *me!*" insisted Robert again. Even after Nick had moved off, as Jacob came nearer with some blocks, Robert asked him, "Aren't you gonna play with me?"

"Yes," reassured Jacob, and they continued to play together until outside time.

Another morning, Kayla found her friendships threatened by being laughed at when she was playing with Sarah and Tracy. As they were walking across the classroom floor, Kayla lost her balance and fell on her behind. Tracy laughed. Kayla looked hurt, and said, "I'm gonna tell on you!" Then she said, "Ms. Stephanie, Tracy laughed at me when I fell."

As Ms. Stephanie moved back over to the bulletin board to continue working on it, she said as an aside to Tracy, who was by then sitting at the art table, "Tracy, when someone falls you see if they're all right. Tracy, if someone falls, check if they're OK."

Tracy looked back, rather sheepishly. She had damaged the fabric of trust that backed up the children's friendships. Kayla joined Hannah, Jim, and Allison in the block area, and played comfortably with them for a while. Kayla was back playing with Sarah and Tracy the next day, however, so the damage to the relationship was temporary. The children seemed to lack a sense of permanence in most of their peer relationships, as I would hear them check with one another, sometimes daily: "Are you my friend?" or "Are you still my friend?" Friendships were viewed as temporary and changeable. Conditions were also readily placed on friendship: "If you're not my friend, you can't come to my house to see my Batman," said Timothy to a companion. The other boy proceeded to play with Timothy and be his friend, accepting friendship almost as a trade for a valuable commodity.

Children could feel betrayed, however, when what they thought was a long-term relationship turned out not to be. I observed outside one day that Travis and Carl were playing together, and sat together on the tire swing. Suddenly, Brian went over and started telling Travis in no uncertain terms, "I'm not your friend anymore! I won't be your friend anymore because you're playing with Carl. . . . I'm not your friend anymore, Travis. I won't be your friend 'cause you're with *him!*" He kept repeating this, as Carl and Travis at first did not seem sure how to respond to his verbal assault. Carl had consistently rejected Brian, and the two boys did not like one another, so he was clearly furious that his earlier playmate Travis was now playing with Carl.

I interrupted with, "You know what? I'm Travis's friend, and Carl's friend, but I'm Brian's friend, too."

"You're—you're everybody's friend," said Carl, happy about that fact but also making the point that my friendship was beside the point in this dispute.

My idea of multiple friends was not welcomed by him. Brian was happy when Carl finally moved off the tire swing to another swing, and then Travis made some room for Brian on the swing. They swung together happily for a while. I thought it noteworthy that, over time, Brian and Carl maintained a poor relationship. Being "enemies" was usually more fleeting than being friends, but Carl and Brian maintained their animosity for weeks. I was not sure of the original cause, but Brian did have a tough time mastering friend-ships and refraining from violence.

While social hierarchies and ongoing friendships were abstract concepts, four- and five-year-olds had some understanding of them and could perceive how everyone fit into the social structure. Outside, I heard Mary say to Amy, who seldom played with the other girls, "Since you have no friends, you can be my friend," and she took Amy's hand and helped her join the girls' play group. "How blunt, but how generous at the same time," I thought. Amy was relatively new to the center and had not developed any longer-term rela-tionships with other children yet.

TRYING OUT ROMANTIC RELATIONSHIPS

Several mornings in a row, I noticed Timothy and Laura spending a lot of time together. This caught my eye because it was rare for a boy and girl to be reg-ular playmates. Most of one morning, Timothy and Laura sat together in the book area. At times they would look at a book together, but otherwise they would sit and watch things going on in the classroom. A couple of times, they asked me in to read a book with them. Laura would sit with her arm around Timothy and lean on him. I was struck by how, at four years old, they were acting like two teenagers in love. They seemed to be a little overwhelmed by this new relationship and all the time they were spending with one another. Their relationship was especially unique among four-year-olds for three rea-sons: First, it was durable—it continued not only throughout one day, but over several days. Second, it was exclusive—the two always wanted to stay near each other, even if they were not playing together. Neither ever "took a break" from the relationship for any significant length of time to play with other children. Most children would do this, even if they eventually wound up playing with their best friend again. Third and finally, their relationship was totally person oriented, not activity oriented. Timothy and Laura were al-ways together, and what they were doing seemed secondary to them.

This relationship was too intense for four-year-olds to sustain, and after Tim-othy and Laura seemed inseparable for two weeks, their "romance" began to cool. Gina had noticed all of the attention Timothy had given Laura. So one Mon-day when Gina arrived, she began playing with Timothy, and they played to-gether, acting silly much of the time, for most of that morning. Shortly after Laura arrived, I noticed her sitting sadly by herself, while Timothy happily played with Gina. Timothy and Gina actively played; there was no quiet sitting together with those two like with Timothy and Laura. Laura still made it a point to sit by Timothy several times that day, and he accepted her presence. There had been no major "break," it seemed; the relationship had just grown more distant.

The "break-up" between Timothy and Laura became more evident as the week went on, and Timothy spent most of his time playing active games with Gina. She clearly was his new "girlfriend," but Laura was still following Timothy around, and sitting near him, and claiming he was her "boyfriend." Timothy seemed to like this incipient competition for him, and I could almost see his head swelling. He looked uncomfortable with Laura's continued attentions, seeming to prefer the more active play with Gina, but I never saw him openly discourage Laura. She sat next to him at circle time and Timothy accepted that. A few moments later, as the children were gathering in the circle area, I noticed Kayla sitting on the other side of Timothy and giving him a big hug. He had become a "ladies' man" at age four! As the day's story was read Timothy would move closer to one girl, see the other follow him, and then move back again, clearly more interested in this testing activity than in the story. As the days passed into weeks, however, as with so many of these "relational fads" among four-year-olds, these boyfriend-girlfriend-like relationships faded into the "normal" background of flexible friendships. Most of the time, the children's closest recurring friends were of their own gender. Timothy and his former "girlfriends" were no exception. However, gender lines were crossed regularly as friendships were struck up and faded away.

Other children also tested the waters of boyfriend-girlfriend relationships. I noticed Gina and Jim playing together a lot one day. "She's my wife," Jim told me later, referring to Gina. He said the same thing to Alex and Laura later when they were talking to Gina. Sure enough, Gina and Jim stayed together playing in the block area most of the morning, and then rode tricycles together outside. At lunchtime, other girls seemed to want that kind of relational pairing, as Bailey announced to her lunch table, "I'm gonna marry David."

"And I'm gonna marry Jim," said Gina.

Bailey had an idea, and turned to David, saying, "Hey, when we grow up, I'll meet you, and I'll say, 'I think you're the David I knew.'"

"Yeah, you'll know me when we grow up, won't you?" said David.

"Yeah, and I'll ask you to marry me and we'll get married," said Bailey.

Gina was pondering this, and said, "But we'll be—we'll be different when we grow up, right? But—but we'll have the same hair. Won't we?" Gina put her hand to her head.

"Yeah," said David. Then Gina said David had asked her not to marry Jim when she grew up. David was happy that Bailey was going to marry him, but seemed jealous of Jim and Gina's longer-term relationship. I was rather surprised by the four-year-olds' sophisticated planning and perception of a distant future.

"If you will marry Bailey when you grow up, then why can't Jim marry Gina when he grows up?" I asked David.

"Well, OK," said David, seeing the inconsistency. "But they can't always be married to each other," he replied. David and Jim often played together, and I realized that David probably saw Gina as competition and an obstacle to his own friendship with Jim.

Outside, Mark got angry when Elena said, "I don't love you," after Mark had told her, "I love you." Mark was furious at this violation of expectations. "You've *got* to love me," he insisted.

"No, she loves *me*," said Nick. He and Elena started moving away, and Mark picked up some gravel and held it threateningly. Nick and Elena started moving faster, and Mark chose not to throw the gravel. But he took Elena's response quite seriously; I had never seen him so angry. How young, I thought, to have one's love unreciprocated.

Almost one year later, a different set of children were discussing marriage at the lunch table. "I'll be nice to you. . . . Will you?" I heard Nick ask Tiffany. "I'll be nice to you if you marry me," said Nick earnestly.

Tiffany sat with her arms crossed like an *X* in front of her, shaking her head. Both children seemed quite serious, yet it was hard to gauge how seriously they really took such discussions. The discussions clearly were meaningful enough that saying one would marry someone was an indicator of liking and a strong relationship. These "marriages" were quite temporary, though, lasting several days at most. More often, they lasted a few minutes to a few hours.

At times, two children developed a consistent relationship that persisted over weeks as they were together at the center. Usually, boys were closest friends with boys and girls with girls, but occasionally a mixed-gender friendship would form. Michelle and Chris developed such a close, ongoing relationship. Over several weeks, inside and outside, they would move from area to area together, build things together, and play games together. One day they worked so hard at cleaning a counter that Ms. Teresa was surprised at the stains they rubbed off. When at times they got busy with something separately, they did not stay apart for very long. Michelle often played with Rachel, her former best friend, during such times. Those two had long been close, playing together often, but after Michelle and Chris struck up their friendship I noticed Rachel playing alone more often. Neither girl seemed upset about this change, and I had noticed no feud, but just an evolution in their relationship to give one another more space while Michelle was closer to Chris. Often, Rachel would join Michelle and Chris in play, and they would form a threesome. Still, Michelle and Chris had the closest relationship among the three for many weeks.

A relationship persisted for weeks between four-year-olds Tanya and Travis. The moment Travis would arrive at the classroom, Tanya would take his hand. "Let's go see that," or "Let's go over in the block area," Tanya would say. They would play together for most of each morning. When given the opportunity to pick another child to wash up for lunch next, Travis acknowledged this relationship by picking Tanya. One morning, Travis was standing by a table watching Ms. Stephanie write the children's names on hearts. Tanya came into the classroom with her mother, and they went over to the table.

"Hi, Tanya!" said Travis.

No response, as Tanya held her mother's hand.

"Hi, Tanya!" Travis said again.

This time, Tanya smiled at him and waved shyly. Soon, I noticed Travis hugging Tanya, and I heard Ms. Stephanie say, "We keep our lips to ourselves; remember, we can hug, but we keep our lips to ourselves. That's the rule." Travis hugged Tanya a few more times. Over several weeks, their relationship continued; they would sit together or play together often, but not always. They could each go off on their own or with other children to do other things, but each retained the other's trust as a guaranteed steady friend. Later, I noticed Travis again standing by the art table, watching Ms. Evie this time. He told her he had eleven girlfriends. She wondered how he could do that and said that he might get in trouble if they found out.

"I won't tell them," he said. "I won't tell Tanya." Travis was clearly modeling his behavior on some ladies' man type. He had told me before that he had multiple girlfriends, and he had given me the "thumbs up" sign with a wink. It was a little shocking, but funny, coming from a four-year-old. He clearly did value his relationship with Tanya, though.

Brian and Amy more briefly followed the same pattern. I was surprised one day on the playground, as the children were walking to the gate, to see them holding hands. They *had* been playing with one another, but clearly this was a sign of something more than happenstance. They held hands all the way inside, and sat next to one another in the circle area. When Amy was allowed to pick someone to go wash up, she picked Brian. They then sat next to one another at lunch. They made an unusual pair—Amy so quiet and well behaved, and Brian more of a "loose cannon." The other children did not trust Brian, due to his past tendency to hit or knock things down, and Amy had some trouble fitting in because she was so shy. Brian looked and acted happier that morning, and I did not observe him creating any trouble at all. Amy received persistent attention from another child she could interact with; the two children seemed to have a positive impact on one another. I noticed that they no longer played together outside after a few days, and at lunch time Brian did not want to sit in either of two chairs that were empty—one next to Amy, and the other next to Timothy, usually a good friend. "I don't want to sit there," Brian told me after I walked with him to the chair next to Amy. He sat next to Timothy, but lunch for Brian that day quickly degenerated into a name-calling match with Timothy. "Timothy called me a baby!" Brian said.

"Well, do you believe him?" I asked.

"No," said Brian.

"Then don't listen to him," I said. This was the best advice I could give on the spur of the moment, but not too useful for dealing with Brian's feelings of anger and betrayal.

Still angry, Brian called Timothy another name, and they started lightly hitting one another. Ms. Stephanie, observing this, separated the two and put Timothy at a table by himself, as he had earlier gotten in trouble for hitting another boy. "I *will* send a note home," admonished Ms. Stephanie sternly, reminding him of their earlier talk. I was sad to see Brian's happy relationship end and his reverting to more violent and unhappy behavior. Once again, he had trouble developing any longer-term relationships with any of the other children.

Amy would interact minimally with some of the other girls, but would more often be found playing by herself. Outside one day, she talked and pretended to be at a beauty parlor with Michelle and Tracy, who played together a lot. On this day, Michelle and Tracy proceeded to comb and style Amy's hair. Nearby, Chris told me he was cooking a hot bowl of soup. "It's not for you," he said.

"Oh. Who's it for?" I asked him.

"Amy. Me and Amy," he said. So Chris, too, had developed a relationship with Amy. When he saw Michelle and Tracy doing Amy's hair, he started growling like an animal and climbing over the girls on the climber.

"What's *wrong* with this boy?" asked an irritated Tracy. She and Michelle kept busy with Amy's hair, and eventually Chris climbed close enough that his boots were close to kicking them. "Hey, he might kick us," said Tracy.

"Come on," said Michelle, "come on," and the girls ran off over to a tree across the playground. Chris continued to walk back and forth on the climber after all the girls had left him. Brian started to get on the climber, as well.

"Get out of here, this is my home," grumped Chris to him. Brian climbed up anyway, and kept on following Chris around. Since Chris had lost Amy's company, he decided to accept Brian's, but he did not seem too happy about it.

The next morning, Chris was playing at a table with some toys and Michelle was playing at the table with him. Chris had brought a small action figure with a horse, and he let Michelle play with it, too. They played together happily for a while, but then I noticed Chris was trying to get Michelle to come with him to another area. "Let's go. . . . Are you coming? Are you coming?" he kept asking, and moved away on a mission with his horseman. Michelle stayed at the table, occupied with something else. At that moment, Rachel walked in.

"Rachel," said Michelle. "Rachel, will you be my friend and not be Chris's?"

Rachel did not answer, as she was trying to cram a big bag into her cubby. Then other things started to fall out.

"Oh, that won't stay," said Michelle, and moved over to help Rachel. They kept pushing the big bag into the cubby, only to have other things fall out. They laughed, and finally got all the stuff back into the cubby. They moved off together to play in the dramatic play area. They played together much of the morning. Meanwhile, Chris was so busy with his own toys that he was unaware that he had been conspired against and abandoned. Later, he let Timothy play with his toy, and he and Timothy played together much of the morning. Children would thus quickly replace one friend with another in a most practical way.

ADULT INTERVENTION IN FRIENDSHIP

With the children's relationships so changeable, I sought to stay out of the discussions of friendship, but I would make clear that I was always their friend, if I thought it was an appropriate time to say so. Indeed, several children seemed to use me as a back-up when they felt rejected by their peers. Kayla, for instance, felt dominated by several other girls in the classroom. After several months of volunteering I was outside one day with the four-year-olds' class when I noticed Kayla sitting on a tricycle and crying. Tanya, Sarah, and Tricia were walking away from her, plugging their ears, and Tricia was saying, "We don't wanna play over there; it's too noisy over there."

I walked over to the crying Kayla and said, "What's wrong?" kneeling by her.

"Tricia won't be my friend," said Kayla tearfully.

"Oh, that's too bad," I said.

"I will," put in Hannah, who had also walked over to see what was happening.

"Maybe you need to find another friend," I told the crying Kayla. "Hannah will be your friend. *I'm* always your friend."

Then Kayla snuggled into a hug, clearly needing comfort. Soon, Sarah came back over and also hugged Kayla. Still sobbing a little, Kayla said, "But Tanya won't be my friend."

"Aw, that's too bad; is she being kind of mean?" I asked.

Kayla nodded.

"Maybe you need to find someone who will be nicer to play with," I suggested. By this time, Tanya had also come over, and was saying she would be Kayla's friend also. Tanya said that Kayla had taken a tricycle that she had been using, and had only gotten off of for a minute.

Playing the mediator, I said, "Maybe Kayla just took a tricycle she thought was free, that no one was using. You think that's what happened?"

Kayla nodded, as did Tanya. Kayla, Sarah, and Tricia started to play together again, and after observing this Tanya evidently decided the feud was not worth maintaining, because she joined back in the game, too. They soon all moved off together to another area of the playground.

One day the next month, Nick was having so much fun playing in the block area that he would not leave the area, even after Lance and Timothy asked him to play with them. "I don't wanna play with you," said Nick.

Timothy clearly felt betrayed. He soon came over to tell me sadly, "Nick won't be my friend." At intervals, he went back to the block area, where Nick, Brian, and Cade continued to play for a long time. "Why won't you play with me?" Timothy asked Nick.

"I'm not your friend," said Nick.

"You can't come spend the night at my house *anymore!*" said an outraged Timothy. Soon, he became so frustrated he threw a pillow at Nick, and Nick went to tell Ms. Teresa. Timothy was asked to move away. The dispute continued as the children gathered on the floor to watch a movie. "I'll beat you up when we go outside," said Timothy to Nick when he still said "no" to being friends. "I have—no one's going to be my friend," said Timothy.

"I will," reminded Lance.

"Only Lance," said Timothy, still seeming to appeal to Nick. They stayed apart until lunchtime, when the group of boys all happened to be at the same table. When asked if he was Timothy's friend, Brian said "yes." Finally, after hearing this, Nick said "yes," too, and the testing of the relationship seemed to be over.

Several weeks later, the relationship was tested again. Timothy and Nick had been playing in the block area and most of the blocks were on the floor. Nick drifted over to the art table to draw. After a few moments, Timothy came over to the table. "Nick, you have to help clean up," he said. Nick continued to draw. "Nick, help me clean up," said Timothy.

"Lance needs to," said Nick.

"*You* were playing," said Timothy to Nick.

"Ask *Lance* to," Nick said impatiently.

Timothy went over and asked Lance to help him clean up, but Lance also refused and moved over to the art table, which was quite popular all of a sudden, with all six chairs now filled. Timothy also came back over to the art table. "Lance won't," he said. "If anyone won't help me clean up the block area, I won't be your friend ever again," added Timothy, sad and pouting.

No one said anything in response. I had been trying not to interfere, but now I said to him, "Why do you think no one will help you, Timothy?"

We both listened, but there still were no volunteers.

"If anyone will help me, I'll be their friend," said Timothy.

Silence. Finally, I said, "I'll help you, Timothy."

He looked very relieved and we walked over to the block area. "Will you help me clean all these up?" asked Timothy, as we looked at the blocks strewn all over the floor. I was a little taken aback, and I decided to be a little cantankerous.

"I don't think I want to," I said hesitantly, as if I were being tricked into doing lots of work I did not want a part of.

"It's too many!" Timothy said, almost tearfully. "I don't wanna pick all these up."

I could see his point. He had had help taking them all down and playing with them, but now nobody would help him clean them up. "You know what, Timothy?"

"What?"

"I don't want you to have to pick all these up, so I'll help you," I said.

He seemed very reassured and went to work cleaning them up with a will as I helped him. Timothy was extra affectionate toward me the rest of that day—I apparently had helped him out in a pinch when he was feeling abandoned and rejected. He and Nick did play together again, but not until much later that day.

GROWING RELATIONSHIPS WITH ME

I was often amazed at how some children, after only one day of my initiating interaction with them, would seek me out and treat our relationship as highly important. This would be followed by many attempts to do things with me. Several children were my friends practically from the first day, but it took some weeks before most children were comfortable initiating interaction with me. Then I would suddenly receive a clear indication that our relationship had moved closer. One memorable day early in the fall, with mostly newer, younger children in the classroom, the teachers took the four-year-olds outside and had them all choose a partner to hold hands with. We walked to a nearby intramural field, where the adults showed the four-year-olds how to play red rover. Then the children were allowed to just run around. This was unusual only because we were out on a fenced, grassy field that was much larger than the regular playground. "Wanna see how far I can run?" Alicia asked me.

"Sure," I said, and she ran far into the distance. The other children nearby also wanted to run far, but they wanted me to run with them. Most had gotten comfortable with me by then, so they wanted me to join their games. I felt like I was in some sort of dream—running with all of these children on a huge, open, newly mowed lawn. Some of the children started to run into me playfully, and others would grab my hand. A few, when I sat down for a rest, sat beside me, and one or two got into my lap. All of this was new for me with that bunch of children. Clearly the threshold to a closer relationship was crossed that day, as afterward the children were more familiar and comfortable with me, and desired more interaction with me.

Brandon was new to the class that semester, and I had never met him before. On my second day in his classroom, after circle time, the children were moving to different spots around the classroom to play. "What are you gonna play with?" Brandon asked me. I sat at a table with him for a while. Later, outside, he grabbed my hand and said, "Wanna go swing with me?" He had learned my name and wanted me as a companion already; within two weeks, the day we all ran around the intramural field, Brandon was one of the children who sat in my lap. I always felt a sense of mystery over the strong connection that children like Brandon were able to form with me, breaking through layers of social convention and relationship development to get close very quickly. One hallmark of my work with children was that their relationship with me was always genuinely felt and clearly expressed, regardless of how long the relationship took to develop. I pondered how crucial relationships are to us as people and how circuitously we adults form and test relationships. The children were learning relational strategies and testing them on one another, but when the four-year-olds found a relationship they liked, they would use all of their expressiveness to show it and keep it.

I noted that, while I had eased into a natural routine of relating to the children as an extra teacher or mentor during my days there, I would get explosions of affection—hugs or excited greetings—on certain days. After a day or two things would settle back into the normal routine for two weeks or so. My relationships with the children—both as a group and as individuals—seemed to develop in a cycle, growing by turns closer and more distant, with an overall evolution toward closeness. This tendency reflects Conville's (1991) helical model of relationships in constant cycles of change, with a distancing followed by a new sense of closeness. I observed this pattern repeatedly, and I soon abandoned my naive sense that relationships would hold steady or evolve in a smooth curve. Sparks of growth in my relationships with the children were followed by times of going about our own business at the center—appreciating one another, perhaps, but not making an extra effort to spend time with one another. Then, a new cycle of strengthening the relationship would begin, and I would notice one child or several children wanting me to sit or play with them more often.

As the months and years of volunteering passed by, I found myself chronicling again and again the growth of my relationships with various children. Such relationships became powerful for me; they held meaning in my own life, contributing to my own happiness and emotional balance. I had few delusions of the children remembering me after we passed out of each other's lives, but I became convinced that our relationships helped in the children's further development. Here was a male adult who was polite and listened to them, who would play with and interact with them, and who was kind and loved them. I would influence them and they would influence me, as we learned and relearned patience with each other's actions and perspectives, finding a balance of dependence and autonomy.

I noted a pattern of phases, listed below, that children and I would pass through as we got to know each other. Some children jumped very fast through several levels and became very close to me, while others passed through only the first one, two, or three before our relationship stabilized. It was difficult to predict which children would get to which level of relationship with me, except that boys more often than girls would get to the closest levels. The staff at the center often pointed out that I was one of the few male figures present there, and in some cases, in a particular child's life. Indeed, during some semesters I was the only male around at any given time. It therefore made sense that, over the years, more boys than girls were interested in relating to me, but there were quite a few girls who showed such an interest, too. The affection could be quite overwhelming at times, and yet I felt blessed.

These are the phases I observed a typical relationship pass through:

First, a child would realize that I was "safe" and he or she would interact normally with other children or teachers in my presence, but would not interact with me. I was still clearly regarded as a stranger or distant adult at this time.

Second, a child would find that interacting with me brought desired rewards. I would listen to, play with, or spend time near the child, and the child would clearly appreciate my initiating interaction with him or her. He or she would often employ nonverbal signals of this appreciation, such as smiling or moving near to me, but would seldom initiate interaction with me.

Third, a child would begin to initiate interaction with me during the course of the day. Usually this would take the form of requests, like "Would you do this puzzle with me?" or "Can you tie my shoe?" or a more commanding "Push me!" on the swing. Children at this level would not greet me, but once my interactions with other children and teachers began, they would feel comfortable talking to me.

Fourth, a child would regularly greet me when I came into the classroom or I was first seen. A child at this level would frequently ask for me to play a game with her or him, and there was usually a comfortable, repeated pattern of interaction she or he enjoyed and tried to initiate repeatedly. This could be a favorite game (several boys would ask me to play hide-and-go-seek every day), or a favorite role-playing activity (several girls would repeatedly tell me, "Pretend you're my daddy"). These children would expect focused attention from me each day.

Fifth, the child would move closer to me physically, often wanting to sit in my lap or beside me. This was often the most noticeable change toward a close relationship. It took me a while to distinguish the first four phases, but a child entering this phase would almost always surprise me with sudden affection. Children at this level were comfortable with asking for a back ride outside, which had become a recurring ritual.

At the sixth or "closest" level, the child would commonly run over for a hug upon seeing me, and give me some kind of effusive greeting. These children would hold my hand and expect me to spend a lot of time with them. Some could not understand that I needed to give attention to all the children and to the variety of activities in the classroom. These were the children who had clearly made their relationship with me a priority of their lives at the center. I might hear that they were asking about me on days I was not at the center, and I found I needed to strike a balance of giving them good attention and responding to their love without becoming their constant companion or personal teacher in the classroom.

Given enough time, it seemed, almost all three- or four-year-old children I interacted with would move up through these levels in our relationship. Most children moved up to level three with me, with quite a few in levels four and five, but each year a memorable few would reach level six. I would be dishonest to say that the growth of such relationships did not affect me, and that I remained the objective observer. I was part of the children's lives, and the teachers' lives, and they were part of mine. I would miss each child more depending on the level of relationship we had reached, and regarding those at levels five and six I found myself going through a grieving process when they moved out of the center and into school. I experienced firsthand the difficulty I had heard elementary school teachers describe—that of missing the children at the end of each school year—but I also learned that my life was much richer for those relationship experiences.

As the children were learning the tools and methods of managing relationships, I found I learned from them about the importance of relationships in life, including how easily we can take them for granted and the importance of being flexible and accepting change as not always bad for relationships. The constant and accelerated pace of change in relationships among children paralleled their high energy and activity levels (and may have seemed natural to them, since a day is a much larger percentage of their lifetime than an adult's). This gave their interactions a surface appearance of unpredictability and chaos, but underneath all of the activity, clear patterns and strategies recurred.

A child-development center's staff should allow for the swiftly changing phases of relationships among children, each of which may be a major event for the children. They begin at age five to show appreciation of long-term relationships, but for preschool children this appreciation is limited; they naturally focus on instrumental goals in relationships. At times, children need some space and time to be alone, while at other times they hover near other children, wanting to join in but unsure how to begin a new relationship (Rawlins 1992). Encouragement of communication with other children unstructured by adults will develop their relationship management skills as they seek ways to meet their own interpersonal needs. Even as children seem to move into and out of relationships willy-nilly, and fight regularly, they are experiencing meaningful relationships with one another as well as with consistent adults. In the process, many crucial communication strategies for relating are being tried; these will be detailed in the following chapters.

4

Are We Friends? Children's Statements, Proximity, and Touch

As we grow, we gradually learn that friendship is valuable, and one should treasure it, work for it, and not give up on or disregard friends on a whim. Before children pass into a stage in which they are capable of such abstract reasoning, however, friendship is clearly viewed as valuable and desirable, but also as a commodity that can be traded for other desirable goods or actions. My observations revealed that the instrumental goals of the friendship dialectic were clearly stressed over simple affection for another child (Rawlins 1992). Five-year-old children would enter relationships initially only for blatantly self-centered motives: to get control, to be included in a group, or to get access to a desired toy or game. At the same time, friendship was given extra value in children's interactions. Open statements negotiating friendship took place among the children regularly. Through such negotiations, children realized that friendships did not have to be tied to the activity of the moment—they could be resumed later and even continue in the face of separation, while each child focused on a different activity. As children became more sophisticated users of verbal symbols to understand and structure relationships, they also became more creative and cognizant of the social order of the classroom (Cicourel 1974). Thus, friendship negotiations often took on extra urgency and importance.

More subtle, highly developed channels were also available through which preschool children could make statements about friendship. Children would use territory or proximity to symbolize and manipulate the social order, especially to show who was liked and disliked. Every culture establishes territories and acceptable uses of personal space, and preschool children's society was no different (Hall 1959). Areas of the classroom designated for convenience for a limited number of children were used by the children to manage relationships: "You can't come in here!" one would say, knowing teacher agreement would be invoked, since a pair or group of friends had filled up an area. This became that pair or group's territory for a time. Additionally, anywhere the children interacted, simple proximity to another would symbolize a closer relationship to that other; conversely, closeness was refused by a child who disliked another. Touching behaviors were also accepted and demanded by children as indicators of affection—holding hands, sitting on laps, and wrestling (usually among boys) were often key communicators of relationships. Such channels reflected the recentness of their development of symbol use from simpler, often nonverbal forms to more verbal and abstract forms (Cazden 1972). The children I observed had been not long before limited to touch, proximity, and simple vocalizations as key indicators of their feelings of affection and acknowledgment of relationships. Their extensive and demanding use of such strategies should not, in retrospect, have surprised me.

Still, on first observation, one noticed most the early signs of abstract, verbal, yet forthright symbol use about relationships. For instance, during one conversation in my first days of observation, Hal asked his friend Ivan: "You have Star Wars sets?"

"Yeah, you could come and play with them!" responded Ivan enthusiastically.

Hal then lined up next to him to go outside, saying, "You're my buddy."

The offer to play with great toys was reciprocated by a verbal statement of friendship.

FRIENDSHIP AS A VALUED COMMODITY

As I continued to observe the children, it became clear that they viewed friendship as a valuable but limited commodity, terrific for getting people to do what one wanted. So if one child did a favor for another, offering a statement of friendship in response was viewed as appropriate. One day, Walker brought some Gak, a slimey, gooey play-dough, to school. Dale saw Walker playing with it, approached him, and said, "Can I play with some Gak?"

"Yes," said Walker, and gave him a piece.

Another child, Neil, was observing this, and asked Walker, "Is he your friend?"

"Yes," said Walker.

"He's your friend?" double-checked Neil.

"Yes, forever and ever."

"I'll be your friend, too," said Neil, clearly wanting to be a part of a group that got to play with Gak. Neil likely had other motivations, too, but his understanding of friendship as doing nice, desirable things for another was clear. A few days later, one little girl, Inela, happened to supply me with a child's practical, commodity-like definition of friendship, when as we ate lunch and talked she told me, "I'm not friends with any boy in this class."

"Really," I said, surprised, since Inela seemed to be one of the most good-natured, if quiet, girls in the classroom. "What about me? Or Zachary? Or Alex?"

"Well, sometimes I play with you but I'm not friends with any of the *little* boys in this class. None of them has ever come and asked to play with me." From her perspective, none of the boys had ever supplied her with friendship as a commodity by playing with her, so she was not going to supply the boys with any on her own part. This sense of being paid by friendship for a good action was reinforced the day Heather was playing with a tricycle and Pearl came up and said, "I want that."

"OK," said Heather, as Pearl moved off with the tricycle.

But then Heather ran after Pearl, saying "Hey! Are you my friend? Hey!" It was as if she wanted to make sure she was paid for her kind act in friendship. And indeed she was, as Pearl and Heather played together for some time after this transaction. Children learned early and applied even at ages four and five the notion of reciprocity—I do for you, so you do for me. Friendship, for many children, related to practical acts like doing something nice for another or spending time playing together. The next week, I saw this dramatized when David was talking to me on the playground after I had joined him to watch a truck dump dirt for a new driveway. "No one will be my friend," he said. "I don't have any friends today."

Wanting to reassure him, I told him, "Someone will be later."

"Do *you* see anybody playing with me?" he asked pointedly. "I don't have any friends."

"Well, you have one person," I said. "I'll be your friend no matter what." We talked a little longer, and then went to find another activity to do. I felt good that I could spend some time with him and make him feel he had a friend, but I also felt I could not adequately supply him with what he *really* wanted—some practical acknowledgment of friendship from a peer rather than a concerned adult.

FRIENDSHIP AS AN ONGOING RELATIONSHIP

Friendship for the four-year-olds did not always have to be tied directly to a concrete activity or gift, however, as I discovered the next day when I noticed Lance playing on his own with blocks for quite some time, while Trent and Stan were sitting near each other playing with toys at the table. Suddenly, Lance came over to the table. "Are you my friend?" he asked Trent.

"Yes," said Trent.

Apparently satisfied, Lance again walked off to play with something else. I noted more of this double-checking of relationships as my weeks at the center multiplied. Providing benefits in the present could translate into a continuing future friendship. The next week, Karl went over to a counter where Neil and Brent were standing. Karl stood close to them for a few seconds, just listening to them talking—a hovering behavior quite common among preschoolers attempting to form a relationship (Rawlins 1992). Abruptly, Karl decided to negotiate openly: "Am I y'all's friend?"

"Yes," the two other boys said immediately, nodding. Then they all went to another part of the classroom and began talking and playing together. An ongoing friendship, reconfirmed, preceded the boys' further interaction.

Sometimes children would see *any* commonality as a reason for friendship. One day, Ed was sitting at the lunch table looking at the kinds of forks other children had. "You have a fork like mine so I'm your friend," he said to a child next to him. Then he went over to the next table, and noted, "All you all can be my friend 'cause we have the same forks."

"Hey Nick," said Neil, hearing this. "You're my friend 'cause we both have big forks."

"Look at my white fork," Nick said to me, indicating his fork's thick, white handle.

"Hey, Nick, we're friends," said Neil. "We have big forks." What interesting status symbols the children invoke, I thought—fork handle size! But the elements of something in common or something done together were clearly integral in young children's invocations of friendship, and they could retain a sense of friendship over time even through intervals of not playing together. Seeking similarities while adapting communication to the other party were basic strategies children learned—and indeed needed to learn—to form and grow relationships (Rubin and Ross 1982). These similarities, children gradually found, could be invoked or repeated again later to indicate continuity of the relationship. Alternatively, such commonalities could be invoked to alter the behavior of another to help a relationship fulfill a highly desired instrumental goal.

FRIENDSHIP AS A COMPLIANCE-GAINING TOOL

During the first few days of my time at the center, the negative counterpoint to the positive rewards of friendship strategies became clear, and actually seemed to be enacted more often than positive expressions of friendship. Conditions were often placed on friendship in a "you-do-this-or-I-won't-be-your-friend" strategy, which I then heard used through all my months at the center. My first observation of this was when one boy was playing with a toy jeep. "Roll it to me," another boy nearby said.

"No," the other responded.

The nearby boy then stormed "I won't be your friend *anymore!*" and went elsewhere. The next day, William told Alex, "We're going to the fair without you."

"If you won't let me go with you, I won't be your friend," Alex responded.

"Hey," interjected Nathan. "I have a great idea, Will; we could go in separate cars, but still go together. Alex could go with us."

"Neato! Great idea, Nathan," William enthusiastically responded. Thus Alex did get his way and was made part of the group. Girls enacted the friendship-withdrawal strategy as well. The next week, several girls were swinging on the tire swing. Alison wanted a turn, and asked Tara to let her on the swing. When Tara would not, Alison exclaimed, "*I'm* not gonna be your friend anymore! When you ask if I'm your friend, I'm gonna say *no!*"

In this case, Tara just laughed, while Dora, another girl on the swing, reinforced Tara by saying, "Good!"

Alison stalked off. Her withdrawal of friendship did not get her what she wanted in this case, but I observed many cases where a threat of ending friendship did work. As Erin arrived at school one day, Allan asked her, "Will you be my friend?"

"Yes, if you'll be Nina's friend," Erin answered.

"OK, come on Erin and Nina," said Allan, leading them over to an area he wanted to play in. Later that day, Allan was hanging on my back to get a ride, but Mary was hanging on to my leg in front of me. "Stand up," they both said to me.

"I can't, with the both of you. That's too heavy," I replied.

"Please, get off," said Allan.

Mary answered, "No."

"Then I won't be your friend anymore. I won't be your friend if you don't get off," insisted Allan.

"If I don't get off you'll be my friend?" asked Mary.

"No, I won't be your friend unless you get off," corrected Allan.

"OK," said Mary. "I'm getting off." Then she did, and Allan got his ride while Mary got chased. The children would try the strategy of setting conditions on friendship on me. After some weeks, I got tired of hearing, "Push me on the swing or I won't be your friend," or "Pick me up or I won't be your friend." I would usually say, "Oh, that's too bad," or "I'll miss you." They still would often persist until they were distracted by something else or I offered to do something different. I sometimes thought I should just say, "I'm sorry to hear that," and leave it at that, but I did want to try to show that I understood their desires. I could sense that my own adult understanding of friendship as a treasured, ongoing relationship was clashing with their childhood view of friendship as a strategically invoked commodity. I strove to stress the value of friendship in my interactions with the children, while avoiding condemning them for their (to me) fleeting appreciation of it.

FRIENDSHIP AS POWER THROUGH ALLIANCES

As my weeks at the child-development center turned to months, it was inevitable that I should see deeper patterns in children's management and
invocation of friendships. Their ongoing interactions suggested that patterns of
small groups or cliques and competitions for power occur among preschool
children just as in any other organization. Children played roles in a cultural
drama that influenced their status within a social hierarchy (Pacanowsky and
O'Donnell-Trujillo 1982). The resulting patterns not only guided future interactions and play (Nervius 1989), but also formulated a pecking order among
the children. The most blatant evidence of this I heard out on the playground
one day during my second month at the center. Brent was on the playground,
and had been provoked to anger by two classmates. "Dummy!" he yelled at
them. Then he noticed Tina looking sad and angry. "Hey Tina," said Brent, "I
wasn't calling you that; I was calling Brian and William that."

"They're my friends," protested David, standing nearby.

"Well, they're *dummies*," stressed Brent.

"But they're my *friends*," said David again.

"Well, they're my . . . they're my *enemies*," stressed Brent, after finding the
right word.

"They're my *friends*," stressed David, and walked away. Clearly alliances
and factions had formed or were forming, and as the days went on, I could
see more and more evidence of this. Wanting friends was normal, and alliances were desired as an indication of belonging and being accepted. Two
boys over several weeks kept reinforcing their friendship by saying, "Hey,
buddy, you're my dog," or "Hey, buddy, come over here," followed by "Hey,
buddy . . . " this or that. They reinforced their friendship over a longer time
period than usual, trying to overcome the tentative and flexible nature of
friendship in the children's world at the center.

Expressions of friendship, in forming alliances, clearly gave the children a
sense of power. Thus, alliances would change as children sought not only
compliance and a sense of belonging, but power over others. A few weeks
into my volunteering at the center, I noted Heath, Jawon, and Timothy standing near one another in the classroom. "Are you my friend?" Heath asked.

Timothy said nothing, thinking.

"I am. I'll be your friend," said Jawon.

"No!" insisted Heath. Apparently that was not the alliance he sought—the
wrong person had answered him. "Are you my friend?" he asked again.

"Yes," Timothy finally said, apparently relishing the power the answer
gave him over Heath. Soon after this I observed a more refined negotiation
of alliances when I was sitting at the art table with Mindy, Allan, and Clay.
Mindy was showing the other two children some pictures she was drawing.
All of a sudden, she said, "Allan, are you my friend?"

"Yes, only if you're not Ethan's friend," said Allan.

"OK, I'm not Ethan's friend," said Mindy.

"Tell him; tell him right now," said Allan.

"Ethan! Ethan, I'm not your friend," called Mindy to Ethan as he passed by. She looked pleased with herself.

Then Clay said, "Are you *my* friend? I'm Allan's friend."

"Yes," said Mindy.

A minute or so later, Ethan, who had heard Mindy but had not said anything, came up to the art table and asked Mindy, "Are you my friend? Are you still my friend?"

"No," said Mindy.

"Why not?" asked Ethan.

"'Cause I'm Allan's friend," explained Mindy.

"Well, I've changed my mind, too. I'm—I'm friends with Jawon," Ethan said calmly, and they all went on coloring while Ethan, as usual, wandered off.

Much energy went into establishing forthrightly, and on many occasions, who was friends with whom. If two children who had been playing together earlier had separated for a while, one might seek reassurance that the friendship was intact by asking "Are you still my friend?" Usually the answer was "yes"; the occasional "no" was met with lesser or greater distress, depending on the situation. If the question produced a "yes," often each child would go on, satisfied, playing separately. But if one or the other felt the friendship threatened, then an insistence on playing together or near each other would result: "Come over here," or "Come on, let's play in the block area." Agreement by the other child reinforced the friendship, but refusal, at times, could endanger it, as one would hear a version of "Then I won't be your friend" or "I'll be your friend if you come over here." Children would often use direct statements of friendship (or the absence thereof) to maintain relationships or gain compliance, belonging, or power.

Teachers could promote friendship while at the same time acknowledging that children would not be friends with every classmate all the time. One day, Nelly wound up sitting at a table for lunch with all boys.

"I'm not your friend," said Lem to Nelly.

"Me neither," said Tate.

"None of us are your friends," said Nick.

"Ms. Samantha said that everyone in this class are friends, so I'm gonna tell on you," said Nelly.

"So, we're still not your friend," said Lem.

"Ms. Samantha!" Nelly called out. "Ms. Samantha!" When she had Ms. Samantha's attention, she said, "They're saying they're not my friends!"

"Well, *good*," said Ms. Samantha in a kidding tone, or a tone that indicated Nelly may have been getting her just desserts. "*Good.* That's all right, Nelly; maybe they'll be your friends later."

Ms. Samantha moved away, and Nelly began to ask who would be her friend, and even asserted, "I'm your friend," to one of the boys. As I came back near the table after a couple of minutes, I still heard Nelly saying she would be the friend of one of the boys, and Tate saying, "I'm not."

I decided to put my two cents worth in, then. "Nelly is trying to be your friend and you won't be her friend. That makes me very sad," I said, and then moved off a little.

"I am," I heard Lem saying.

"I am, too," said another boy. I believe the tide had already been turning in the friendship and alliance testing, but maybe I helped it along a little. Nelly and the boys continued to talk as lunch progressed.

My impressions of forthright statements of friendship by the children were that they primarily involved seeking practical, enacted behaviors by others. An ongoing relationship was viewed as valuable, but most tentative, fragile, and flexible, and at times the children would spend time checking up on it with the other party and trying to maintain it. At times, though, a friendship valued at a certain level would be "traded" for the sake of gaining influence over others as well as their compliance. Additionally, alliances would form and change based on attempts to belong to groups and gain power over others. A set of sophisticated strategies was invoked by children to form a clear—though always malleable—social order. While five-year-old children may not have fully developed the idea of an ongoing friend to whom one is always loyal, the concept was forming and frequently tested in terms of practical behaviors and statements. Several more powerful relating strategies I found, however, did not involve verbal symbolism at all.

FRIENDSHIP THROUGH PROXIMITY

One of the most powerful ways of communicating about relationships for children was the use of proximity, or closeness. Being near or next to someone for any length of time communicated a strong or strengthening relationship to them. As adults, we get used to mingling with others in elevators, in stores, and in line for things, and lose our sense that being next to someone implies a close, friendly relationship. Children at ages four and five clearly retain the idea that being close *physically* goes along with being close *relationally*. The use of space and territory could be viewed as a key cultural difference between preschool children and adults (Hall 1959). Adults leave a larger personal space around individuals and hesitate to intrude too much on another's territory. For five-year-olds, a natural way to state or reinforce liking for someone is to get right next to her or him, regardless of location. Young children have not yet developed the complex sense of territoriality that adults have. For children, anyone close is at least potentially a friend, and someone disliked is necessarily someone to stay far away from. Five-year-olds seldom alter these basic nonverbal symbols based on varied social contexts; this kind of sophisticated adaptation comes later. The commonly accepted meaning of proximity for the children was made clear to me early on. The first day at the center, I noticed Mary saying to Jawon, "Sit here!" He did so, and when she noted another boy, Lee, sitting next to Jawon, she said "You're *his* friend."

Jawon nodded. All parties took for granted that Mary was merely confirming an obvious fact: since Lee was next to Jawon they must be friends. This worked negatively, also. If one child was mad at another or did not want to be a friend to the other, a refusal to sit near that child would result. The next day I did indeed observe this kind of situation: Tiffany saw Yolanda starting to sit down next to her, and instantly yelled out, "No, I don't want to sit close to you. Don't!"

"Why?" Yolanda asked.

"Because she's my best friend," Tiffany responded, and moved closer to Tanya. Not only did this event demonstrate the limited-commodity view of friendship children possess, since the notion of being friends with *both* girls apparently never crossed Tiffany's mind, but it certainly showed in no uncertain terms that Tiffany wanted to sit next to only the girl she considered her best friend, to symbolize and reinforce that relationship. One child moving away from another would also communicate disapproval or unfriendliness. Yolanda was sitting down on a carpet square preparing for circle time one day, and Cheryl bumped into her. "Ow!" said Yolanda. "That hurt! I'm not sitting by you!" She abruptly moved away to sit on another carpet square. Later, Mary kept trying to sit near Jessica during circle time, but Jessica kept moving. "I don't want to sit with you," said Jessica.

"I want you to be my friend," said Mary. The norm was consistently and strongly enacted that being next to or close to someone communicated friendship or approval, while being distant from someone meant an absence of friendship. In this case, the teacher suggested some manipulations of power in their relationships: "She doesn't want to be your friend right now," said Ms. Samantha to Mary. "Find someone else to be your friend for awhile. If you play with someone else, and she sees that, then she'll want to play with you." The teacher advocated letting go rather than pursuing an undesired relationship; putting some distance between Mary and Jessica could make Jessica realize the value of the friendship after all.

As circle time ended one day during my second week, David's name was called by the teacher for him to go to lunch. "David, save me a seat next to you!" said Allan as David went to wash his hands.

"OK," said David. He washed his hands and went to a table with plenty of chairs. Several more children's names were called, and seats began to fill up. Brent took the seat next to David.

Allan, still sitting in the circle area, said, "Hey, next to you!"

"Well, I'm still your friend, OK?" responded David, rather than asking Brent to move.

"OK," said Allan, and after washing his hands he contentedly went to the next table. The potential problem posed by not being next to each other, in this case at least, was resolved by verbal confirmation of their friendship.

Sometimes a verbal confirmation was not enough for one party in a friendship. A couple of months later, Timothy had gone to sit at a table for snack, and noticed his regular friend Lem moving toward another table. "Lem!" Timothy called out. "Lem! Over here! Lem!" Lem appeared distracted by someone talking at the other table, but he had not yet sat down there. "Lem!" Timothy called again. Lem moved toward sitting at the other table. "Lem, I'm not your friend anymore if you don't sit over here," said Timothy firmly. This caused Lem to sit across from Timothy at his table and they ate together. At that point, Timothy seemed determined to accept only close proximity as evidence of their continuing friendship, threatening to end it if Lem went elsewhere. This influenced Lem to stay close to Timothy.

A few days later I was part of a group of children sitting in a circle on the playground rolling a truck to one another. Katie, Benjamin, Tina, Matt, and I were in the circle. Samantha approached the circle. Katie said, "No, Tina doesn't like you. You can't play."

Samantha continued to stand there, just outside the circle.

Matt suddenly and graciously said, "OK," and started moving over to make a space for Samantha. "You can play with us."

"No," Katie insisted. "You can't sit here; Tina doesn't like you."

Matt and others then moved the other way, and Samantha was allowed to join the circle sitting in a spot farther from Tina than the first one Matt had offered. Her nonfriendship with Tina was maintained by distance, but she still was allowed to play with our group.

When more than one child wanted to demonstrate friendship by closeness at the same time, some negotiations were necessary to prevent conflict. Even at four and five, children often proved themselves capable of fairly sophisticated managing of the spatial symbolism of their relationships. A few weeks after starting observations at the center, I saw as circle time ended and lunchtime was approaching some friends saving seats at the tables for others still waiting to be called from the circle and wash their hands. Neil was saving a seat for Brian at the table. Matt came over and said to Neil, "Can I sit here?"

Neil said hesitantly, "Well, OK."

"I'm your friend, right?" queried Matt.

"Yes," said Neil.

Brian noticed this while he still sat on the floor and said, "Hey, I thought you were saving that seat for me!"

"I was," said Neil, "but then Matt came over."

"I know," said Brian, "I'll sit in front of you; then we can talk."

"Yeah," agreed Neil, and they did so with all seats arranged for. Not only did these negotiations show some surprising flexibility and intelligence on the part of these five-year-olds, they also showed the importance to them of proximity and spatial relationships as symbols of their friendships. I also noted that one child going over and sitting near to or starting to play with another child could spark a friendship without a word being spoken.

For the children, friendship was something concrete and enacted, and a primary aspect of that action was clearly being near one another and spending time with one another. I noted one day that Matt and Hannah suddenly discovered they could be friends, and they went around the classroom playing with toys together and holding hands, and then during circle time they made sure to sit next to each other. When Hannah rocked her feet back and forth, so did Matt. Both seemed happy to discover someone they could get along with and enjoy playing with, and they enacted those feelings most strongly by being near one another for an extended period. Loss of proximity could endanger a relationship, as shown when I heard Allan questioning Mary one day: "Hey, why do you keep walking away from me? Aren't you my friend?"

"No—yes," said Mary. "We're your friend, but—"

"Then why do you keep walking away from me?" pursued Allan.

"We're just going over here," said Mary, and she and Hannah walked to the other side of the room. Allan eventually joined them and played with them there.

The message proximity conveyed for children also applied to their relations with adults, as I quickly learned. Because they saw me as a nice presence in the classroom, most children wanted me to stay near them and not move away. One morning I came in and sat down at a table next to Christopher to build with him a while. I said, "Hi, Alex," to include him, as he was sitting at a table right near us. Then when Christopher and I went to do a puzzle at the puzzle table, Alex followed and sat next to us. Later, we all went back to a bigger table to build with toys. When I went to get another chair Alex said, "Please stay over by here."

"I will," I said, and helped him, Christopher, and Stan build castles for a while. I had a pleasing sense of being wanted. Over my weeks and months at the center, children wanting to be near me was one of the strongest and most common signs that they liked me and valued our relationship. Sometimes, as an adult interacting with the children, I found myself part of the competition for who would be close to whom. At times, when it looked like one of a set of friends playing together was getting interested in joining me to do something, another would say, "Come on, Mary. Over here," or in some other way get the child to stay with the group. Any diversion or separation, including one that I might cause, put the friendship in question. The children saw closeness—both literal and figurative (which in their eyes may have been inseparable)—as limited and guarded it jealously, whether it was with other children or with me.

Adults, I found, should maintain awareness of the importance of proximity to children while modeling and teaching them flexibility about interpreting its symbolism. Children must and do learn that we cannot always be close to the ones we love or want to develop a strong relationship with. It could be difficult to balance the demands of twenty or more children in the classroom or on the playground; the challenge was to do something that allowed everyone who wanted to be close to me to have a turn and be part of things. My observations reinforced the notion that simply spending time with children was among the most powerful ways to develop a close relationship with them. Indeed, the most effective methods for teaching younger children involve continued close interaction with them, rather than simple explanations or controlling directions (Cazden 1972).

FROM "DON'T TOUCH ME" TO "HUG ME": CHILDREN AND TOUCH

Physical contact is one form of communication that retains a strong symbolic meaning throughout our lives. Many studies reveal that being touched by others improves our health and can be crucial to the development of infants and young children (Vargas 1986). Witness the growing popularity of massage treatments in our day! However, all of us fear touch in the form of violence—hitting, kicking, or other forms of abuse. We need to touch and be touched, but we may hesitate or shrink from physical contact at the same time. In the child-development center where I observed, there was a departure from the restrictive attitude toward touch one sees more and more of in adult organizations. Still, there were clear limits to touching. As in many centers, the dangers of abuse from too much or inappropriate touching were cited in written employee guidelines and evident in the staff refraining from touching too much—and they were prohibited from ever touching in a punishing fashion. The ambivalence I found at the center toward touching others reflected North American culture. Ours has been called a low-tactile culture, meaning we touch others only in very limited situations. For many Americans, interpersonal touch may mean very few things: usually greeting, hostility, power, or sex (Vargas 1986). As children grow out of infancy, they learn that their natural desire for touch as a key indicator of affection must be restricted. They learn, in essence, *not* to touch.

Indeed, at the child-development center one of the few basic rules posted on the wall was to remind children and adults to "Keep your hands to yourself." While this represented a positive form of the command "No hitting or kicking," it also implied that physical contact in general should be refrained from. I noted that preschool children resented touches as hits or intrusions unless the context clearly indicated affection—then touch was prized and highly desired. The children saw touching or holding as a natural and expected form of affection with anyone they liked; these behaviors were restricted in a larger organizational context like the child-development center. The dominant attitude at the center, however, acknowledged that children often needed to be touched affectionately, and teachers would seldom hesitate to hug or pick up the children, especially to comfort them, but also at times just for fun.

I needed to adjust to being touched from the time I first began working with children. I soon learned that I come from a relatively distant family in terms of touch or affection. At first, I was rather uncomfortable with children suddenly hugging me, grabbing me, or getting into my lap. My discomfort reflected North American adult culture and my own upbringing (I believed and knew I was loved, but it was expressed to me in different ways). Yet in my early days of observing and interacting with preschool children I was quite moved by these strong indicators of love and trust, as one suddenly wanted to hold my hand, or get a hug, or sit in my lap. In later months, I came to take being touched for granted. When a child wanted to be picked up or to sit in my lap, my early reaction of "What a special, blessed child to reach out and want to relate in such a way" had changed to "Well, OK, another one; here you go." At times I would catch myself and remind myself how special each child was, and how rare and precious such gestures of affection are in most of our lives (certainly in mine, before I began working with children), and to transfer that special feeling to other people I love (especially my wife and to my own son when I became a father).

Physically violent touch also had seldom been a part of my life, and a most serious violation when it was, so I found almost no tolerance of it within me. Children's acts of hitting one another, kicking one another, or biting another were alien and unacceptable to me. It took me some time to realize that some of this activity inevitably goes on among children, and not to feel mortified if a child acted in such a way toward me. Fortunately, my own strong opposition to such negative touches was shared by the staff at the child-development center. Negative touches were viewed as among the most serious violations of the rules children could commit, and were punished by time-out accordingly. One of the most frequently stated classroom rules was, after all, "Keep your hands to yourself." Clearly, however, touch was used to communicate the strongest feelings children had relating to one another (just as it generally is by adults). Positive feelings generated holding hands and hugs, and negative feelings would generate hitting, kicking, and once in a while biting or throwing things.

A few months into my observations at the center, a child arrived who more quickly than most resorted to violence to get his way or when angered. I wrote the following entry in my journal about two weeks after his arrival:

> One boy in the four-year-olds' class too easily moves to hitting, pushing, or even biting at times if he is grabbing me or does not get his way with another child. He can be a very nice boy, and even polite, and will at times get focused on a toy or activity. Other times, he wanders around the room, picking up things out

of other kids' cubbies, or bothering and breaking what other kids are building. Most of the staff has agreed that these are ways to get attention, and teachers have to fight the impulse to quickly punish or avoid such a child due to constantly bad behavior. Even as I have been hit (at times playfully, a few times angrily) or bitten (lightly) by this child, I've had to try to keep in mind that he needs positive attention, and perhaps we can help model for him better ways of interacting.

The response of the center staff to the boy's behavior was to gently and positively guide him to a preferred activity. Time-out was used as a last resort, but the above child caused an increased stress on timely, consistent use of time-out. At times, children wanted too much positive touch or affection, as this entry from two months later indicates:

> Today was an unusually quiet day, as few kids were in each class. Paul came over when I came in and wanted a hug. So did Ed. Then Paul wanted me to read him a book, then Ed did, and then Paul wanted to hear a couple more. I seemed to spend a lot of time in the book area this morning. One aspect went well, at least—they were good about taking turns and not pushing or squishing other kids in my lap. Paul pushed on Gabe once when he felt Gabe was getting in his space next to me. Paul soon found a spot in my lap, which solved that issue. Actually, today each child who wanted to hear a book would sit in my lap to listen to it while I read, and then would move for another child to get a chance. Paul's doing this let Ed and John have some turns. For a while, I felt monopolized by Paul, but fortunately the other kids were by then busy with other things and not trying to push him out of my lap. There are days when Paul tends to cling to one of the teachers, and wants a lot of attention. Today was one such day, and I was the one. He wanted several books read to him, and cried outside when I would not give him a second ride on my back. I finally took him over and sat with him on the playhouse until he felt he had enough attention for a while outside, and he went to play something else.

Children who overused positive or negative forms of touch required extra guidance and energy from teachers, and thus became noted and often considered "problems." But the staff at this center tried to pursue positive guidance techniques to get such children to moderate (or end) their inordinate use of touch for communication.

The importance children placed on proximity and touch as symbolic of a close relationship became more and more central to my observations due to my role as participant with the children in their classroom and on the playground. Within my first month of spending time at the center, the children were gathering for circle time, and one girl said to me, "Sit by *me*," and then many others chimed in, saying, "sit by me . . . sit by me."

"I'm not a giant," I remember saying kiddingly. "I can't sit next to all of you!" I eventually sat behind the circle, as usual. As the weeks passed, when I did try to sit with the children on the floor (as other teachers and staff often did), I would find one or more children wanting to sit in my lap, and others scooting over beside me. At times, the teacher would ask all the children to sit on the floor—especially during circle time. I came to enforce this "rule" also—the children, I realized, were being distracted during circle time by trying to be on or close to me. Other times, though, when the children were more casually sitting on the floor, I would sit with them and let one or two sit on my lap. Often, only those one or two seemed interested, and such affection was not a problem.

That touch could be perceived positively or negatively was made clear one day when a teacher tried to touch and comfort Jessie, who normally liked that teacher. This day, Jessie pushed the teacher's hands away, clearly indicating her anger. The teacher's touch, which normally would have communicated affection, now seemed to communicate unwanted control when filtered through Jessie's anger. On the other hand, the ultimate, affectionate, taken-care-of gesture the children often wanted from me and other adults was simply to be picked up. I tried to accommodate this as the other teachers and aides did, without letting it interfere with classroom activity. The children's requests were even rather bossy: "Pick me up!" But I was moved by the requests and was often a pushover, I admit.

One day, David asked me to read to him. He liked being in my lap. He did not like it, though, when two other children sat on either side of him. He soon got up and left. Later, he asked me to pick him up, and outside he sat on my lap again for a while. I noted this because it was unusually affectionate for him. As the months went on, I realized that kind of desire for extra touch happened when a child felt he or she had grown into a more trusting relationship with me, as a confirmation of our new closeness.

One aspect of becoming closer to young children was the removal of the barriers of politeness and discourse that we as adults normally operate behind. I was gratified when children learned to trust me and became willing to interact with me, but then the breaching of such barriers could be taken too far when children hit or kicked or grabbed at me and would not let go. On several isolated days, some children grabbed my pockets and held on, and threw small rocks or pine straw at me outside. On a few occasions a little boy started punching me, not really hard and seemingly in a friendly, playful manner. I tried to respond in some way to object to that kind of behavior.

"You're hitting [or kicking] me. I don't like that. . . . Rocks stay on the ground. They are not for throwing at people." Those comments were typical of how the staff members would correct the children. Some days, my most effective lines were "You're hitting me, so I need to move away," and "You're being mean, so I can't play with you." These got quick reactions: "We won't be mean," or "I won't hit anymore." And then the children did improve their behavior, avoiding undesirable touch. But these incidents showed me how children around age four will throw out many social barriers against touch once they decide they like and trust an adult. Such ready touching behavior made the children unpredictable—they might start talking extensively to me, or follow me everywhere. I could get mobbed by four- and five-year-olds as they piled onto my lap or hung on me. Acknowledging the children's desire for closeness and affection while redirecting their behavior to a more socially desirable channel seemed to work the best to maintain my relational equilibrium with the children.

At ages three, four, and five, children would also communicate with their peers through touch, at times overwhelmingly. Girls, especially, would hug and hold hands with each other, but such behaviors were still quite common among boys as well. One day, Hunter came into the classroom in the morning with his mother, and Charlie ran over to say, "Hunter!" and gave him a big hug.

"Leave me alone!" said an overwhelmed Hunter after a few moments of this. Mike had also come over, and then he hugged Hunter, and Hunter did not seem to mind as much. I had noted that Mike and Hunter had maintained a closer friendship over several weeks than Charlie and Hunter ever had. A child would often hug another he or she sat next to when getting ready for circle time. Children would readily invoke touch communication with one another in a way similar to that with adults they knew and trusted.

I also noted that the desire for affection through touch seemed to be expressed in waves, much like the ebb and flow of relationships described earlier. and then the cycle would repeat. The waves involved getting closer and letting go as expressed by the amount of touch in an ongoing cycle.

In a way, the order of my observations was the reverse of that of young children's symbol development in relationships. While touch and caressing are vital to infants (Vargas 1986), consistent proximity to others is important once a child becomes mobile. Playing in tandem without much direct interaction with another child is commonly observed in two-year-olds (Selman 1980). Once a child masters language use, whole new systems for managing relationships become available, and forthright, abstract negotiations about how much and how long friendships will develop can begin. These latter are what I first observed; but, not surprisingly for preschool children, proximity and touch continued to serve as crucial indicators of affection or its lack.

Anyone working with preschool children should encourage verbal interaction, of course, but it will do little good to insist that all children be friends all of the time. That abstract ideal is not going to happen, and young children are too concretely focused on meeting instrumental needs anyway. Adults can encourage friendly relations and discourage unfriendly ones, but all children must learn to negotiate both. While preschool children are learning to restrict proximity and touch communications in more sophisticated ways, adults may unwittingly send very rejecting messages by often or abruptly refusing proximity or affectionate touch between children and adults. Successful adult teaching with preschool children requires adult openness to more touch and proximity than may be the adult's norm, while children can profit from adult interaction that models ongoing relationship talk. Differences in the meanings of touch, proximity, and friendship negotiations between those of preschool age and adults point to cultural differences that may be difficult to bridge; but such differences also make communication—and life—more fun.

5
Revealing Culture: Invoking the Rules

At the youngest active ages, starting around age one or so, children begin to interact with one another in a preverbal way. These nonverbal messages include proximity or touch. Young children often play near one another without any forthright contact or acknowledgment of the other (Selman 1980). Once children learn to talk to one another, a whole new range of communication strategies opens up to them. No longer must messages be limited to playing near one another, actual physical touch, or yelling, crying, and other vocalizations. Yet, though children may talk, they may not know what exactly to say to deal with an issue or manage a relationship the way they want to. I observed that, in those situations, children would invoke taken-for-granted social rules in place of trying to figure out a more creative verbal way to influence another person. A child would invoke the rules to remind another child (or even an adult) of what to do.

Since the social context played such a crucial part in shaping young children's communication (Allen and Brown 1976), preschool children would often use appeals that directly referenced that context. Such appeals would also be used by adults to remind children of key rules and expected routines. Invocation of such rules reinforced the shared reality for members of the child-development center culture (Pacanowsky and O'Donnell-Trujillo 1982), and could serve as social correctives for undesired actions or a "safe" and clearly understood basis for further communication. Children often seemed to need verbal reinforcements of norms and rituals they could follow without prompting. Such communication strategies served as the foundation for recreating social order through interaction, and developing for children the idea of a "generalized other" always concerned with individuals' behavior (Mead 1934). While all communication served to create culture, forthright statements about rules and expectations provided an essential base for maintaining the culture.

SIMPLE RULES

At the child-development center, adults facilitated this process by keeping rules clear and simple. Teachers would remind their classes regularly about rules like "use inside voices" or "make sure to clear your place at the table." Even commonplace rules like those, however, were subsumed for most teachers within four or five key guidelines that were posted in each classroom in giant letters and often referred to. When I started spending time at the center, the following classroom rules were posted in Ms. Stacey's four-year-olds' classroom:

1. Be safe. Walk inside.
2. Be kind. Keep your hands to yourself.
3. Be neat—turn off the water and dry your hands.
4. Use good table manners.
5. You are loved.

Ms. Stacey would, at least once every two months or so, review these rules with the children. The first time that I observed this came during a morning circle time with the children sitting on their carpet squares and the teacher facing them in her chair. She asked them what the rules were in the classroom.

"Don't hit," said one child.

"Don't run," said another.

"Clean up your area," noted another.

"Don't talk with food in your mouth," said a fourth. Thus, inductively, Ms. Stacey had the children themselves review all the basic rules and further specific rules that followed from them. While all of the children seemed to know the rules firsthand, they would often forget to *follow* the rules. I decided that situational and relational factors overrode the children's natural desire to follow the rules at times. Teachers often invoked rules through questions like, "Do you wipe hands on your clothes?" These would demonstrate that the children *knew* what they were supposed to do, even if at times they forgot to follow the rules. Keeping the rules simple and clear genuinely helped the children choose their behavior and interaction methods. I noted very little capricious or inconsistent guidance from adults as a result of this, and even the children could readily invoke a classroom rule when provoked to do so.

The center staff placed a strong emphasis on allowing the children to make choices, as long as they were within the rules, and so teachers would seldom vocalize repeatedly what the children should do. New activities, like clean-up time or circle time, were announced, and the children would proceed to reorganize themselves for the new activity. Teachers would, of course, have to remind one or two individuals what to do, but the class as a whole would already know. On my third day of volunteering, one child sat in the circle area and told a friend, "Be quiet! Let's be quiet. Get on your carpet square."

Ms. Stacey, observing this interaction and its helpful result, responded with a "Good, thank you for making a good choice. That was a good choice."

There were limits to what teachers would tolerate, however. One day, after lunch, Ms. Stacey turned off the lights and called all the children over to the circle area. The children had been milling around the classroom, talking rather loudly, supposedly getting ready for naptime. The children had finished lunch, but Ms. Stacey still was eating hers. In a quiet voice, she gave them the following speech:

> I needed to call you here to sit with you so I could finish my lunch. Sit with your hands in your lap. You all need to be here to calm down, settle down. I hope one day you'll know what to do, and you'll go to your cubby, and take your things out, and prepare your area for your rest. I called you here because this time, this time after lunch, is quiet time. You need to get your mat out quietly. If you're going to talk, talk quietly and get your things out. OK, now listen for your name, and if you haven't got your mat in its place, go to your cubby quietly and get your things out. . . . When you go, you'll go quietly; no talking to the person next to you.

She said all this slowly, with lots of pauses for her to eat and for the children to sit quietly. Once the children, one by one, got on their mats, they seemed quiescent. But when Ms. Stacey left the room for a time, many got back up, talked or made noises, or walked around again. Ms. Stacey came back in, and they soon got quiet again. I noted a major difference in rule compliance when the lead teacher was present in the classroom.

At times, I found that I needed to reinforce rule following and could not, as an adult, maintain a neutral observer role. Both children and other adults expected some rule reinforcement from me, and I complied. One day, on the playground, Neil told me, "I was going to be Evan's friend but the teacher won't let me play with him."

"Oh," I said, "Why not?"

"We were going in the bushes," Neil answered.

"Well, it's good to be friends with him, but it's wrong to go in the bushes. You're not supposed to be there."

"We like to go in the bushes," Neil added, somewhat uncertainly.

"It's good to be friends with him," I reiterated, again playing the teacher-reinforcer part, "but if he does a wrong thing, you don't have to do a wrong thing, too."

He moved away, thoughtfully. Inside, when I would sit behind the children during circle time, if one or two were talking rather than listening, I would remind them to "please listen." Ms. Stacey at least once suggested that I "encourage them to listen," clearly indicating that my help was desired and that I should not stay in a passive role. Usually, the children were attentive during circle time, but some days they seemed more distracted than others and would need more reminding about the rule to listen.

Teachers would often note that school rules might be different from home rules. Gun play was not tolerated at school, and most children internalized that rule rather quickly. Still, some of the children, boys especially, needed frequent reminding. One morning, several boys were playing with guns they had constructed out of some toys. Ms. Judy, observing this, said, "Guns stay at home. Bring all your guns over here and put them away. Take them apart and build something else." The boys did so, reluctantly, but I noticed some playing guns on other days. Another rule that needed more consistent reinforcement than most was the washing of hands. Kenny came out of the bathroom one day, and Ms. Judy, observing him, said, "You need to wash your hands after you go to the bathroom, Kenny."

"I already did," Kenny said.

"No, you didn't," said Ms. Judy. "Every time you go to the bathroom you need to stop and wash your hands."

"At home I don't," explained Kenny.

"What you do at home and what you do at school are two different things," stressed Ms. Judy. "Now wash your hands. Use soap."

Kenny reluctantly did so. School rules were reinforced with the message that it was irrelevant whether home rules were the same. Basic politeness rules were also reinforced, and the children who had more trouble with them clearly had not been expected to be so polite at home. One day at snack time, Michael said, "I want more crackers."

"That's not the way you ask," gently responded Ms. Stacey.

"Could I have more crackers . . . please?" attempted Michael.

Then Ms. Stacey got him some more.

USE OF RULES TO MANAGE RELATIONSHIPS

Children would use understood rules to structure their interaction, for instance by invoking the limit for the number of children allowed in each classroom area. These limits were posted by each area and reinforced by teachers and children. One morning, Kenny and Timothy were playing at the counter. Timothy was playing with some sand in a box, and Kenny was playing with some shapes. Brian came over and tried to join them at the counter. "No, only two here! Only two are supposed to play here," insisted Kenny.

"I'm gonna play with this," insisted Brian, grasping a toy abacus.

"I'm gonna tell on you," said Kenny. He walked over and told Ms. Lisa, "Brian won't leave and he was the last to come in." So Ms. Lisa told Brian to move to another area, and he moved off and sat by a wall, looking disgusted. "I'm not Brian's friend," said Kenny to Timothy. "I told teacher on him. Are you Brian's friend?" he now asked Timothy, who had silently continued playing with sand all this time.

"No," said Timothy.

"Hey, let's go somewhere else," said Kenny.

"No," said Timothy. "I'm your friend, but I don't wanna play with you right now."

"Are you my friend?" Kenny asked almost simultaneously.

"Yes," said Timothy.

"I'm gon' to walk away, OK?"

"OK," said Timothy, and he stayed playing with the sand for quite a while. The rules and teacher confirmation of them were invoked to keep Brian away from the pair, but then when Kenny wanted to leave it required some negotiation about the normal "rule" that friends play together and stay together. He and Timothy agreed that the current "violation" was acceptable. On another morning a couple of weeks later, I realized that a child was invoking rules to keep me all to himself for a while. I was sitting in the block area with Michael and Carl one morning, and Timothy tried to come in to the area with us. "No, Timothy, there are already three here; you can't play," said Michael.

"You don't have to count me; you only have to count kids," I explained to Michael. He reluctantly left Timothy alone, but clearly was not happy with him joining us in the area. The next morning, Michael and Carl were playing in the block area when David came over to join them.

"Get out!" asserted Michael. Then he appeared to notice only two boys were in the block area, while three were allowed. "OK," he corrected himself. "You can come in. Don't mess it up! Build with us."

David joined them, but soon Debbie walked over and entered the block area. "No, you can't come in here!" insisted David.

"Only three can be in here," added Michael.

Debbie, aware of this rule and apparently concluding that it was not worth arguing over, tossed her head and walked huffily away. A few days later, this issue became more complicated and a child decided to argue about it. Timothy and Alex were building in the block area with Jawon. Jawon left to go to another part of the classroom, so Brent went into the block area. "Get out!" said Alex.

"There can be three in here," asserted Brent.

"Jawon is fixin' to come in here," said Alex.

"He left," persisted Brent.

"Move, we're trying to build here," said Alex.

Brent slowly moved away, but stayed in the block area. Alex and Timothy accepted this, and went on playing with each other. The number limit on each area could be invoked to exclude undesired playmates, even though this strategy did not always work.

RULES AND POWER STRUCTURE

Rules not only served as tools to manage children's relationships, they also created and reinforced the power structure that formed the backdrop for their conversations. Sometimes children who had internalized rules practiced invoking them during their interaction to the point where they became funny. David and Nicki were walking all around the classroom one morning and playing together, and I overheard many invocations of classroom rules by Nicki. She sounded like a teacher, humorously so at times. Once, David pulled out a box to look at some transformer toys he saw in it. "Put those back; that's not your cubby," Nicki correctly told David, and soon he reluctantly did so, apparently to stay in Nicki's good graces. Then Nicki said, again sounding like a teacher, "Let's find an area," and they headed over to the block area. Building with lots of blocks was not apparently on Nicki's agenda; she told David, "Don't take any out," as he reached for some blocks on the upper shelf. "You know, you take 'em out, you put 'em up." David continued to take some blocks out, and Nicki accepted this and started to build along with him.

A few weeks later, at the lunch table, I heard Sarah admonish Patrick: "Don't talk with your mouth full. Isn't there a rule on the wall that says 'Use good table manners'?" she asked, looking around. Patrick seemed to know she was right; he looked quietly contrite. A few minutes later, Sarah was talking with a few other girls sitting nearby about talking with one's mouth full. "You're not supposed to talk with your mouth full," she said.

"I didn't," Shelly said.

"*I* don't talk with my mouth full," said Laura.

"You showed your food," Sarah said.

"I did not," insisted Shelly.

"She showed her food," insisted Sarah to her colleagues. This dispute continued, but after the children explored this issue for a while, the conversation moved on to other topics. The enforcement of that particular rule was Sarah's focus for several days, I noted.

Things became more humorous when a child would attempt to enforce a rule with an adult. One day, a teacher fairly new to the classroom, Ms. Rebecca, took two paper towels to dry her hands. The children had been told repeatedly that they should use only *one* paper towel when drying their hands. Alex saw her and said, "You only use *one* paper towel!"

Ms. Rebecca looked somewhat taken aback, but recovered her poise and said, "Well, my hands are bigger than yours, so I need two."

Alex still looked put out; he seemed quite serious about that particular violation of classroom rules.

"Alex, Mr. A-lex," sang Ms. Rebecca in a light, kidding tone. Yet she too seemed a bit put out over this scolding by a four-year-old. Both parties moved on from there and that was the end of the incident. I was glad to see that Ms. Rebecca did not take serious affront to Alex's attempt to enforce a rule that had been enforced on him.

Decisions about what to do and what kind of behavior would be expected from others were assisted by appeals to rules. During my first week at the center, two boys were considering trying to sit on a table, which was against the rules. One, Brian, did sit on the table, but got off very quickly on seeing his friend Kenny's look of surprise. Though he had gotten off the table, Brian insisted, "I don't care about going to time-out."

"You don't say 'I don't care' to the *teacher*," said a shocked Kenny in response.

"I didn't say it to the teacher," returned Brian.

"Oh, you said it to a kid," said Kenny.

"But I don't care about going to time-out," insisted Brian.

I couldn't help interjecting, as I sat nearby, "You want to go into time-out?" I found myself compelled to enact the "adult power" role.

"No, I just don't care," returned Brian to my comment.

"OK, I'll go tell the teacher," said Kenny, clearly testing for a response.

"No! Don't go tell," pleaded Brian.

"I won't," said Kenny, and they moved off and played together for a while. I witnessed a similar incident a few weeks later, when Kendra and I were sitting at a table building with LEGOs. David was also at the table. Evan came over and knocked over Kendra's construction, and she started protesting in a whiny tone. Evan proceeded to make a toy gun out of some LEGOs. "We don't make guns at school," said Kendra firmly, as Evan pretended to shoot with his toy.

"He's gonna get in trouble," said David.

"No, I'm not," said Evan.

Then Kendra and David began repeating together, "You're gonna get in trouble."

"No I'm not! Leave me alone!" said Evan, after a couple of rounds of this. He messed with Kendra's creation again.

Again, I could not resist, as the potentially powerful adult, interjecting a comment. "Whether you get in trouble or not depends on you," I said.

"No, it depends on you," Evan said.

"No, it's what *you* do that decides that," I corrected.

"Well, I wanna get in trouble," said Evan petulantly.

"Well, I don't give a care; that's *you*, not *me*," put in an irritated David. Evan got distracted and moved elsewhere, and Kendra, David, and I continued building for a while. Evan had clearly been "managed" by the three of us through the invoking of several classroom rules: being kind and keeping one's hands to oneself, not playing with guns at school, and making good choices to avoid getting in trouble. He seemed to tire of the onslaught of rule invocation and moved off. Kendra and David seemed happy with this result.

Rules were also invoked by teachers to manage children seeking too much or too close attention. Alex and David were sitting on their carpet squares on either side of me during circle time before lunch. After teaching the children about leaves, Ms. Stacey had started to call names of children to wash their hands and go to lunch. Alex and David then wanted to sit in my lap, and moved toward me. "I'm looking for leaves that are on their carpet squares. David, Alex, you're not on your carpet squares," said Ms. Stacey. So they moved back to their carpet squares. It was a clearly understood rule that children needed to be on their individual carpet squares during circle time.

Rules and teacher authority were often directly associated with one another. About a year after I began observing at the center, Alex went to the table where Ms. Stacey was sitting and said, "Teacher, David and Jawon have their shoes off."

"Tell them to put their shoes back on," calmly responded Ms. Stacey as she filled out some forms.

Alex walked back over to where the boys had been playing and, with the additional authority provided him, said, "Ms. Stacey said to put your shoes back on!" Eventually, the two boys did comply. A few months later, Timothy, Lance, and Kenny were building in the block area, and Timothy inadvertently kicked a block so that it hit Lance. Lance looked angry. "Ow, stop it," he muttered angrily. When Timothy did nothing more, Lance said, "I'm gonna tell on you."

"I'm sorry," said Timothy then.

"I'm gonna go tell Ms. Stephanie on you."

As Lance made his way across the classroom, Timothy kept repeating, "I'm sorry, Lance. Lance, I'm sorry," from his spot in the block area. When he saw that these apologies were not going to prevent Lance from talking to the teacher, he said, frustrated, "I'm not Lance's friend. Don't be Lance's friend, all right?" he added to Kenny, next to him in the block area.

Lance came back and said, "She said don't do that anymore."

Timothy responded, "I'm not your friend."

"I'm not your friend either," added Kenny. "You can't come over and see my remote control car," he told Lance.

"Can I?" asked Timothy.

"Yeah, you can," said Kenny, and he continued to tell Timothy about it as they played in the block area. Lance played nearby, separately, for a while. I wondered if he thought telling on Timothy to Ms. Stephanie had been worth it. Maybe he felt a sense of justice, but he at least temporarily had lost two friends. They were reconciled later, as the children usually were.

More dramatic power assertions occurred, as well. One day, Ms. Stacey was going outside, and Jana and Charline were coming toward the door to go inside.

"I need a drink of water," Jana said.

"I need a drink of water, too," echoed Charline, and both walked inside through the door.

Firmly, Ms. Stacey said, "Come back, Charline! Jana, come back out here. Now, you can *ask* to go get water."

Both girls stopped and came back through the doorway. "I need some water," said Charline.

"Say, 'May I go get some water, please?'" suggested Ms. Stacey.

"May I go get some water?" Charline echoed politely.

"Yes," said Ms. Stacey.

"I don't wanna do it again," protested Jana.

"OK, then go play," said Ms. Stacey.

"No! . . . I need some water," insisted Jana.

"Then ask me if you can go get some; I'll let you," said Ms. Stacey firmly but gently.

Jana finally asked, very softly, "May I have some water?"

Ms. Stacey responded, "Yes, you may go in and get some water." Then, to me standing nearby, she said, "Rules."

"Manners," I responded approvingly.

Ms. Stacey mused, "She needs to learn to ask, not tell us what she will do. She tries that at home, and her mom gives in. I tell her, 'Don't give in to her,' or she'll come here and do it. She needs to let her know who is the parent. Then when she comes here, she'll know we're in charge."

RULE DISRUPTION AS CULTURAL EDUCATION

When a classroom's lead teacher went on vacation for two weeks, her absence was an adjustment for all and an education in the taken-for-granted norms established as part of the center culture. Classroom management became tougher for the staff and me for a while. Without a lead teacher there, the children seemed naturally more antsy. Ms. Kathryn, the temporary replacement, usually worked with infants or two-year-olds, and so her guidance in the four-year-olds' classroom seemed lackluster and unfocused. She spent a lot of time waiting for the children to get quiet instead of asserting herself or starting an activity that would capture their interest. The student assistants and I would stand around, trying to guide the children to the next activity and generally keeping them from flying all over the place. I remember thinking, "Tell them to *do* something. Let's *start* an activity—if we're going to go outside, let's go." I responded with dislike to her strategy because, being honest with myself, she took my more passive, less controlling attitude toward the children to an extreme that did not work for a lead teacher. During those two weeks, I could certainly see the need for control and consistency around children to go along with love and affection for them. A few days later into Ms. Kathryn's stint as substitute lead teacher, there was more disarray in the classroom, with children talking loudly and ignoring classroom routines.

One of the assistant teachers, Ms. Janet, apparently out of impatience, took over the group activity for the class; Ms. Kathryn was present but did not object. Ms. Janet was forceful and moved the class along in activities much better than Ms. Kathryn could. However, as the day wore on, Ms. Janet became more controlling—insisting the children get in line, making a child who talked go to the back of the line, and waiting until the children were completely quiet before allowing them inside for lunch. I had never seen these kinds of behaviors at the center before. Ms. Gina, who was waiting outside with us, said to me, "The longer you wait the more active they get." She had a point—the control was getting extreme. But Ms. Janet did get the children quiet and talked to them about lunch, and the day then proceeded in an orderly fashion. After the lead teacher, Ms. Stacey, had returned from vacation, I noted that the regular routine resumed and the standard rules were questioned less and followed more.

Observing the children's interaction, I discovered the basic cultural rules of the classroom always in the background, guiding their communication with each other and with adults. From time to time, children would follow the teachers' modeling by invoking rules in order to get the outcome they sought. Through such recurrent rule evocation, the social order of the classroom was maintained, as all parties acknowledged and yielded to it. Once adults created a center and classroom culture, the children used it as a basis for communication and built upon it their own expected rituals and behaviors. The necessity for a solid routine upon which to build strategic communication was aptly demonstrated during my observations at the center (Anderson 1989; Haskins 1985). An effective child-care center culture requires adult agreement on basic values and expectations, so they can be clearly conveyed to the children (Palmerus and Hagglund 1991). The taken-for-granted nature of these values and expectations led to a notably open and comfortable communication climate at the center. Extrapolating beyond my own observations, I could only imagine the conflicts and defensive communication that would occur at a center where various adults insisted on widely divergent rules, or expectations and routines were changed randomly and often. Consistency with clear central social norms will be a valuable premium at any well-run child care center. A clear routine, simple rules, and a tolerance for varied forms of interaction appeared necessary for a comfortable child-care center culture.

6

Discipline Dogma

While observing and participating at the child-development center, I could not help but imbibe a strong dose of the philosophy of child discipline advocated by the center director and staff. Their focus was always, "Tell kids what to do, not what *not* to do." The rationale was that a child may not know what to do in place of an undesired act. The stress on positive discipline was strong and reinforced. The center director, during staff meetings and in employee handouts, stressed the need to eliminate the words "don't," "stop," and "can't." The word "no" was frowned upon. Lead teachers, who had worked at the center for several years, enacted this strategy of positive redirection effectively, even in conversations with adult assistants. New employees, however, were at times hard-pressed to replace "old" norms of child discipline with the new ones desired by the center culture. I once observed a new teacher aide outside see a child turn on a water hose he should not have been playing with. "No!" said the teacher, out of habit, immediately followed by, more softly, "Oh, 'no' is not a word." She seemed somewhat at a loss as to how to respond to this rule violation other than going over and turning off the hose. Fortunately the child had already moved off. Phrasing requests positively got more difficult the more outrageous or anger provoking the child's action was. Still, staff, students, and observers at the center were repeatedly coached on positive guidance techniques. "Keep your feet on the ground" and "Keep your hands to yourself" replaced "Don't climb," or "Don't kick," and "Stop hitting." While the reality of discipline situations did not always measure up to this ideal, the center staff members worked hard to uphold positive discipline strategies.

At times I would observe the children and teachers with a focus on methods of discipline. The most favored strategy was to ask a misbehaving child to leave an area, and suggest something else for him or her to do at a different table or in a different place. Since "don't" and "can't" and "not" were to be avoided, the staff did try to request positively: "*Walk* please," to those running; "keep your hands to yourself," to those hitting; "keep your feet on the ground," to those kicking. If a child threw something, the teacher would ask the child to pick it up, and keep asking and insisting until the child did so. Ms. Carla used the counting method one day: "I'm going to count to three, and by then I want you at the door." This worked almost magically, I believe because it was used sparingly by teachers who the children knew would enforce their power. Once, on the playground, Ms. Stacey observed children spiraling a large, metal swing around in an unsafe way, and she told them, "That's the wrong thing to do," which was one of the most negative statements I heard. The teachers' most serious threats were sitting a child down in time-out for an interval, sending a child to another classroom (usually with younger children), and sending a child to sit in the director's office (the center's equivalent of being sent to the principal's office). Another final threat was to speak with or write a note to a child's parents.

TIME-OUT OR NO TIME-OUT

When a child misbehaved, failed to follow directions, or broke a clear classroom rule, the pattern of discipline was fairly constant. The standard procedure was to redirect a misbehaving child to another area or activity. The next step was to take the child aside for a talk about why a certain action was a poor choice. The last resort, short of sending the child out of the classroom, was to have the child sit down quietly, off to the side in time-out. Ms. Debra, the director, had made it clear that she did not like the use of time-out except in extreme circumstances, so when I began volunteering there its use at the center was limited. The classrooms at the center were orderly and controlled, for the most part, thanks to involved and concerned teachers who consistently used positive requests and insisted on them. At times, the lack of "punishments" did lead to more chaos in the classrooms, as a select few children would fail to respond to positive redirection techniques.

On the other hand, time-out could be overused or ineffectively used, eventually leading to its falling out of use again. Children would rarely be left sitting too long, or not be clearly told why they were being placed in time-out. I did observe adults seem to forget about children they had placed in time-out. During my time at the center, two children had such recurring behavior problems that the discipline strategies short of time-out were not working, so a clear, systematic use of time-out was reinitiated. The teachers involved expressed their relief at getting approved the use of such a "discipline tool." The problem behaviors decreased quickly and dramatically.

The striving for balance in discipline was ongoing, with many teachers wanting to use time-out as a tool (perhaps at times too frequently), and the director wanting to avoid time-outs if at all possible (even, at times, at points of near chaos). This shaky balance was pushed to the extreme by one child, who presented one of the most memorable discipline problems of my time at the center. I first noticed Evan as an affectionate boy who was full of energy and fairly cooperative with teachers and the other children. As time passed, I observed that Evan could play nicely for long intervals, but most days he would have an interlude of throwing blocks, skidding them across the floor, or messing up the creation of another child. One day, Alex was working hard with LEGOs when Evan came up to the table and grabbed a bunch of the LEGOs. Alex yelled and cried, which was unusual for him. The usual teacher reaction to this kind of behavior was to ask Evan to give the toys back and suggest that he go to another area. If Evan had committed a larger rule infraction, a teacher would sit him down and talk to him about it. Evan did seem to have a shorter attention span than most of the other children, and would always be seeking additional stimulation; when he found this by violating the rules, he got into trouble.

After two weeks of such behavior, it became clear that Evan would only listen to and obey Ms. Stacey, the lead teacher. His propensity to knock over things, take toys, and throw things had earned him a bad reputation among his peers. Most of the children did not want to play with him. One morning, Evan tried to go into the block area. "No," the other children kept saying when he would take or move a block, though they accepted one another's moves readily. After a few minutes of this, Alex told Evan, quite sincerely, "We'll be your friend if you'll get out of here." This turned on its head the norm of friendship being shown by proximity and playing together. A vicious cycle seemed to develop. Evan would seek friendship or play with other children, but they no longer trusted him and would say "No!" to his attempts to join in, even when other children would be welcomed. Evan, of course, would be angered by this, and so he would engage in even more negative attention-seeking behaviors.

I knew that things were getting worse for Evan when one day he would not lie down for his nap after Ms. Stacey had left, and Ms. Jennifer tried to sit with him in her lap to settle him down, and he spit in her face. This got him sent to the main office for a talk with Ms. Debra. A few days later, he was playing in the block area near some other children, who were tolerating his presence there. After they were asked to clean up the area, he began "spanking" Jill, who was wearing a short dress. Then he apparently pulled Jill's underpants down. Ms. Stacey, scolding and angry, took Evan to Ms. Debra's office, and then returned and helped Jill put some pants on. Ms. Stacey was soon called to a conference in Ms. Debra's office, and Evan's father took him home. It had become clear to all that his problems stemmed from more than attention-seeking at school. The presumption always was—and nearly always it was borne out—that children with extreme discipline problems were facing some serious problems at home.

As time went on, Evan's tendencies to hit or push other children, take other children's toys out of their cubbies, and wander around during naptime continued to be problems. He could participate and listen well when he wanted to. For example, during a field trip to a music store one day he behaved very well. Once he became interested in something, he could follow expected class norms. His bad behavior seemed to be a combination of negative ways to get adult attention and frustration at not being able to develop solid relationships with other children. His routine at naptime, for instance, varied from theirs—most children would automatically get their mats out and lay on them without being told to (even as they played, talked, and got distracted). Evan always had to be told, several times, to get his mat and get on it. He would keep on wandering around the room, bothering or playing with other children, even after most of the others were settled on their mats. The teachers often had to resort to the threat of sending him to the office or calling his father to get him (one day Ms. Jennifer made the latter threat while holding him down on his mat). Evan would eventually cooperate, after a fashion.

With only the lead teacher and ultimate threats getting through to Evan, the staff seemed to be growing more distressed about the situation. Outside help was presented in the form of a woman working on her dissertation in the area of managing difficult children. She came in and became a sort of consultant on techniques for effective child management. As a result of her presence, all center staff were guided in giving consistent and effective discipline to Evan—and thus to all the other children—through the use of time-out. The focus on positive redirection and reinforcement at the center had been so strong as to discourage time-out, and a child like Evan had stressed this system to its limit. The four-year-olds' classroom had become more chaotic thanks largely to his refusal to respond to normally effective positive discipline tactics by the adults.

On the first morning of the consultant's presence she put Evan in time-out immediately when he disobeyed or seriously misbehaved. The new routine was to briefly sit the child down and ignore him, *right* after he misbehaved. The consequences were swift and sure, as when I asked all the children to come inside, and Evan, who did not immediately join the other children at the door, was put into time-out. After that, he came when I called him, and Evan had been notorious for *not* coming when he was called to come inside! I was struck by how effective quick, consistent use of time-out was with Evan, and with all of the children in this new atmosphere. The classroom seemed more controlled and peaceful over the next few weeks.

THE AWKWARDNESS OF POWER: DISCIPLINE FROM A VOLUNTEER

As I got to know children, they would test my tolerance for naughty behavior. I would feel disconcerted and uncertain, but over the first few weeks of volunteering I realized that I needed to be forceful and at least make my feelings on behavior clear. I desired mostly to interact and form relationships with the children, and because of that I became, at times, too much of a "softy." I lost some power or credibility with the children, since I would not, like other adults, give commands and expect them to be obeyed. The children grew to *like* me, but never to *fear* me. While I generally did not want them to fear me, when they were determined to disobey I found my influence over them to be quite weak. As a researcher and volunteer, I was not in a position to deal with major matters of discipline anyway, and I deferred these matters to the teachers.

One day, after a few weeks at the center, I observed that four-year-olds Jeremy and William were *determined* to fight. They would take other children's toys, knock over the blocks they were building with, or pour milk in their food. The other adults and I kept telling them to stop, but I found that my power was limited. I even pried them off of one another, but it seemed that before long they were getting into more trouble. One of the assistant teachers, Ms. Kendra, would threaten them with a time-out but did not follow through. It made her seem mean but less powerful. I tried not to make threats because the children knew I would not follow through, and I often felt it was not my "place" to do so. As a result, I had developed a tendency to avoid discipline situations. I would make my feelings clear, saying, "That is wrong," or suggesting something else for the children to do, but then I would leave the area (almost as if that in itself were a punishment). At times, that was effective at ending the fighting or misbehaving, but not always. The lead teacher, Ms. Stacey, had the most power over the children. When she got involved they would then shape up quickly, as they *knew* that she would sit them in time-out or invoke other consequences if they did not comply.

Later in my time at the center I decided that when a child misbehaved I needed to try to get the problem solved instead of moving away. This was tough and required creativity, as I lacked the legitimate power of a lead teacher and did not want to get into a confrontation with a child that would call for that kind of power. Ms. Stacey's discipline style was quite effective: if a child was asked to sit out, she would talk to him or her about *why* what he or she had done was wrong, and her position of power reinforced her message. Her key strategy was to deal with the issue immediately and not avoid it.

I would reinforce my own role by spending extra time with "problem" children. I would refuse, however, if they were misbehaving. I was giving Evan a back ride one day, and he started trying to kick other children who were chasing us. He slid off my back, and I said, "I can't have you on my back if you're doing that." As I chased the other children, Evan moved off and started to cry. He soon found me again.

"I want the rest of my back ride. I only got a short turn," he said.

"Well, Evan, you were trying to kick the other kids, and that helped you slide off. I can't have you on my back if you're doing that," I responded.

"I won't do it. I want to get back on your back," pleaded Evan.

"You can finish your turn after Paul gets his," I agreed. Paul got a back ride, and then Evan got one, and he was nicer the rest of that day. I found that I did have influence over the children, after all, though it was not as direct as the lead teacher's. I could refuse to play with the children when they were breaking some rule or mistreating someone. My doing this, in tandem with the staff's using time-out more frequently and quickly, had a calming, steadying effect in the four-year-olds' classroom.

A few weeks after starting observations at the center, I had to work on my resolve to be more assertive. I had taken Kenny, William, and Tanya inside to get some water. On the way back outside Kenny came with me onto the big playground, while William and Tanya started to play on the two-year-olds' playground. "Come on, you guys aren't two," I said. "Come back on the playground with us." They ignored this request twice; in a playful or natural adult tone I was clearly not being listened to. "Do I have to come carry you?" I said, deciding to stand my ground. They still would not come. I finally went over, picked them up, and *carried* them into the four-year-olds' playground, telling them I was disappointed in them. I did not enjoy doing this, but I finally did solve a clear discipline problem without having to wait for a teacher to step in. I valued my relationships with the children so much that I would discount the tasks of learning and discipline at times, and the children would then push to see how far they could misbehave with me.

Two weeks later, an assistant teacher, Mr. Tony, dealt with two boys who had pinched a classmate. They knew they were in trouble, it seemed, because they had quickly moved off behind some bushes on the playground. "I see you hiding back there. I even have my glasses off and can still see you. Come over here. Come out here, *now*," said Mr. Tony firmly. William, Chris, and Alex began to run away. "Get back over here! I'm going to count to two, and you'd better be back over here. One . . . ."

The three boys returned to stand near him.

"Have you been pinching people? It's *wrong* to pinch people," Mr. Tony told them.

"I *didn't* pinch anybody," said Chris.

"I'm not talking to you," returned Mr. Tony. "I'm talking to these two. It hurts when you pinch and people don't like it. No more, or you'll have to sit out." The boys moved off, and the problem appeared resolved. I enjoyed seeing a male staff member handle the situation, but I was also a bit envious of the ease with which he did so. He could credibly invoke the power to make them sit out, while I almost never did so and generally did not feel it was my place.

LOVING DISCIPLINE AND SHARED CLASSROOM RULES

Ms. Stacey and Ms. Stephanie, the lead teachers, had a very firm hand with the children, combined admirably with a strong, loving touch. Ms. Stacey once gave a girl who was having a rough day from misbehaving a hug, saying, "Hey, you're a hugging child today, aren't you?" Dora smiled, clearly feeling loved. Ms. Stacey said, "I was observing you do some things I didn't like to see. I don't want you doing those things to those other children. You were being mischievous to those children. Now when they say, 'Stop it,' you *stop it*, OK?"

Dora smiled and nodded.

"I love you, but you can listen good and be a good girl, I know it," Ms. Stacey concluded. Dora had been hitting and climbing on things that day, and she acted better and calmer after this conference.

The lead teachers Ms. Stacey and Ms. Stephanie would, at intervals of three months or so, have a gathering of the children to remind them of basic classroom rules—more often when there was a younger, newer set of children in the four-year-olds' classroom. One morning a few months after I had begun volunteering, several of the children were having repeated trouble listening and getting settled into their activities. Ms. Stacey asserted unusually tight control over her classroom that day by having the children sit quietly on the floor before lunch. She lectured them about needing to listen and follow the rules. She said she could and would call their parents if she had to. That stood out as unusual. But the classroom rules were posted on the wall and regularly enforced; they were no mystery. One of the posted rules—"You are loved"—set the tone for the enforcement of the others; they were positively phrased and consistently—but lovingly—enforced.

After about a year at the center, I witnessed a solemn lecture to the children after they had come in from outside. Ms. Stephanie told them, "I have some children who are fighting, and wrestling, and it's too much. Fighting is *out*. With this pushing, and kicking, and wrestling, somebody will get *hurt*. I don't usually do this, but if you are fighting, you will be put in time-out. If you are fighting, you will have to *sit down*. It's important to listen to your teachers, 'cause if one child is talking, *Alex*, then other children might want to talk too. Hannah, see, she saw Alex talk and she wants to talk back. I'll bet if she didn't see Alex talking she would stay quiet and listen. It's important to follow the rules, or someone will get hurt. The fighting, hitting, and kicking will stop. In this classroom, Power Rangers are *out*."

"Power Rangers can be at home," piped up Randy.

"If your parents say it's OK, that's fine," said Ms. Stephanie. "But here you need to listen, and if me, or Ms. Carla, or Mr. John find you fighting, they have the right to sit you down, too." I wondered if Ms. Stephanie was talking to us adults as well as the children with that comment. I believed so. It might have been a hint to us to be more forceful than we had been, or reassurance to us that we *could* be!

"Now, let's get ready for lunch. Timothy and Alex, you may go wash your hands," finished Ms. Stephanie. The day's routine proceeded, but the stern lecture had refocused the children on the rules of desired behavior.

TESTING DISCIPLINE

As four-year-old Timothy grew more comfortable in the classroom setting, I noted he would ignore rules or teacher directions more often, to see what he could get away with. This was fairly typical behavior. One day, Timothy's mood was such that things were the way he said they were, and he would hit or push another child who contradicted him. He would wrestle in fun with another boy and would ignore anyone other than the lead teacher. Ms. Stephanie told him, "Please stop and sit down," or "Stop." Ms. Stephanie sat him down in time-out twice that morning, and usually she avoided that action except as a last resort. Timothy was normally fairly well behaved, so his stubbornness on this day stood out. The lead teacher and the assistants consistently stood their ground to enforce the rules and prevent him from finding no consequences for his violations.

On another day, Jill and Trevor were climbing and sitting on a wooden railing of the playhouse. I did not realize that was against the rules until Ms. Stephanie, from a distance, told Jill, "Please get down." She said, "Mr. John, encourage them to stay down." She had internalized the antinegative philosophy of the center to the extent that, even with other adults, she often made comments like "encourage them to make the right choice." Both the children and other adults like myself learned the limits of permitted behavior through such tests.

Expressions of dislike or not including another child could also, at times, push the limits of discipline. One day, Vicki joined Rachel and Michelle in the block area, and the three girls played house for quite a while. Shortly, Michelle was sitting at the play table with a very sad expression on her face. Ms. Jennifer wandered over and asked her, "What's going on, Michelle?"

"They said they hate me," said a teary Michelle, referring to Vicki and Rachel.

"Vicki!" called Ms. Jennifer. "Come here. Vicki . . . you like each other; you shouldn't say we hate anyone."

"I didn't say I hated her," said Rachel, who had also come back over.

"I know, I'm talking to Vicki. I want you to hug her neck and tell her you like her," said Ms. Jennifer. Vicki did so, though reluctantly at first. "Good, now we're all friends, and sisters, OK?" said Ms. Jennifer, and she joined in as they resumed their play roles.

That day at lunch, Chris and Ivan were looking for a place to sit together, and Brian was too. When Chris and Ivan found two seats at a table with all boys, Brian started to cry and walked off and sat down on the floor. Ms. Stephanie walked over and talked to him, concluding her remarks with "*Tell us what is wrong.*" She then let him move a plate to sit and eat lunch at the table next to Chris. After eating well together for a while, Chris and Brian were fighting and slapping at each other. They caused Chris's milk to be spilled all over the table in front of him and onto his pants. Brian would laugh and call Chris "baby," and then Chris would hit again. Soon, Ms. Stephanie took a crying Chris to another room to talk to him. Shortly after he and Ms. Stephanie had returned, there was another name-calling and hitting match with Brian. Ms. Stephanie then took Brian's plate away, since he was not spending much of his time eating lunch. Crying, he got onto his mat. Chris and Ivan, as they passed Brian, would get into "sparring matches" with him involving light hitting. This continued so long that Ms. Stephanie finally asked Brian, Chris, and Ivan to sit in time-out on the floor before going to their mats. In spite of teacher responses, Brian and Chris could not behave within accepted limits. "Rough day," Ms. Stephanie told the children as they got quiet for naptime. "We'll do a whole lot better tomorrow." The children had clearly tried her patience that day, but her optimistic spin was typical of the communication climate at the center. The limits might be tested, but desired behaviors would be reinforced gently, firmly, and consistently.

DISCIPLINE AND OLDER CHILDREN

The class of school-agers, older than the four- and five-year-olds I spent most of my time with, provided interesting examples of how discipline problems evolved as children aged. Six-to-eight-year-olds seemed to have trouble following directions—they required several repetitions, and I could see the older children refuse to follow them at times to test the response from their teachers. With Mr. Calvin they showed more respect, as they knew he would enforce time-out or other sanctions (like no game of a certain type). They paid less attention with Ms. Dena, who was much nicer and warm with them, and tested her requests more. I could see that it took a firm and consistent hand to teach and enforce correct behavior—almost more so, it seemed, with older children than with younger. As time went on and the school-agers seemed less and less controllable, Mr. Calvin and Ms. Dena gave negative sanctions more readily to the children. A child heard immediately "Move out of that area," or "Sit down," when rules were violated. The teachers of the school-agers also resorted to a firmer use of redirection and then time-out to enforce order. This had the desired effect.

The most difficult time for the school-agers was after lunch, during the hottest part of the day, when the younger children were all napping. Due to the heat, the older children also stayed inside, but they were expected to have quiet time in their classroom, whether they were watching a movie, reading, or playing games. Typically during this time, especially while the children played games, the noise level would get louder, and louder, until Ms. Dena would have to repeat, "It's getting too loud!" or "No talking." Finally, card games were banned, and quiet reigned once again. On one Friday, the noise level got so loud three times that Ms. Kathy, who worked in the main office, came into the school-agers' classroom twice and talked to them about being too loud. Finally, she had them all put their heads down on a table—even those who had been quietly watching the movie. I noted that quiet and control had been achieved, but justice had not. Not all days involved so much confrontation between the staff and school-aged children, but the basic pattern of rising volume leading to a reminder or actual sanctions repeated itself on most days.

After a couple of weeks of summer, Mr. Calvin mentioned that he had been "called on the carpet" and talked to by the director about "telling them to shut up all the time" and making a loud group of children lie down one afternoon. Apparently, the tale had been exaggerated and lamented when one of the children told her parents. From my observations of the elementary-age children, though, I could see that such firmness was needed to hold them together and in control. The children would push "softer" teachers to the limit. Mr. Calvin told me he was now saying "Zip it!" instead of "Shut up!" That did seem less harsh. "Maybe that will be acceptable," he remarked rather bitterly to me.

Zach (age nine) and Darryl (age eight) were good friends, but then a pretty little girl named Anne (age ten) joined the school-aged group for the summer. Soon after this, the two boys were no longer friends, as first Zach and Anne and then, the next week, Darryl and Anne spent lots of time with one another. Never did I notice the three of them playing together. Even the other school-agers would tease first Zach and then Darryl about having a "girlfriend." Then, one Friday, the words "I want to have sex with Anne" had been scratched onto the wood of the playhouse with a rock. Zach and Darryl, of course, were the primary suspects. I had to leave that day before the issue was settled, but I left with a sense of innocence lost for them, and idealism about childhood lost for me.

After the weekend, when I returned, I found that it had been Darryl who carved the graffiti. Ms. Debra's first reaction had been outrage at the staff for not monitoring the children closely enough to prevent such a thing. The parents had echoed this criticism. On the other hand, I thought, it was a big playground. The boy had been talked to, along with the parents, and the punishment was that he had to sand the message off of the wood. That was appropriate, I thought, but nine- and ten-year-olds should *know* such an act is wrong, whether there is a teacher watching or not. I believed there should be a clear, unified rallying behind punishment to show the child responsible that it *was* wrong, not a focus on distractions like parents blaming teachers or staff members.

The next issue that came up with the school-agers that summer involved movies that the children could watch as a break in the middle of long, hot days. It turned out that one parent had complained that the children were watching too many "Ninja Turtle" movies. The director and staff decided that the children would watch only "G"-rated movies from then on. "PG" movies had been a large part of the selection thus far, and I wondered if the staff could really stick with their restriction. They did so for several weeks, but as the summer went on I noted more "PG" movies slipping in, and no one mentioning anything more about it.

The final major discipline restriction with the school-agers that summer involved ball games. Kickball was one of their favorite outdoor games, and one day I was told that there had been a violent fight over a ball game. Wesley (age ten) had been involved, and Ms. Dena told me she had been scared by his level of anger and violence. I had often noted him reading while the others played games, and I had seen no evidence of a hot temper. Evidently, several fights over ball games had gotten so intense and seemingly out of hand that the teachers were both afraid and furious. So several children had been involved, not just Wesley. I had noted that the longer the children were outside in the intense heat, the more angry and conflict prone they became. I could picture an argument on a hot day about a ball game escalating to high levels of anger and violence. The staff's response, though, struck me as an overreaction: all ball play was banned. It seemed a shame that all were deprived of a normal, key recreation activity because of the violence of a relative few. The school-agers' class did stick to the ban for several weeks, but as new student teachers and volunteers, who were unaware of the rule, spent time with the school-agers, the ball-playing ban lapsed.

ADULT CONSISTENCY ON DISCIPLINE

One inconsistency I observed several times at the center regarded the question of how controlling to be with the children. One day I observed for a time in the three-year-olds' classroom. Ms. Tori was a student teacher for the semester, and was overseeing a transition from snack time to sitting on the floor for an activity. She had a forceful personality, and she liked order. She could have fun with the children, but it often seemed that she played the part of drill sergeant. "It needs to get quiet in here," she would say. "Thomas and Greg, sit down! We have a game we're gonna play, but we're not playing it until everyone is quiet." The noise level would generally decrease, but not to Ms. Tori's desired level. Ms. Tori continued to insist on everyone getting quiet, and the delay in the start of the next activity would lengthen. After a point, I could not help noting that the focus had moved from beginning a new activity to testing the teacher's control. Finally, after all the three-year-olds were quiet enough, she began calling their names to come sit on the floor. When the children were all on the floor, once again Ms. Tori waited, insisting that everyone be quiet before starting the activity. Then she got down on her stomach, saying, "Now we're gonna crawl like caterpillars." Enthusiastically, the three-year-olds began to imitate her, but she said, "Not now! Sit up and watch me. Not now, sit up and watch me—we're not doing this until everyone is sitting," she added harshly. She seemed to be focusing on control at the expense of the fun of a learning activity. Finally, after more delay waiting for the children to sit back up, she finally sent them around the classroom crawling on their stomachs.

At heart, most discipline issues revolved around how much control adults wanted to have over children. Adults must decide what basic values and routines will undergird a child-care culture. Most important to this culture, I found, was adult agreement on forms of discipline, so that children did not receive mixed messages about who is in charge or about consequences for actions (Palmerus and Hagglund 1991). At times, the lack of favor for *any* negative consequences to bad actions (in this context, usually time-out) led to near-chaos and lack of control in classrooms. Once swift, sure time-outs were reinstated, however, classrooms were calmer and more controlled. Very few children, I noted, needed frequent time-outs once they were consistently enforced. Yet, even as time-out as a discipline strategy fell into and out of favor, the director insured consistency throughout the center, especially among the verbal preschoolers and school-aged children. This child-development center left children with a wide latitude for choices and actions, which provided a strong foundation for communication development. While every day needed structure, and the functioning of the organization required rules, the staff generally used as few control strategies as possible—until problems with individual children's lack of control forced the staff to refine their discipline strategies. These strategies, though they seemed to increase staff control, actually calmed the classrooms down enough that life there for children and adults was quite pleasant. A few inevitable conflicts over discipline were observed among the staff, but this center staff was admirably consistent and flexible, ensuring a fun, creative atmosphere. I believe my time spent volunteering there was enriched because of such a flexible approach to control and discipline.

7

Power and the Use of Control

Everyone wants a sense of control or power in life, and thus people like to get control over others. As shared meanings emerged at the center through interaction, all parties to a greater or lesser degree sought to assert control over those meanings. As children mastered verbal symbols in the form of language, they also mastered an understanding of social structure (Cicourel 1974). Through structured and repeated interactions, even preschool children could establish and reinforce power differences at the center (Mumby 1993). Adults took as a given the fact that they must be in control in a child-care situation (Leavitt and Power 1989), yet often exercised that control with subtle verbal guides replacing direct and forceful commands. The result was a constant undercurrent of negotiation about who would control and who was where in the hierarchy. This changing power structure was most evident between the children, while at times also refined between a child and an adult.

In the constant resurfacing of control issues at the child-development center, the key issue was usually how a child could gain control of a relationship or an activity. At first, I noted primarily attempts by children to control other children or the toys they wanted to play with. A promise or threat to "be your friend" or "not be your friend" were very common resources used for control. Further rewards would at times be offered: "You can come to my birthday party," or "I'll let you play with this," or even, by one boy, "I'll give you a dollar." Children seemed to forthrightly enact the social exchange theory, which holds that in any relationship, some behavior of value to both parties must be exchanged for that relationship to continue. Friendship itself was an acknowledged, basic value, and the children would openly trade based on it. At times, they would seek control even at the possible expense of a friendship.

Control was a major issue, also, for the teachers and staff at the center. They saw control as necessary to guide and teach the children, as well as to keep everyone safe. At first, I took adult control in the classroom for granted, as the children did. As time went on, I became more aware of different styles and strategies adults used for control. Some teachers were happy with a fairly free-wheeling chain of events in the classroom, as long as basic safety rules were observed. Other teachers sought more "toeing of the line" by the children, insisting that all rules be followed nearly all of the time, and more often and forcefully correcting the children. While adults could be flexible with control strategies, they consistently sought to make clear that adults were in charge at the center and there were symbolic boundaries beyond which children would not be permitted to go. With less power distance between children, they enacted a greater variety of strategies to assert control over one another.

CHILDREN'S CONTROL STRATEGIES

I encountered an issue of control my very first day at the center. Apparently sensing that I was a nice adult who was not a teacher, Michael told me shortly after I was introduced to him, "I'm your boss." He seemed serious about it.

I responded, "Well, I don't need a boss. But I could use a friend." We continued to interact, but Michael clearly wanted someone who would play with him and do what he wanted. I found myself trying to balance being kind to him and spending time with him with not letting him be too bossy or completely monopolizing my time. Oddly enough, when he played games with his peers, he would accept being controlled. On the playground a few months later, I observed him playing with Alex.

"Michael, come over here. Get over here. Michael, get over here. Michael! Go everywhere that I go! Michael, we need to be over here," Alex told him by turns. While Michael seemed reluctant to yield to all these commands, apparently he thought the relationship worthwhile enough to continue to play.

Soon after this, one of Michael's own games on the playground allowed him to assert control. He started playing school, and acted the part of the principal. He would boss me around and put me in time-out. I played along with him for the sake of the game. I found I did not much like being ordered around by anyone, but there at least was an element of humor in being bossed around by a four-year-old boy. Janice approached us and asked Terri, who was also playing school, "Terri, wanna play restaurant with me and make desserts?"

"No, I'm playing with Michael," Terri said.

"What are you playing?" asked Janice.

"School, but I'm not a teacher," said Terri.

"I want to play," said Janice.

"OK, you can," said Michael, who was clearly in charge of the game.

"I want to be the teacher," said Janice.

"OK, you be the teacher," said Michael. "Now, *get out your mat and get on it!*"

At this point, Michael sounded so much like stern teachers at the center at naptime that I broke out laughing. The children looked puzzled yet thrilled. "Why are you laughing?" asked Janice. I explained to them that it was because Michael sounded so much like a teacher. The children seemed to feel good that I was laughing, as if they knew I was laughing *with* them, not *at* them. All of our feelings of control over the situation seemed enhanced.

Children learn young to use rules and procedures as a form of control over one another, as I observed one morning within my first two months at the center. Michael and Neil were playing with some toy airplanes that Ms. Kim had brought. Michael was showing Neil how to fly them.

"Here, you can play with this," he said.

"I don't want to," said a hesitant Neil.

"But it flies like this," said Michael. Neil took up the plane and flew it. "Yeah, try," encouraged Michael.

Then Carl approached and said, "I want to play with one of those."

"You have to ask Ms. Kim," said Neil.

Carl went off and did so. "Yes, sure," said Ms. Kim. "When one of the other kids is finished, you can." Carl then quickly returned to the two boys flying toy airplanes.

"Could I play with that?" asked Carl.

"You have to ask Ms. Kim," repeated Neil.

"I *did* ask Ms. Kim," said Carl.

"You have to say please," stalled Neil.

As Neil and Michael continued to play with the airplanes, Carl repeated his journey over to Ms. Kim, asked her again, and got almost the same answer. Returning to Neil and Michael, this time he said, "Could I please play with that?"

"I'll trade you," Michael offered, indicating a pink car Carl was holding. They traded, and after some delay all three boys continued playing with airplanes and cars. But Neil maintained a noteworthy control over Carl's behavior by appealing to adult authority and politeness norms, and in the end it was Michael, not Neil, who let Carl play.

Later, outside, Ellen found a beetle and cupped it in her hands. Lori and Jennifer followed her around the playground to watch the beetle and watch her showing it to other children. "I found a love bug," Ellen would say.

"Let me see! Let me see!" the other children would exclaim. Ellen would then uncup her hands and let them peek at it inside. "Can I hold it?" some children would ask.

"No," said Ellen. Eventually, she released control of it by letting it go through a hole in the chain-link fence, so no other child would gain the control of it—and the other children's interest—she had enjoyed.

Age differences were a natural source of power differences for children. About a year after I started spending time at the center, one day before lunch, the older children who were part of a summer school-age program came out on the playground where the three- and four-year-olds were playing. So, for a time, children from three to nine years old were all together on the playground. The younger ones, especially the three-year-olds, were quite attracted to the older children. They would follow the older ones around and want to do what they were doing, like playing with a basketball. Sometimes the older children would ignore the younger ones, but more often there were some interactions. Four-year-olds Timothy and Alex were looking for fossils, and two eight-year-old boys played along. The older children took the games less seriously, but participated for the benefit of the younger ones. Sometimes the older children would pick up younger ones so the latter could make a basket with the ball, or give little ones rides on their backs. I was surprised at the number of friendly, almost mentoring relationships that emerged between older and younger children. It gave the older children a chance to be in a powerful role for a change, and they seemed to enjoy it.

On a different day, I saw how an older brother could have positive control over a younger one. Timothy was four-and-a-half, and Trevor was three, and so they were in separate classrooms at the center. Often, both classes played on the same playground. On this particular day, Trevor ran to Timothy when he saw him come outside and grabbed his hand. From then on, Trevor followed Timothy around the playground, and usually wanted to do whatever his older brother did. As time went on that day, the two brothers would play on different equipment or play different games with various other children, but continued to play in general proximity to one another. A strong brotherly bond was associated with the power the older brother retained over the younger.

One day, playing near one another at a table, Carl and David got to talking about older brothers. Carl invoked his brother's power: "My big brother is eight."

Not to be outdone, David said, "When I'm ten I'll beat your big brother."

"No, you won't; he'll be eleven," said Carl.

David kept claiming he would be older than Carl's brother, and Carl kept denying it.

"When were you born?" asked Carl.

"When I was younger," answered a somewhat uncertain David.

Unsatisfied, Carl asked again and got the same answer. This went back and forth a third and fourth time, until Carl said, "You don't know when you were born?" in frustration, and the topic changed to the blocks they were building with. Carl was trying to assert control by using his knowledge of age differences, but David's inability to comprehend them stymied Carl, and he gave up.

At times, children would stress something in common as a basis for friendship and control of others at once. Hannah was sitting at the lunch table near

Kelly and Emily, and as she looked at the food on her plate, she said, "whoever likes this and this and this can come to my house."

"I like potatoes," said Kelly.

"Me, too," said Hannah.

"I don't," said Emily.

"Whoever likes them can come to my house," said Hannah. In this situation, the conversation went on, and there was no confrontation over liking potatoes between Hannah and Emily. Several of the girls would often appeal to a commonality of food preferences as needed for a friendship to continue, and they treated it fairly seriously during the time the conversations would last.

Overseeing an activity or initiating one desired by other children would also give a child more acknowledged control. One day, Lem and Justin had built an elaborate construction out of all the blocks in the block area. Jimmy joined Lem in the block area.

"We used *all* the blocks in the block area," said Lem.

"You sure did," I said.

"Do you like it?" Lem asked me.

"Very much so; yes I do," I said. Then, Lem knocked over a small part of the structure. Jimmy, seeing this, imitated him and knocked over a larger part of the structure.

"No, don't do that!" said Lem hotly. "Fix it up right now!"

"I don't have to," said a nonplussed Jimmy.

"Yes, you do; I'm in charge," insisted Lem.

"No, you're not in charge," responded Jimmy.

"Yes, I am!"

"No, you're not. Mr. John," said Jimmy, appealing to the nearest adult, "is Lem in charge?"

I did not want to take the "I'm an adult so I am in charge" route, so I merely said, "I don't know. Did someone put you in charge, Lem?"

"Yes," he said. "Ms. Michelle."

"You're lying!" insisted Jimmy.

"No, you're lying! 'Liar, liar, pants on fire!'" sang out Lem.

"No, you're not in charge," said Jimmy.

"Yes, I am!" insisted Lem. I continued to observe, not sure where Lem's assertion of being "in charge" came from, but the two boys soon tired of the debate and decided to turn their attention back to the blocks. Lem rebuilt the structure with help from Jimmy; both were happy. They found a way for Lem to feel in control, while Jimmy did not have to yield unquestioningly to Lem.

Lem continued to assert control over his friends in the block area, as I observed two days later. This time, he and Justin were building with blocks and putting toy animals on top of them. Lem started putting small animals on the blocks; Justin put some big animals on them.

"No, don't put those animals on there," said Lem.

"Yes," said Justin.

"No, they're stupid. Aren't they?" asked Lem assertively.

"Yes," agreed Justin. "We don't need them." He put the big animals back in their container. Then he took one back to put on the blocks. "Hey," he said, "this one we could put . . ."

"No, that one's stupid," insisted Lem. Justin put it away, following Lem's dictates. Evidently, Justin decided that continuing for the time being in a good relationship with Lem was worth more than wresting control from him. This was typical of their relationship, with Lem controlling what they did, for the most part, and Justin following along. Each relationship seemed to arrive at its unique "control ratio" between the parties.

One kind of control the children relished stemmed from their bringing a toy in from home. Teachers discouraged this, but there were still exceptions, especially on show-and-tell days. Ellen brought a toy to school one day that was full of little nails she could press things into; the nails yielded to make indented shapes. The other children, naturally, all wanted to try it. Ellen was in charge of letting each child have a turn. "Look at this," she said, and made a shape of her hand and then her face.

"I want to try it," said Malcolm.

"OK," said Ellen, and let him.

Hannah and Brent wanted to try it next.

"OK," said Ellen, keeping track. "It's your turn after hers," she said to Brent. Then Lem came into the area and wanted to try it.

"I want to play with it," said Lem.

"No, he's next," said Ellen, indicating Brent.

"I won't be your friend anymore," said Lem.

"Oh well," said Ellen, acting unconcerned but clearly thinking about the situation. After a few seconds, she said, "Hey, you can have a turn after her and him, OK?"

"No," said Lem, and walked away. Ellen shrugged her shoulders. A little later, when Malcolm was trying to pull the toy back from Brent, Ellen said, "Share! Share!"

Malcolm let it go, saying, "You're a *mean* girl!"

"If you don't share, I'll have to put it back in my cubby," she explained to him. She repeated this line to several other children in the next few minutes. "Share," she kept insisting earnestly. She clearly liked being in charge of something many of the children wanted, even as she played the role of teacher by reinforcing a classroom value.

Brent got a similar sense of control when he brought an orange toy car to school three days later. "Can I play with it?" asked Alex quickly.

"OK," said Brent, but after a couple of minutes he took it back.

"I wanna play with it!" screamed Alex.

"It's mine," said Brent, who then came over to me.

Alex followed, pulling at Brent and screaming.

"Alex," I said. "That is Brent's; it's up to him to say who plays with it."

"If I say no kids can play with it, no one but me can," said Brent. He handed the car to me. "Keep this," he said, "and don't let anyone play with it." I put it up high on top of the cubbies.

Alex still wanted it. Whining, he said, "I wanna play with it!"

"Can you *ask* Brent?" I said.

Calming down, Alex said, "Brent, could I please play with that?"

"Oh, OK," said Brent. "For a little while." I got the car down for Alex to play with.

When Brent later refused to let any other children play with his toy car, Ms. Stacey said, "Share, Brent. If you can't share then the car goes back in your cubby. Go ahead and play with it, Alex." Brent yielded his control until Alex asked him, "Does it open up back here?"

Brent took it, saying, "No, it doesn't open back there. I'll play with it."

"Hey," Alex said. "I didn't get to play with it long." But he seemed less frantic after having been given an opportunity to play with it earlier. Alex regularly would get upset when *he* could not play with a toy another had brought. "He won't share! He won't share!" Alex would insist, invoking the classroom rule. Yet he seemed to take advantage of this rule, as he always wanted to be the one who was shared with first or most. Several times he cried when he felt his turn was not soon or long enough. Due to conflicts like these, the teachers prohibited bringing toys to school from home, except on show-and-tell days. Sometimes parents would let children bring toys on other days, however, especially on Mondays, to help get them to school or overcome separation anxiety. While the teachers may have been displeased, they often did not want to interrupt activities to confront the parents. When it came to bringing toys from home, children, teachers, and parents all seemed to want control over the situation.

A bit later, Brent told me, "All the kids want to fight over this, but if I say, no one can play with it; only me, 'cause it's a very special car."

"Well, Brent," I said, "why don't you put it away in your cubby where it will be safe? Then no one will take it or play with it, and it will be your special car." Shortly, he did just that, and the verbal and physical battles for control of the car ceased.

As my months of observation turned to years, the most usual persuasive tactic for asserting control by the children was an appeal to friendship as a commodity to be traded. A child would say, "I won't be your friend if you don't. . . ." One time, Lem told two other boys with him in the block area, "I won't be your friend if you won't help me build this." Yet friendship would also be used as a positive inducement, as in: "Will you do this? I'll be your friend." This clear, basic use of the social exchange theory was quite a normal pattern among the four- and five-year-olds. During my extensive interactions with them, it became natural for them to try this persuasive tactic on me, attempting to get me to do what they wanted. I usually would say, "Oh, I'm sorry to hear that," and the children would try another strategy. I took to insisting on being asked nicely, with "please," retaining my control through respect and the enforcement of politeness rules, but if the children followed those guidelines I would agree to anything reasonably asked. The children seemed to appreciate that I would let them have control of our interaction in such ways; with me, the control was not always the one-way adult-over-child variety.

Children's appeals to friendship did not always work with other children, either. One day Alex and Timothy were in the block area, and Brent sat down at the art table to color. "Brent! Brent!" Alex and Timothy kept calling. When Brent finally looked over at them, Alex said, "Aren't you gonna play in the block area?" Timothy pointed to a "boat" they had made out of blocks.

"Come over here!" responded Brent. "If you come over here I'll be your best friend." At this, there was a pause. No party seemed to want to move. All three boys simply dropped the interaction with each other and continued to play where they were.

Some children would yield easily to control attempts, but others would not. I saw this dramatic contrast in an incident one day when John, Kenny, Timothy, and Tyler were sitting at a table punching holes in cards with hole punchers. John found that the hole puncher he had worked, but the cover would easily fall off. He tried to get Kenny, sitting in the chair next to him, to trade with him. "Wanna use this one?" John asked Kenny. Kenny continued to concentrate on punching holes out. "Kenny, wanna use this one?" asked John, louder.

"No," Kenny said softly, shaking his head.

"I'll be your friend. . . . I'll be your friend forever," said John.

Kenny turned sideways, away from John, continuing his work punching holes.

"But I'll be your friend; I'll be your friend forever. . . . You can use this one," continued John.

"No!" stressed Kenny.

John then left Kenny alone and thrust his hole puncher at Sarah, who was now sitting across from him. "Here, you use this one," he said in an insistent tone. "I'll use that one."

After a brief hesitation, apparently deciding against resisting John's persuasion, Sarah relinquished hers, and then all continued quietly hole punching for a while.

As the children got to know and trust me (or almost any adult), they tended to get more bossy. After I had been in the classroom for several weeks, Sarah was telling me firmly, "Sit here. . . . Come over here. Come on." It seemed natural for the children to grow less polite with and more demanding of all caretaker adults over time. I wondered if this illustrated the basic truth behind the phrase "Familiarity breeds contempt." The teachers accepted this pattern as normal and responded as desired to such control messages often. Especially at the lunch table, phrases like, "More ketchup!" or "I want more fish sticks," were responded to matter-of-factly and cooperatively by the teacher serving lunch. If these commands were shouted, they would usually elicit a response like "Can you ask nicely?" or "Use an inside voice." When I felt a child was getting too demanding of me, I would respond with, "What's the word?" or "What do you say?" which usually elicited a "please." I could understand why the teachers did not always insist on polite phrasing, however—at times it did not seem worth the effort.

"Mr. John! Come get your dinner! Sit here," Alex said to me twice one day from the dramatic play area. Alex liked to be in charge, and as long as he had other children to interact with, he would be highly involved with them. When he found himself without peer companionship, however, rather than playing alone he would often ask me to play with him. He and Jennifer both liked to control their playgroups by making suggestions and commands, and they had enough influence that the other children would often play along. When he and Jennifer played together, though, it usually was not long before Alex went to play somewhere else. They would not always fight, but clearly both wanted control over what the group was doing. Since I was cooperative and nice, and would play along with the children, Alex could always count on me as a back-up companion. At naptime one day, having shown more interest in spending time with me than normal, he told me, "I didn't get a back ride."

"Well," I said, walking near his mat, "I can't give you one *now*."

"Sit down here. . . . I want you to sit here," Alex said. I sat with him for a few minutes and rubbed his back. While I did not want him to always get his way, I strove to help children find a sense of control through their communication.

A child who had been at the center the past year but had moved came back to visit one day. His name was Jimmy. John had been his best friend, the one he usually played with during his days at the center. So when Jimmy returned, John was naturally thrilled to have his old playmate back again. Several of the other children remembered Jimmy, and gave him friendly greetings, too, and their excitement evolved into a game where Katie and several other girls were chasing Jimmy, Brian, and John and kissing them (they especially tried to kiss Jimmy). Jimmy was having fun with this game, as were the other boys and girls involved. John, however, would drop out of the game and sit by himself. He did not seem happy about his classmates usurping his time with his friend. After a little while, he went over to Jimmy and said, "You're hurting my feelings." John told the girls, "I don't want you to kiss him anymore," trying to pull Jimmy along with him. Jimmy kept running away, along with the girls, leaving John sitting alone. Shortly after, though, the other children tired of the game, and John finally got his one-on-one time playing with Jimmy.

FAILED CONTROL STRATEGIES

Children would often fail in their attempts to get or to keep control, even of themselves at times. I'd been observing about eight months at the center when I noticed Will get angry because he wanted to use the taller sink to brush his teeth, and he knocked Alex out of the way. Seeing this, Ms. Dana took his toothbrush away and made him sit down briefly. At this point, he knocked over the trashcan. Ms. Stacey took him out of the classroom and into the darkened observation room to sit until he calmed down. I happened to be sitting in there writing, but I did not speak to him. Very soon, Ms. Stacey returned and asked Will, "Are you ready to come back now?"

"No," he said, still pouting a bit.

"Well, OK; next time I come back I want to hear you say, 'Yes,' you're ready to come back and do what you're supposed to."

After she had left again, he ventured a comment aloud: "It's my muscles that did it. My hand muscles did it."

"Well, someone has to *control* those muscles," I said.

"Sometimes I lose control," he added.

"You've got to try to keep control. Practice that," I said, and very soon Ms. Stacey returned again and brought Will back to his mat. It was compelling to see a five-year-old working forthrightly on an issue of self-control.

One day, I observed Laura directing a "movie" outside, telling sisters Jennifer and Nell to do certain steps and act out certain sports. The two girls happily played along, accepting Laura's direction. "Why don't they take some pictures of you?" asked Ms. Christina, passing by.

"'Cause I'm the boss," Laura said. She often took this role during play, and often the other children would accept it. If Laura tried to push this role too far, though, it could backfire on her. One day, she became impatient with Mary, and suddenly Laura exclaimed forcefully, "Move! Move, Mary! You have to do what I tell you."

"You're not the teacher," protested Mary.

"Move!" said an unfazed Laura. "When I tell you to do something, you're to do it," she added, sounding like a small impatient mother.

This was too much for Mary, who quietly refused to move. Laura herself had to move over, in the end. Several weeks later, I saw Laura and Jennifer playing together in the home living area. They had been playing there for quite awhile when Jennifer exclaimed, "I'm not your friend *anymore*." Laura had been asking Jennifer to do something (or, more accurately, *telling* her to), and Jennifer had had enough. "I'm not your friend anymore, 'cause you're always *mean* to me."

"Why won't you play?" asked a nonplussed Laura.

"Because you're *mean*," answered Jennifer. "You're always the boss."

"Will you be my friend if we're both the boss? We're both the boss," asserted Laura. This agreement to share control seemed to work, as Laura and Jennifer continued to play together for a time.

Boys, too, would get used to a controlling relationship with other children and push their attempts at control too far. Carl was playing with Matt outside, and Matt, five years old and about to go to kindergarten, was telling four-year-old Carl, "Here's that big block; get it, Carl." Carl picked up a big plastic block and carried it a little way toward the tree. He quickly tired of its heaviness and awkwardness, and let it drop. Matt had to go get it and carry it the rest of the way himself. Matt was clearly enjoying playing with and commanding Carl, however.

After a little time of following Matt's orders, Carl tired of the game and ran over to tell me Matt and he were "trying to get those two acorns down from the tree. But we couldn't." Carl started to climb the monkey bars nearby.

Soon, David, another four-year-old, came over and said, "Carl, Matt wants you." Carl just went on climbing. David left, but quickly returned again. "Hey," said David. "Matt still wants you."

Carl went on climbing, got down, and said nonchalantly, "I'm never going back over there," and walked on.

David suddenly looked determined, grabbed Carl in a hug, and said softly, "I'll bring you over there." He began hauling Carl, but that only lasted about three steps before Carl took off running, with David in hot pursuit.

This chase lasted for a couple of rounds of the playground. After David tired of it, sitting down, Carl ran closer to him and said, "You still can't get me," trying to get the chase started again. David would not comply, and both boys moved on to other areas. None of the three managed to get their control established with the others that morning.

Jimmy and Rob had been friends over several weeks, playing together regularly each day I observed them. On one particular day, when Jimmy arrived, he stayed away from Rob. "C'mon, Jimmy," Rob said. "Let's play freeze tag. I got you."

"I'm not playing freeze tag," said Jimmy. A little later, Jimmy was sitting on the tire swing and Rob came and got on with him. "No!" said Jimmy. "I don't want you on here. I'm not your friend anymore." Jimmy reinforced these comments by getting off the tire swing himself. "He's just a crybaby," Jimmy added. Apparently, two days earlier, Rob had gotten hurt and cried. Jimmy had somehow caused the accident and had gotten in trouble; now he was still angry. Outside, soon after Jimmy had left him on the tire swing, Rob came over to me and complained, "Jimmy won't be my friend." Rob's strategy as the day continued was to stay near Jimmy and to make sure to sit with him at lunch. Jimmy came to grudgingly accept Rob's presence and companionship. Rob clearly was struggling to maintain the relationship between them, but Jimmy was now accepting Rob only conditionally or temporarily. Jimmy was beginning to realize how much power he had over Rob.

Other failed attempts at control occurred when many of the three-, four-, or five-year-olds wanted to play ball. They would be unwilling to release control of the ball by throwing it to another. One day, Alex threw a ball to me, and I threw it back toward him, but it flew just past him to Carl. Carl liked this, and so he kept asking me to play ball with him. Any time I said "Yes," he would refuse to let the ball go. He also asked other children to play ball with him, and again would not let it go. Evidently, he did not trust that he would get it back. So no ball game would get started, and soon Carl would be asking us again, "Will you play ball with me?"

"If you want people to play ball with you, you have to let go of it, and throw it to someone," Ms. Stephanie told him. Shortly after, he did throw the ball to me and to some of the teachers. He seemed to trust adults to throw the ball back to him, but not other children.

After another year, Carl had mastered the idea of playing ball. At that point, he was organizing kickball games. The number of bases the four- and five-year-olds used when playing kickball was flexible; it could range from three to seven. "No, stay there," said Carl to a child who had gotten to the second base. "Don't run till somebody kicks it," he added. He was clearly in charge of the game as the organizer, and making sure the other children knew the rules.

Meanwhile, in the line of children waiting to kick the ball, Brian was trying to join the line anywhere but at its end. He went and stood in front of John, who was at the front. John looked downcast and uttered a word of protest. Then, Brian tried the middle of the line, getting words of protest and shoves from other children in line. They were collectively maintaining control of the kickball "system," and all playing were expected to conform to its rules. When Brian stood in front of Derek, near the back of the line, Derek too protested. "I'll be your friend if you'll let me in line here," said Brian, and he stood in front of Derek. Derek still protested, moving back in front of Brian. "But I'm your friend now," Brian insisted, still hoping his strategy would work.

At this point, I decided to use my adult influence. With Derek now in front of Brian, I moved to the back of the line. "I'm in line behind Brian," I said, but at that moment Brian once again moved in front of Derek. "Oh, wait!" I added quickly. "I'm in line behind Derek," I said. Derek looked up at me and smiled, and seeing this, Brian moved back behind Derek and in front of me again. Then, my attention proved the ultimate distraction and his attempts to assert control over his place in line were forgotten.

ADULTS KEEP CONTROL

The staff at the center generally promoted choice making by the children and gave them the flexibility to try to gain a sense of control through communicating with one another. However, there were limits beyond which adults would reassert their own control. For the children, one fun form of control was to start an activity that other children would imitate. One day, Carl started a parade around the classroom, and Timothy, Kelly, and Brian followed him, doing what he did—walking, kneeling down, and jumping at intervals. After a few rounds of the classroom, Ms. Stephanie decided to reassert teacher control, saying, "OK, now, find a place at the table." Taking two boys gently by the shoulder, she said, "You two sit here; you can talk to Mr. John." She gently but firmly moved the two other children to tables, where they started to build.

This adult reassertion of control was also evident one week after I started volunteering at the center. The children were getting loud in the classroom, with some crawling on the floor and playing animals. This was an "outside game," but Ms. Stacey tolerated it for a few minutes before saying, "All right. I want all animals to go to a table. We do that outside. Go to a table, we do that outside. Neil, stand up, now." As she said this, the children did find places at tables to play, and the noise level and animal play died down. The distinction between outside and inside activities was maintained, in the end, by an assertion of control by the teacher. But she had let the play go on inside for a short time, rather than insisting on full control immediately. Too, she had incorporated the children's game into her own directions by saying "I want all animals to go to a table," using a child-focused message to reassert adult control of the classroom.

Of course, the teachers would assert extra control if they felt the need. One day, Ms. Judy had all the children sit down in the middle of the playground before we all went inside. This was so outside of the normal routine that Michael asked, "Why are we all sitting down?"

"Now, I want to see how we can *walk* to the gate and inside," said Ms. Judy. When three children did not walk, she had them sit down outside and try it again. Implicitly acknowledging the break in routine to me, she noted, "If there was some catastrophe, we need to have them under control. We can't just have them flying all over the place." The children knew that their teachers and other adults had control, and such overt assertions of it were normally not needed and thus were infrequent at the center.

A few weeks later, several children were blowing bubbles that a teacher had brought out. Brent did not want to give Ellen a turn at blowing bubbles, even though his turn had gone on a good long time in comparison to most. I tried to help Ellen persuade Brent to let her have a turn, but none of our verbal suggestions worked. Ms. Katie eventually had to firmly take the bubble toys from Brent and give them to Ellen. Having no better choice then, Brent yielded and moved away. In this case, force by the teacher worked to reestablish control, while persuasion had not.

One day Alex was crying because he was sitting alone at a table during lunch. Ms. Stacey said to me, "It's gotten so he needs to be separated from the other kids; he's teaching them bad habits and I can't tolerate it." Soon, she went to Alex and said, "It's all right. You can eat your lunch, Alex." She knelt down by him. "I'll tell you why this is. When you've been sitting at the table, you've been telling the other kids to do things wrong and use bad manners. When you can make better choices and not teach the other children bad things, you can sit back at the tables again." When Alex kept up his crying, she took him out of the room. Ms. Stacey soon returned him to his little table, and though he had stopped crying, he did not look happy. This incident showed that teachers would not permit certain boundaries to be crossed without reasserting control and insisting on different behavior. But this extent of control stood out because of its rarity at the center.

Children naturally model their own power relations on those of adults, and so I observed how the teachers and the center's director interacted. Ms. Debra, the director, would often drop into the classrooms and chat with the adults and children present. She knew the children's names, and they did not seem to fear her the way students sometimes fear an elementary school principal. Ms. Debra treated staff members as equals, bantering and joking with them. While teachers noted her presence, there was no sense of hustle or shaping up when she came into the classrooms. The director's power seemed well understood but muted, a part of the chaotic daily atmosphere, with teacher aides and student observers coming in and out of the classrooms regularly.

The most powerful person for the children was clearly the lead teacher, who was in charge of their classroom and the most constant adult presence each day. Even with three-year-olds, the absence of the lead teacher made a difference. When Ms. Tanya went on an errand, Mr. Ted, an older gentleman, was left with the children, who had been inside all morning due to cold temperatures. They seemed to have missed their outside time. After Ms. Tanya left, the noise level gradually increased and several fights broke out. Kim and Tyler had built a tall tower out of LEGOs on the floor. Lauren and Todd knocked over the tower and took some of the blocks. The four children grabbed at each other and the LEGOs until I separated them. "That was not nice," I told Tyler. "I'm sorry they weren't nice to you. They want to play with the blocks, too." Tyler cried about the situation a little, and eventually moved away to play in the block area. By this time, several other boys were using the small drawers from the home living area's dresser as seats on a train. Several other children were walking in line as a train around the classroom. Their voices grew louder and louder, and they brushed blocks from the tables onto the floor. Mr. Ted, mellow and unassertive (as well as being fairly new), and I managed to get the children to replace the drawers, but still the noise seemed to grow louder. With a feeling of relief, I saw that Ms. Tanya had returned and was having the children start cleanup time. I was struck by the contrast between the three-year-olds' response to Mr. Ted and me and their response to their lead teacher.

When I accompanied the children on a field trip my sense of authority was enhanced by both adults and children. Each adult going along was assigned several children to guide and keep track of. A couple of times, I went to the local zoo with the four-year-olds, and they did a good job of staying with me and doing as I asked, which I found quite rewarding and fun. But my power and control in those instances was directly reinforced by the presence and guidance of the lead teacher and a teacher aide or two. The lead teacher maintained control during the field trips, with comments like, "Hold someone's hand. Get a partner"; but that control was individualized by the adult group leaders. I felt rewarded to have my own sense of power respected by the children and my on-staff colleagues at the center.

It was an indicator of the lead teacher's power that I always felt a sense of relief when I knew Ms. Stephanie, or Ms. Tanya, or Ms. Stacey was around. If the children got rambunctious, we could count on the lead teacher to use her credibility and forcefulness to reassert needed control. I was less sure of myself and my control, given my ambivalent situation as a volunteer; it was exhilarating when the children would listen to me or respond to my suggestions. Other staff members, too, who were not around full-time, had to strive harder to maintain control over the classroom. We would echo and reinforce each other's decisions. About two years after I had started spending time at the center, the lead teachers were absent, and the student teacher in charge had planned a field trip to the post office. Ms. Eva had the children sit on the floor, preparing for departure. She and Ms. Jane were making sure the van was ready and other details were wrapped up before we left. It was time to assign each teacher or adult chaperone three to five children to shepherd during the trip, a procedure usually done by the lead teacher. On this day, Ms. Eva decentralized this process, letting each adult choose some children to guide. I felt adrift. Which children did I favor by picking? It got harder when Timothy said, "Mr. John, will you pick me? Pick me," and then Kenny said the same. Michelle said, "Pick me and Christy," while Neil said, "Mr. John, pick me."

It was tough to pick some and not others, so I said, "We'll see who's on my list."

Timothy kept persisting. "Pick me. I want to hold your hand." So, I let him do so for the moment. "Please pick me," he kept saying, so I tapped him on the head. Then Kenny came up and grabbed my other hand, and I let him remain. All the children had now been asked to move toward the door, so the process of dividing the children up this time seemed rather random and chaotic.

Seeking guidance about who I would be shepherding, I asked Ms. Eva, "How are we dividing them up? And how many do we each take? I don't know." She and Ms. Jane were now getting children, one by one, into groups of three.

"How about Amy?" Ms. Eva said.

"OK," I said. "Amy can come with me." Thus were we finally and more chaotically than usual divided into our groups, and we proceeded out to the van. I wondered how the field trip would go without a lead teacher, but once we were under way the children did fine, and Ms. Eva stayed in charge in her quiet, mellow way. As long as the children had a sense that someone was in charge, they would cooperate. It was in the transition times, especially when the next activity was uncertain, that the absence of the lead teacher's control was most noticeable. I was perhaps more sensitive to these situations, since my own ambivalent status and tentative sense of control with the children were more apparent at such times.

In terms of control, I once found myself asking, "Which came first, the chicken or the egg?" As naptime began, I would often rub the backs of a few children who asked me to, while other staff members would do the same. One day, Evan came over and asked me to rub his back while I was rubbing Jennifer's. "OK," I said. "If you lie on your mat quietly, I'll come over and rub your back."

He went over to his mat, but did not lie quietly. He squirmed around and made noises. Other teachers in the room asked him to rest quietly. "Mr. John can't come over and rub your back if you aren't on your mat," Ms. Stephanie said to him a couple of times. Finally, I went over to him.

"Rub my back!" he ordered. Usually, the children would quiet down when their back was being rubbed, but I thought Evan needed a lesson in listening.

"If you can lie quietly here on your mat for *one* minute, I'll come back and rub your back. I'll be right back," I said.

"OK," he said, finally.

I walked around the room, and when I returned I asked Ms. Stephanie if he had been quiet. "Yes," she said.

"That's good! That's the way. Now I can rub your back," I said, and did so for a few minutes while he stayed quiet. Sometimes it was hard to decide whether to rub the children's backs to help them get quiet or to insist that they get quiet before rubbing their backs. There seemed to be a battle for control between children and adults as naptime began. This would generally last only a short period of time before all the children would get quiet, with many sleeping. Occasionally, a child would not be still during much of naptime. The teachers would have to think of creative ways to maintain their control, and the child would be removed from the classroom in extreme situations.

One year the combination of the lead teacher's and the teacher aide's personalities led to tighter control of the children's behaviors. It was manifest in several small ways. For instance, normally lunchtime talk was tolerated and even encouraged as long as it stayed out of the hollering decibel range. Shortly after a particular day's lunch had gotten under way, two boys and two girls were talking at a table, and I heard, "I'm gonna marry Alice," from someone.

Then, Derek said, "I'm gonna marry Charline," smiling. Charline shook her head, but Derek kept saying, "Yes, I am," and smiling.

Ms. Chaundra overheard this and said, "Let's not start this conversation; on Friday it led in a bad way."

Soon after this, Ms. Stacey said, "Let's eat without talking." When a few conversations continued, she said, "Excuse me. Eat your lunch without talking. Derek, you are talking with your mouth full. Let's eat our lunches without talking."

Then Ms. Chaundra walked over to the table where some of the children had been talking about marriage. "About this talk about marriage—no one is marrying anyone in the four-year-olds' classroom, or the fives' classroom."

Then Ms. Stacey chimed in, "We are all friends in this classroom; no boyfriends or girlfriends, but just friends." Silence was enforced for a while, which seemed most unusual at lunchtime. Then Ms. Stacey said, "If you need something, raise your hand, and then you may talk. Alice, eat without talking."

"Yes, ma'am," responded Alice, and the silence continued as lunch finished up.

"This is new," I thought, and I put it down to the increased stress on control that year by Ms. Stacey and Ms. Chaundra. At times, it seemed almost like a contest between them to see who was most in charge of the children. I never had seen so much control not only of what children did, but of what, how, and when they talked. A few days later Ms. Stacey said, "Remember what I've said about talk about girlfriends in here. We're all just friends." I had heard talk about girlfriends and marriage by the children at intervals before, and it just faded away naturally. This time, for some reason, Ms. Stacey and Ms. Chaundra made it into a control issue. Soon, the topic died away among the children once again.

One day that December, the children were distracted by reports of possible snow. When it did start to snow, the movie the four-year-olds were watching was interrupted as all headed to the door or windows to see. Ms. Stacey let them all take a brief run around in the snow outside, but quickly called them back inside even though they wanted to stay outside and play. "It's too cold," she said. Back inside, the children were restless and talking during the movie. Finally, Ms. Chaundra stopped the movie and said, "You need to sit still and listen before the movie starts again."

"Either the TV talks to you, or you talk. We can't have both," Ms. Stacey added, reinforcing the adult reassertion of control. Watching videos at school was rare for the children, and they usually paid close attention, so clearly the weather was distracting them. After that year, when Ms. Stacey and Ms. Chaundra no longer worked together in the classroom, adult control seemed to return to its previous, more tolerant, levels.

ADULTS AND POWER DIFFERENCES

I noted during my time of observation at the child-development center that adults and children lived in different worlds in terms of power and face maintenance. One incident struck me as inadvertently illustrating this power difference. Matt and several other children were at a table playing with plastic blocks of various shapes, and I talked with them briefly. Matt, as he was leaving the table, tossed a toy plastic star that hit me lightly in the stomach. I was torn between surprise and an inclination to chuckle at this seemingly boyish, playful act, but Ms. Stacey, the lead teacher, had observed the incident, and to her eyes it was an unacceptable act of disrespect.

"Matt, wait," said Ms. Stacey. "Come back here and think about what you did to Mr. John. What happens when you hit people with things?"

"It hurts them," Matt answered in a small voice.

"And what do you say when you hurt someone? What should you tell Mr. John?"

"I'm sorry," Matt said in his quiet voice.

"Good," said Ms. Stacey. "Now let's don't throw things at people."

Matt moved away, looking sad and mad, and stayed by himself for a while. I think he was treating me playfully, almost as another big child, and was shocked to find he had violated the respect and power rules between adults and children, which he normally knew well enough. I understood Ms. Stacey's point, seeking to maintain the power structure, and in my surprise at having a small toy thrown at me I certainly did not contradict her. I did make it a point, though, to spend extra time with Matt later that day and reassure him that I still liked him.

I did notice through the years that, with some exceptions, the older the child, the longer it took him or her to open up to communication with me or trust me. It seemed that the older children had learned the social norm of self-control in terms of expressing feelings or communicating with others, and the dangers of trusting another in a relationship. The older children also seemed more conscious of the "power barrier" between children and adults. The young four- and five-year-olds were more willing to disregard this barrier as I interacted with them, and they would quickly play games or want to pretend with me. With the three-year-olds, spending even an hour or so in their classroom would lead children I barely knew to want to play with me, run up and embrace me, or ask me to help them. Simply being near them and apparently benign led them to trust and approach me. When I visited the after-school program regularly, it would take several days or even weeks before children older than six would easily talk to me or want to involve me in their play. They were reluctant to pretend with me until even further along in the relationship. The children seemed much more concerned with their self-image after the age of six, and they seemed to have more of a sense of the social hierarchy and the expected behaviors of people at each level of it.

Even the younger children I observed often encountered hierarchical power differences, though. For instance, one of the children would often have to say, "Ms. Brenda!" to a teacher three or four times before being acknowledged, while adults might have to repeat themselves once at most to get another's attention. The children, at times, would reciprocate this—they would not respond at first even when I was fairly sure they could hear an adult addressing them.

The children would sometimes treat me as a power-rich adult, telling me about some behavior other children had engaged in. They assumed that, as an adult, I must have the power to immediately respond to an infraction, or to provide permission or supplies for something I had no knowledge of. It took the children some time to realize that, while I moved in the adult "power world," I chose to join them in their world much of the time. Thus, I was accepted fairly quickly by three-, four-, and five-year-olds into their world of pretend and games, and would often hear "sit beside me!" as they gathered on the floor for circle time. Most children did not bother to try to get individual attention from the teachers in the room as much as they would seek it from me. After I had known Paul for a few months, the three-year-old would see me and call out happily; but then he began calling me strange names: "Mr. Johnny, Mr. Ponny, Mr. Mommy." They were cute rhymes, but there seemed to be an undercurrent of disrespect in his familiarity. I chose to regard the names as an expression of affection, but was struck by how as an adult I was still sensitive to potential symbols of disrespect coming from a young child.

A child's trustful disregard of the power difference between himself or herself and adults could be disconcerting or even irritating. One day I got carried away interacting with a normally quiet, cooperative Daniel and found myself shocked at our mutual attempts at control. This occurred on the playground about two years after I started at the center. I felt comfortable in my relationships with all the children, and they and the staff all seemed comfortable with me. I had found a tricycle abandoned and sitting near the sidewalk outside. Unthinkingly, playfully, I stood on it and started moving it down the sidewalk. Suddenly, Daniel came over and climbed on it. Somewhat taken aback by this assertiveness, I started to joke with him. "Why are you taking my bike?" I asked.

"I want to ride it," he said.

"No, don't take my bike," I said, still kidding but getting angry.

"I want to *ride* it," he said, growing more strident.

"How can you take my bike?" I asked, growing genuinely concerned at his disregard for my standing on the tricycle.

"Get *off* of it. . . . Get *off* of it. Get away from it," he said, also growing angry.

I usually avoided or gave in to fights like these, but now I was genuinely angry. Daniel started to yell, "No! Get away from it!" which was out of character for him.

"I'll stay away from you *forever*," I said firmly but softly (after looking around to see if another adult was around). I knew what I did was wrong even as the incident unfolded, but it reinforced for me that adults have feelings in their relationships with children, and must find appropriate ways to acknowledge and, if needed, communicate them. Then I did walk away, as Daniel said something else—I missed it in my anger. I felt badly, but I thought, "I've made my stand; I don't want to overcompensate now, so follow through." I went elsewhere; I did not seek Daniel out though I was tempted to do so, and I casually moved away when he rode the tricycle toward me and said something. From his perspective, I'm sure that I was being unreasonable—tricycles were for the children, after all, not the teachers. He probably did not see his action as taking the tricycle from me.

Soon after this, Daniel ran over to me, saying in a worried tone, "Mr. John, I took turns. I took turns."

I picked him up, saying, "Oh, Daniel, that's so nice. I'm so glad you took turns, I'm going to give you mine, too." And I put him back on the tricycle he had yielded up, and said, "Go ride again." To our mutual relief, things between us were fine. The incident was a quick education for me on power differences, as well as emotion taking over when one feels a loss of control.

Even as I moved often into the lower-power world of the children, I found I had power currencies I could spend, having some talents that were appreciated. I even found myself defending and bragging about a particular talent one morning. Andrew and Jimmy were sitting on the tire swing outside, and as I passed by Andrew said, "Mr. John! Will you spin us around?"

"OK," I said. "Hold on tight! You'll go real fast!" I spun them, to their obvious enjoyment.

A little later, after they had slowed down, Andrew asked a passing Will, "Will, do you want to get spinned around fast by Mr. John?"

"Yes," said Will, and he got on the tire swing.

"Ready?" I said. "Hold on."

"Yes," the boys said, and I spun them.

"No! Stop! I'm scared!" said an alarmed Will.

"No, it's not so scary. It's not scary," reassured Andrew, as Will got off anyway. "You're too little to spin around yet. You're too little. Hey Jimmy, do you want to be spun around by Mr. John?"

"Yes," said Jimmy, and stayed on the tire swing. I spun them again.

Soon, Andrew said, "Mr. Max can spin faster," apparently to see how I would react.

"No, he can't," I replied, half jesting but feeling a little defensive.

"Why?" asked Andrew.

"Because no one spins faster than I do," I said, and kept on spinning them as they showed their enjoyment.

"You both spin the same," said Andrew. Andrew clearly saw himself as more powerful than Will, who was scared to get spun around on the tire swing, but less powerful than myself or Mr. Max, who could spin them on the tire fast. My place in the power structure for him seemed to be as a friend who had some of the power of an adult without all of the distance in relationship he normally expected to go with it. I found myself not wanting to be viewed as secondary to Mr. Max by a child, even though Mr. Max was a staff member and I was not. I should not have minded that he was higher in the children's hierarchy, but I found myself demanding equality.

Another power currency I had with four- and five-year-olds was sports prowess. It was not hard to excel as a reasonably fit adult playing with little children, but for me it was new, as during my growing-up years I was not very athletically inclined. One summer day, some of the children organized a softball game, and Michelle asked me, "Would you be our pitcher?" I did this for quite a while. Michelle acted as catcher and announced "Strike one" or "Strike two" or "Strike three; you're out!" helped by other children in line. Most of the children in the class joined the line to play for a while. I tried to keep the pitches easy to hit, but even at four and five it was quite a challenge for some of the children to hit the ball. As a child who had always found it difficult to hit a baseball or softball, I found it ironic to now be in the power position of pitcher. I tried to encourage those who had trouble as much as I could with phrases like, "Almost!" or "I know it's hard," or "Hit it; hit a home run." All seemed to enjoy trying in this communication climate, though Tina seemed rather frustrated when, though she was one of the older girls, she still could not hit the ball. I sought to make them feel like they were having fun, even though I could have mocked them or made it impossible for them to hit the ball. I wanted to equalize our adult-child relationship somewhat for the sake of playing the game.

One day after about a year at the center, I observed a humorous instance of the power distance between adults and children, made interesting by the involvement of an adult not normally part of the child-care environment. A maintenance man entered the classroom to change the filter in the air conditioning unit. I was sitting with some children at the coloring table near the door, labeled "MECHANICAL," behind which the unit sat. Like myself, the children had never seen that door open. "So *that's* what's in that door," said Mary, watching.

Alex and Timothy came over to see what was going on, and started to ask a whole bunch of questions. "What are you doing? Why are you in here?" asked Timothy.

"What is that? What are you going to do with that?" asked Alex.

The maintenance man ignored them completely (though his task did not seem so complicated that it needed his full attention).

Getting frustrated, Alex turned to me and asked, "Why doesn't he answer us?"

I shrugged. When the man produced a new air filter, I finally volunteered something for the sake of their insatiable four-year-old curiosity: "Time to change the filter," I said.

"That's the old one," said Timothy as the man took it off.

"Yep," said the man, his only word during the ten-minute procedure. At one point, Ms. Stephanie told Kelly and Alex and Timothy to move back to give the man room to work. It was fascinating for me to observe one of many adults who seem to have no clue about how to interact with children. The man's discomfort and reluctance to communicate almost made the children seem like the powerful ones temporarily.

Children took the power difference between themselves and adults very seriously. One day, I heard Ms. Jill say several times in her joking but forceful way, "Watch yourselves! We don't want any accident reports. No accident reports on Fridays!" Later, Carl approached me on the playground whimpering. He had scratched his arm on top of the fence. While the scratch was not deep, it was long and bleeding slightly. It turned out that Carl was not hurting much, but he was afraid to tell Ms. Judy or Ms. Stephanie about the scratch because he'd heard "No accident reports on Fridays" repeated. I went with a reluctant Carl to talk to Ms. Stephanie (the staff had to know about and respond to all injuries, of course), and she was sweet and reassuring to Carl. He was more worried about getting in trouble for his accident than about the pain of the scrape itself!

An older child once verbalized the perceived power difference between adults and children quite directly. I had agreed to go on a field trip that included older school-aged children, and I entered the room that morning to hear discussions among the children about which adult's group they would be in. Ten-year-old Sarah asked me, "Could I be in your group with Hannah and Alex, and Mandy and Laura, 'cause Laura will cry if she's not with Mandy?"

Not yet knowing what the situation was, I jokingly said, "That would make one group with only two families."

"Could we?" persisted Sarah.

"I'm not sure of the groups," I responded honestly.

"Well, could you ask?" said Sarah. "You're an adult so they'll listen to you; they won't listen to us 'cause we're kids."

"OK," I responded, taken aback by that forthright statement. Sarah did not sound whiny or complaining, but was just matter-of-factly stating her view of the situation. I thought she had neatly verbalized the perspective—and complaint—of many children as they grow up and seek attention and respect. I did her the favor of bringing up the issue with the lead teacher, but the groups had already been chosen, as I had suspected. Sarah and her sisters traveled with me, and were delightful companions, following my suggestions and staying near me. Laura wound up traveling with Mandy in another group.

Control issues could arise between adults as well. Ms. Stephanie, the lead teacher, was out ill one week, and the assistant and student teachers were filling in for her. Mr. Sam, a part-time worker at the center, came in to "visit" that day, and wound up filling an extra teacher role for an hour or so. During his interaction with the children, he let several children follow him onto an adjacent (and empty) playground, which meant the teachers needed to round them all up and get them back on the right playground. He did this in fun, and none of the regular teachers protested it, although they looked a little taken aback. Mr. Sam had a forceful personality and could make the children listen well, usually. Still, this time, he was reduced to carrying and lifting some of the playfully reluctant children over the fence while I held the gate closed against attempts by some other children to get back on the alternative playground. Mr. Sam tended to add an element of "craziness" when he was in the classroom, and other staff members seemed to laugh at it while viewing it with some uncertainty as "outside the norm" and a little out of control.

The next day, I realized that not all staff members were pleased with Mr. Sam, as he returned to the four-year-olds' classroom to substitute for Ms. Stephanie, and the assistant teacher, Ms. May, made plain in side comments to me that she did not appreciate his style or his usurpation of control of the class. He never spoke to Ms. May or let her know that he would be substituting for Ms. Stephanie as the morning began. He was just there. Later in the morning, he made a classroom announcement that a little girl had lost her ring, while Ms. May had been more discreetly helping her look for it.

"Now she'll feel worse if we can't find it," Ms. May said to me. "You never want to make these things a big deal." They eventually found the ring, fortunately, in the little girl's own shoe! Mr. Sam could be more directive and somewhat overbearing in his relations with the children (he was in the military reserves, and I think this showed). "He is a stranger in this classroom," Ms. May said to me later. "I wish he would act like it. I hate to say it," she said, "but people should 'know their place.'" Ms. May clearly did not appreciate the forceful taking of control by a newcomer, or part-timer, who was a "stranger" in the classroom. Mr. Sam clearly violated some norms of control for teachers during his visits to the classrooms that month.

ONE RESEARCHER'S AMBIVALENT POWER ENACTMENT

I, too, started out as a stranger at the center, and had to figure out my position in the power and control hierarchy. One day, shortly after I began spending time at the center, I was walking around the playground and came upon Alex and Carl digging in the turf. Matt also had approached them and was talking to them. As I approached, Matt said, "They're digging up the grass—make them stop!"

"Are you digging up the grass?" I then asked the two boys.

"No," said Alex, "we're digging up mud."

"No, that's grass!" insisted Matt. "We need grass to live. Don't dig it up."

"We're only digging up mud. We're digging for mud treasure," explained Alex.

Having seen Alex often playing a game of looking for treasure, I put in, "Did your treasure map tell you this was the spot?"

"Yes," said Alex. I was not thrilled with them digging on the playground, but I was faced with whether to interact about it casually or make it a control issue by asking them to stop digging. I hesitated to do the latter, and chose to observe what transpired after this dialogue. Matt still was not happy, even though he often had played treasure hunt with Alex.

"Stop, you're digging up—cows eat grass; how would you like it if you didn't have milk to drink?" asked Matt with some inspired creativity.

Alex did not know what to say to that, and remained silent, continuing to dig in the dirt. Matt then went off to find Ms. Stacey, the lead teacher. It dramatized for me how little control I had over the children, due to the little control I would exert. They knew I would not force them to do much of anything. In a way that was good—I persuaded by force of reason or by my good relationships with the children—but it would not be good when I encountered a child determined to do something wrong. In this instance, by the time Matt found Ms. Stacey and told her, Alex and Carl had moved on somewhere else in their treasure hunt, so it worked out all right for me not to have asserted control. I was learning I would have to choose my battles for control in my ambiguous role at the center.

I often found difficulty in balancing communicating one-on-one with the children and the need to discipline and be more commanding toward them. There were times when my ambivalent role pulled me in opposite directions—talking empathically with the children on one hand, and assertively directing them on the other. One day, several four-year-olds wanted to ride on my back, as usual. I had gradually adopted a policy of giving each child who wanted a back ride only one each day. In doing so I had conceded spontaneous play to a rule that allowed each child a turn and prevented back rides from taking over all my time with the children. On another day, Paul wanted me to chase him and started running down the wooden steps of a large playhouse. In his haste to get away, he stumbled and rolled down the stairs (almost in slow motion, it seemed). Needless to say, I felt terrible. It had not occurred to me that he might try to run away while we were up there. I wanted to pick Paul up, but I knew if he was seriously injured that could make it worse. So I tried to comfort him and let him get up by himself. He finally did so, as an interested nearby Jennifer said, "We shouldn't run down the stairs."

"Yes, we'll have to remember, huh, not to run down the stairs," I added to Paul. He soon stopped crying, and was OK. But I was struck by the irony: myself, the adult, feeling guilty like a little boy for playing too rough with Paul, while Jennifer, the four-year-old, voiced the teacher's lines. Later that same day, I was near the swings having an enjoyable interaction with John and Jawon when they started shoveling gravel at one another. I had to put my teacher/disciplinarian hat on. "Rocks need to stay on the *ground*," I said firmly, using the positive direction favored at the center. They paused only briefly, since they viewed me more as a "companion" than as an authority. I finally decided to playfully chase John away. This diverted him from the gravel, but I still did not feel taken seriously and was frustrated. Yet, I needed to remember that I wanted interaction with the children more than I wanted control over them, so I had to accept a lower level of power and influence than most adults on staff at the center might have had. One reason I avoided conflict was that if I kept trying to tell the children what to do and was disregarded enough times, I would wind up with even less credibility.

A few times I did intervene and try to take adult control too soon. Timothy was outside on the playground one day, rolling a tire up the wood ramp and letting it roll back down. Neil tried to assist with the tire, but Timothy said, "No! I'm gonna do something with it!"

After Timothy rolled it down again, Neil said, "Can I try?"

"No," said Timothy.

"You never share," said Neil.

"I just got it," said Timothy.

"Hey, another tire," said Neil, and he pulled it out from under the play platform and began to stand it up. Soon, I heard him protesting at Ramon, who had knocked the tire over and was sitting on it.

Seeing Neil getting frustrated again, and with a sense of injustice, because Neil had worked on getting the tire out and Ramon was now keeping it from him, I firmly pulled Ramon out, saying, "Neil was trying to play with that."

Ramon started crying and said, "You hurt my arm!"

"I didn't mean to hurt you," I said.

Ramon moved off, sat down, and flung a few rocks around. After pouting for a while, he got up and started interacting with the other boys again. A bit later, I noted that Neil had tired of the tire and Ramon was rolling it. I could not help but wonder: Would they have resolved the issue to their own satisfaction if I had not intervened?

As time went on, I began to realize that it was up to me to set the tone for communication between a child and myself, especially on first meeting or arrival. By trying to let the child set the tone by initiating communication, I may unintentionally have snubbed or seemed to ignore a child at times. I decided I would make sure in most instances to give a friendly greeting, and *then* sit back and let the child respond or communicate as he or she saw fit, which produced the richest observations.

Having faced this ambivalent state of power for several months, I reflected on one day's events:

Today the main issue for me was communication and closeness versus control and distance in relation to the kids. It was one of those days where they did things that were quite endearing and reminded me that I love them, but also pushed my frustration and temper to the limit.

On the one hand: Shaun came over and wanted to sit in my lap for a while and build a city out of LEGOs at the table. David wanted me to build blocks with him, and John wanted me to read him a story. Among the three-year-olds, Neil came over with a fish he had made and wanted to sit in my lap for a while. "Time to go to sleep," he would say, and curl up. "It's wake-up time!" he'd say after I closed my eyes. Greg also came over later and grabbed onto my back playfully, even though we were not outside.

On the other hand: David and Jawon were throwing pine cones at me on the playground; Shaun and John threw mud balls, and Mary kept trying to grab my belt buckle as I walked around outside. Paul kept wanting to get on my back and would not let go. I find that while the kids trust me and love me, they (at times) do not respect me or listen to me when I ask them to stop something. I need to work on preserving the relationships while being firmer when necessary. If the kids have a right to their feelings, I have a right to mine as well. I also find that I need to use talking to Ms. Stacey about them as a threat, though I'd rather handle it myself. As an adult, I should not have to threaten to "tell the teacher," yet today it did work. The lead teacher is respected because of her constant presence and consistent discipline; I'm just a fun guy who shows up a couple of times a week. While that basically is the role I want, I would like some respect. I need to realize that kids will recover after I get angry with them, as long as I don't lose control. I certainly can tell them how I feel and that they should stop doing something. I also warn them they will get in trouble. I also need to work on being creative and suggesting a different game or activity with them, though some can be stubborn.

Throughout my time at the center, I tried to balance my role as "honorary staff member," accumulating some of the power and respect of that role, with being a playful extra-big peer of the children.

I could become too involved with the children, seeking too much control by communicating with them at the expense, I came to feel, of my own observations and study of communication in their child-care environment. Nearly two years after I began my work at the center, I reflected on these feelings in my journal:

> At intervals during this work I find I have to work on "letting go," or not intruding on or demanding participation in the children's interactions. This gives me some quiet times sitting in the classroom, which over the past few weeks I have cultivated. It is partly the notion of letting the kids come to me if they want to, and otherwise simply observing their interactions and not interfering or speaking unless spoken to. I have found that when I get too involved in volunteering here, I circulate around the classroom, seeking confirmation, affection, and participation, rather than just seeing what kind of interaction is going on, and per-

haps being drawn in naturally. The key issue for me is patience—gratifying interactions with kids will happen if I make myself available for them and wait. I know I must avoid being a "busybody" or seeking my own reward and acceptance among the kids; instead I seek to observe their interactions and relationships and become involved and accepted more naturally. Inevitably, it seems, when I focus on "letting go" a little, special events happen and relationships grow. For instance, today, Sarah colored a picture for me, and many kids came over to talk to me without my even trying. I don't always need to start a conversation when none is really needed. The kids come to me on their own. I only need to be present.

Reminding myself to simply be present more was an attempt to moderate my own desire to guide relationships into good growth. Taking a laissez-faire role resulted in strengthened relationships while allowing me to focus more on my observations and research.

Control and structure were necessary at the child-development center, yet adults could create and reinforce a wide range of strategies for their maintenance. Uninterested or inconsistent adults could promote tolerance of disorder, or too much control of interaction by adults could lead to a stifling of flexible communication strategies enacted by children. With a more defensive communication climate, less communication would take place and messages would become more assertive, as children followed the adult lead and regularly sought a teacher to assert control. Generally, in the center where I observed, there was a looser and more varied exercise of control by adults. Such flexibility allowed a wide variety of control strategies to be attempted by the children, and more experiments with and learning from communication resulted. The need to control and to be controlled within a social order is basic to all individuals, and a child-development center staff can serve a crucial function in helping children learn to establish social control through sharing meaning.

8

Uncertain Relationships: Power Differences and Seeking Adult Support

Both among themselves and with adults, children at the child-development center were more or less sure of themselves, their competence, and their value to others during their interactions. Yet their effectiveness with peers seemed to depend on their effective communication with adults. All of the children tried to reassure themselves of adult support, whether by doing what was expected of them in the classroom for teacher approval, misbehaving to test teacher response, or getting attention through conversation or play with adults in attempts to develop relationships. Some children would pursue adult attention even further, asking for a story to be read, climbing into a lap, asking for a back rub at naptime, or, at the extreme, telling adults they loved them or giving a spontaneous hug. Most of the time, teachers would attribute preschoolers' low or high need for adult contact and support to their family background and their interaction with parents.

While differences in desire for adult help and contact were tolerated and appreciated, unusually high needs were considered problems, since disruption of classroom activities would often result. Children with such needs might constantly desire adult interaction or touch, or they would continually break rules or disrupt others to test adult response. The key to such attention-seeking behaviors may stem from an infant's development of attachment (or lack thereof) with the primary caregiver, usually the mother. As reassurance in life, and especially in times of stress, an infant seeks closeness to a consistent caregiver (Solomon and George 1999). Development of this sense of attachment leads to a secure attachment style, and most likely leads to balanced expectations for adult support in later years. Deprivation of attachment, however, can impact later relationships in various ways. A preschool child may avoid adult contact, showing detachment and not trusting such contact to be consistent; alternatively, a child may seek adult attention but then quickly reject it, showing an approach/avoidance pattern (Solomon and George 1999). I saw instances of both behaviors during my observations, and even more often observed anxious children desperately cling to interactions with a teacher or with myself. As I was one of the few males in the setting, many of the four- and five-year-olds, especially boys, worked hard to stay involved with me.

Different children would use more or fewer of these strategies depending on their need for adult support (their goal) and their view of the appropriateness of such actions (their assessment of the situation). Some felt included enough in class and were content with being a part of classroom activities and playing with their peers. Others found certain activities or individual teachers provided them with relatively rare or cherished opportunities for a closer relationship. For me, the most emotional situations involved children for whom establishing a closer relationship with me clearly was one of their highest priorities during our times together at the center.

AN UNCERTAIN POWER DIFFERENCE

At first, the children (and I) needed some time to understand who I was and what my role was in the classroom. After a few weeks, Evan was comfortable enough with me to approach me and ask, "What are you?"

"What *am* I?" I said.

"Not like a man or woman, but like are you a policeman or a businessman?"

"Oh," I said, "I'm a teacher."

"What do you teach?" asked Kenny, standing nearby.

"I teach at the university; the big school," I said. "We learn about communication; how people talk."

"Do they get to ride on your back?" asked Kenny.

"No," I said, stifling a laugh, "they are too big; they don't want rides on my back." I got a big kick out of this question, and so did the other teachers when I told them about it later. I could also tell from the question what was key to some of the children in our relationship.

Children took varied amounts of time to get used to my presence in the classroom and trust me enough to respond to or initiate interaction with me. One factor was what other children were doing with me. After weeks of seeing me give children in "my" four-year-old classroom back rides outside on the playground, four-year-old Andrew asked me for a back ride. Even though he was in another class, he had finally decided to trust me and try to join in a relationship like the children I was closest to. After Andrew took that first step, Anna, Nina, and Marcus, who also were from the class that did not see me as much, also asked for back rides. While Andrew had interacted with me briefly over several weeks when both classes were on the play-ground, the others had very seldom even talked to me. Yet when Andrew took the risk to initiate further interaction with me, he showed the way and made it more comfortable for the others to try it.

Several weeks later, Evan had a tough day of throwing things and pushing other children aside, and he was placed in time-out several times. At nap-time, he asked me to rub his back, and said, "I wish you could stay all the time. I wish you were the teacher, and not Ms. Stephanie."

"I'm a teacher, too," I said.

"But you're a helper, and my dad said you're not the teacher, she is."

I responded with, "She is the lead teacher; you are right about that." I fig-ured Evan wished I were around more because he could get away with more with me than with the teachers—but I also hoped that perhaps I was having some positive influence. I would, at times, have a child ask me, when it was near time for me to leave, "When will you stay in here all the time?" or "Will you stay in here every day?" The best that I could say then was that I would come into their classroom every day I was there. They wanted my presence and attention more than I would have guessed when I began volunteering and observing with them.

Some children, I noted, were always shy early in the morning when they first arrived at the child-development center. They might listen to adults greeting them or talking to them, but they would not talk back, even to adults they knew well. Later, they would open up and talk just as normal. I also found that if I refrained from greeting children, most would not greet me. They seemed to wait for the adult to make the first conversation move, especially as the day was beginning. When I did say, "Good morning" or "Hi," they might not respond immediately, but they would grow talkative and affectionate toward me faster. I gradually decided that it was part of my role as the "high-power" adult to initiate interaction by greeting the children, and then let each child follow up on the greeting as each saw fit. The ex-ceptions to this general rule were those children who had made a relation-ship with me a priority. From them I could count on an often effusive greet-ing when they first saw me arrive in the morning.

At first, since I was simply observing and interacting with the children and very seldom disciplining or asserting power over them, I would forget how much relational power they perceived me to have. One morning, Brian and I had been coloring at the art table, and I had drawn some fish of different col-ors. I spontaneously gave my fish picture to Brian. "Thank you," he said, very sincerely, and at clean-up time he took it all around the classroom, saying, "Look what Mr. John made for me." I had no idea it would become such an event for him. Later, at naptime, he took the picture out again and kept it next to him on his mat. I was reminded that simple adult acts can communicate great relational messages to children. Another morning several weeks later,

Brian was yelling, refusing to move, and causing a disturbance in the class-room. Brian was generally a well-behaved child. On this day, however, he had cried and jumped up and down in a mini-tantrum when his mother had left him, even though he usually did not show any separation anxiety. At lunchtime, Brian wanted me to sit next to him. I gave Ms. Stephanie a mis-chievous look as she told me I was welcome to eat the extra lunch that had been set out. "I don't know if I want to sit next to Brian," I teased.

Brian's face grew sad as he started to take me seriously. "Oh, he can be that way," remarked Ms. Stephanie, observing this. "Oh, look at that face!" she added, as she saw Brian looking so sad.

Feeling rather badly that he had taken me so seriously, I quickly said, "You know what? Brian's my buddy. I want to sit next to him." He looked so happy with me eating lunch next to him; I was glad to make him feel better, and re-alized that time with me could be seen as a valuable, desired commodity.

I also grew aware that attention from me could be perceived as a scarce resource to be competed for. Brian asked me to push him on a swing one day outside, and I walked over to do so. Before I could, however, Hunter and Michael asked me to push them. "Push *me* first," they each said. I went ahead and pushed Brian, because he had asked me first, after all. The other two boys were then quite put out.

"I'm not your friend anymore, Mr. John," said Hunter.

"I'm sorry to hear that," I responded. He still wanted me to push him. I did so, and then Michael got mad. "I'm not your friend, Hunter," Michael said, choosing to focus his anger on the pushed child rather than on me. Michael still wanted me to push him, and he was happy after I did so. But I noted that even being pushed first could indicate some sort of extra status or attention. On another day, I sat with Ivan as he built with small blocks at a table for over half an hour. He worked long and hard creating buildings, taking them down, and putting little "people" around and on them. Chris, following Ivan's exam-ple, sat next to him and built an even taller tower out of the blocks. Michael and Ryan, at times, passed by our table and would take a block from the other boys or even knock a tower down, on no provocation that I could see. I won-dered if they were jealous of Ivan and Chris and the praise and attention I gave them. Yet Michael and Ryan did not dwell on the situation and quickly moved away each time. I was not certain how much competition for adult attention and approval sparked their brief disputes, but I had a strong suspicion that it was at least a partial cause. In spite of these irritations, Ivan maintained his co-operative posture, giving Chris blocks that he wanted at intervals and asking before taking blocks nearer to Chris. I was impressed by Ivan's and Chris's civ-ilized behavior in contrast to Michael's and Ryan's raiding, "barbarian" behav-ior. These roles were not permanent and would switch over time.

On another morning, I was in the four-year-olds' classroom and I saw a newly arrived and quiet Mark in the room. "Hi, Mark," I said, and sat down at a table near where Ryan was building with big LEGOs. "Hi, Ryan," I said. "Whatcha building?"

"A big tractor," he said.

Soon, Mark came over and climbed on my lap, which surprised me, as this was a first for him. "I wanna go with my nanna and pappy; they brought me today," he said.

"Oh, will they pick you up today?" I asked.

Mark shook his head. Soon, he started building his own "big tractor" out of LEGOs. Ryan came closer and touched Mark's creation. "Noooo! Keep away!" said Mark. "Get out of here!"

"Ryan can build with his own LEGOs," I reassured them, and he did for a while. A couple of times other children would come over and talk to me, and Mark would attempt to push them away and say, "Get out of here!" He clearly wanted some time alone with me that morning. I seemed to fill a gap for him left by the adults who had dropped him off at school that day.

RELATIONSHIP AMBIVALENCE WITH ADULTS

Some children remained unsure how to react toward me as an adult; at certain times I seemed to be viewed as a threat; but at other times as an opportunity for a new relationship. One morning a few weeks after I began volunteering, I walked into the classroom and Ivan said "hello" to me as he often did, and as I passed the block area I said "hi" to Greg and Ryan, who were playing there. Ryan said "hi" back, but Greg said, "I'm not your friend anymore." This was the second time in two days that Greg had reacted to me this way, and I was unsure of why. We had never been particularly close, but I was unaware of any negative incident between us.

I chose never to make a big deal out of that response, however, and said, "Oh, that's too bad. Well, I'll be your friend anyway." I paused with them and watched them in the block area briefly, and then moved on. Kayla wanted me to read her a story, and I sat down with her and did so. Before long, it was Greg who came over, sat beside me, and got a book for me to read to them. They both kept me there reading to them for a while, alternating books chosen by each. Greg, that day, clearly overcame his dislike for me or his seeing me as a threat, and spending time with me became desirable for some reason. I felt my strategy of not being "set off" by his expression of dislike had paid off!

Children could, I found, clearly yet strategically indicate their dissatisfaction with our relationship. Vicki asked me one day to build roads with her in the block area. I did so for a little while, but was soon called away to another area. When I got back to the block area, I saw that Evan and Sarah had joined Vicki there. I randomly picked a block up from the shelf, and Vicki insisted, "No, we don't need anymore of those!" as she grabbed my arm.

"Oh, you're finished?" I asked, nonplussed by her sudden harshness with me.

"Yes," said Vicki, as Evan and Sarah continued to work on their road. I moved off, since I was encountering some mild hostility. A few minutes later, I saw Vicki at the art table coloring.

"Whatcha coloring?" I asked her.

She did not answer, but continued to color. After finishing with one crayon, she would throw me an angry look, get another crayon, and continue to color. Seeing that I was "in the doghouse" with her, I decided to just sit there and watch the classroom and not go any further toward taking this apparent bait for conflict. Soon, Amy came over and got a magazine out to cut. Vicki then took the initiative, asking, "Do you know what these are, Mr. John?"

"They look like a flock of birds," I said.

"Yeah, they are," Vicki said, and suddenly things were back on friendly terms between us. I was never sure what had made her angry. In her perception, perhaps I had abruptly left her in the block area.

Over a longer term, one girl named Tina at first was very sweet toward me, but in later months seemed to develop a love-hate relationship with me. One minute she would be loving and smiling, but then the next minute she could be stern and angry, and it seemed more than playful. This became a frequent pattern for her, and I wondered if it was caused by jealousy of my attention to other children or something stressful going on at home. She moved on to kindergarten before I got more insight.

Other children, at times, would also seem to alternate between seeking affection and cold rejection toward me. Alex was sitting on the tire swing with David and Brent one day, and out of the blue he said, "I'm gonna take care of my mommy."

"Oh? That's great," I responded.

"Sometimes my dad gets mad and is mean to her," Alex added.

Alarmed, I tried not to overreact, and simply said, "That's too bad," sympathetically.

"And she uses bad words," said Alex.

David then piped up, "My Daddy tells me to shut up."

"That's a mean thing to say," I said.

"I'm gonna protect my mommy," reiterated Alex. "Even when there's a storm."

"That's good for you to do that," I said. "Are you gonna stay with her when there's a storm?" I asked.

"Yeah, and I won't even let her be scared." I wondered what family episode had prompted this sudden description, and I also wondered if that explained Alex's ambivalence toward me at times. Usually, he was a happy child who asked for attention ("Mr. John, look!" or "Mr. John—rub my back!"). But other days, if I was even nearby he would say, "Leave me alone," or call me some mildly mean name, or say some other variant of "get out of here." I wondered if troubled relationships with adults at home (perhaps especially with his father) were affecting his relationship with me.

There were other children who seemed uncertain whether to approach a relationship with me or avoid one. A few months later, a newer boy in the classroom, Nasser, developed a similar alternating kind of relationship with me. At first, he always wanted me to watch him do things or show me things he had done. Then, he went through a phase where he always acted angry with me and sad to be in school altogether. He would hit or kick me at times, a little too hard to be playful. Then, one day out on the playground, I was chasing some children and included Nasser in the game. He loved that and wanted me to chase him the rest of the time we were outside. That day at naptime I was talking with James about friendship, and Nasser said from nearby, "I'll be your friend. Thank you for chasing me today."

"You're welcome," I said, very surprised. "It was sure fun."

"Will you chase me again?"

"Sure."

"Are you leaving?" Nasser then asked.

"Yes."

"Will you hug me?"

Even more shocked, I did so. We seemed to have crossed some kind of relational barrier that day. He was then quite friendly again; he was angry from time to time, but the anger no longer seemed directed at me. I had noticed some children got angry at times when they seemed to want to get me alone, but found that nearly impossible in our classroom or outside settings. I wondered if the children were angry at the lack of total attention they wanted from me, or from others in their lives I might represent for them. Most, out of necessity, learned to "share me" with the others.

OVERCOMING POWER DIFFERENCES: STEPS TOWARD CLOSER RELATIONSHIPS

Many children indicated a leap to a closer, more trusting relationship with me by initiating or joining in a game of chase on the playground. This pattern would repeat over and over through the years as new children came to the classroom: I would spontaneously start to chase a child outside, and others would join in. Soon, one or several children would be saying, "Chase me!" The mock hunt with the benign outcome of me grabbing them or letting them get away seemed to allow the children a way to build a basic friendly relationship with me. Often, the four- and five-year-olds wanted to be pushed on the swings, also clearly a way to get adult attention. This was illustrated when some children wanted to get the tire swing pushed. Some other four-year-olds started to push them, and they quickly protested. "No kids pushing," said one boy. "We want Mr. John to," insisted another. There was a clear relational indicator being sought above and beyond getting a ride on the swing. I also noticed five-year-olds like Garrett or Timothy swinging very high on their own, but then when I got close, I would hear them ask, "Would you push me, Mr. John?" It certainly meant more to them than simply getting their swing going, as they could do that themselves. Once Ms. Danielle was pushing three girls on the tire swing, and as I passed by she told me, "Mr. John, they want you to push them." I did for a while, until they got tired and were replaced by Holly, Katie, and Ivan. When Mr. Eric started to push them, Ivan insisted, "No, Mr. John; I want Mr. John to push us."

"I want Mr. Eric—I want Mr. Eric to push us," insisted Holly. So Mr. Eric pushed them briefly, with Ivan looking none too happy, and then I pushed them again, to Ivan's delight. Being pushed by a grown-up was more than a practical act of compliance for the children; it was an indicator of closeness and a good relationship for them.

With one three-year-old I inadvertently sparked our closer relationship when I walked into the classroom and finally saw a group of children that I had missed outside. "Hi, Mr. John," said David, as he had begun doing regularly.

"Hi, David," I said. "I was looking for you outside, and I could not find you. Where were you?"

At this he looked intrigued and delighted, and said, "We went inside." And for weeks after this incident, when I came into his room he would greet me and ask, "Mr. John, were you looking for me outside?" The idea of having me look for him enthralled him and led him to initiate more conversations with me.

Sitting on my lap was an expression of a close relationship that children, once they felt comfortable with it, clearly coveted. Children having me read to them in the book area would quickly and forthrightly enforce the two-child rule in that area when additional children would drop by to see what we were reading. "Only two can be in here!" they would insist, clearly not wanting our book time interrupted. One day, fights over my lap wearied me after Elena asked me to read her a book. I went with her over to the book area and sat down. Then Steve suddenly crawled onto my lap. Elena was clearly frustrated. "He won't let me sit on your lap," she said.

"Will you move over and let Elena sit here?" I asked. Steve moved a little, and there was some room for Elena on me then. "Good," I said. "You both can."

"No, we can't," protested Elena. "It's too crowded." She clearly was not willing to share my lap with Steve, but she did sit next to him, none too happily. We all read a story and then moved on to other activities. Later in the week, Amy came over to me in the classroom and asked me to read a book to her. I went with her to the book area, and Nicki followed. Amy said, "I want to sit with you," as Nicki tried to sit in my lap. "No-o-o-o!" said Amy.

"Here, it's Amy's turn," I said, since she had asked to be read to first. I helped Nicki sit beside me.

"She's squishing me!" said Amy. Though she was on my lap, Nicki and Janet were now sitting on each side of me, and Amy clearly resented everyone else invading our reading session. We proceeded to read for a while, and then Amy said, "I want to get up 'cause they're squishing me." So she moved off, and Nicki took her place. At the end of the next book, Nicki got up to get another, and Janet moved next to me. When Nicki returned, a loud argument ensued. Nicki yelled at Janet that she was in her spot and yanked and pulled on her arm, insisting, "I was sitting there!"

"You left! You got up!" was the angry response.

As they yelled and grappled with one another almost on top of me, whatever I said was lost in the commotion. Now that all occupants of the classroom were looking at us, Ms. Stephanie came over and separated them. "Nicki, you and someone have to leave, because there are too many in this area. Move away," she said firmly to several children who had entered the book area as the conflict was beginning. David, Janet, and Rachel were left in a quiet book area with me. Somewhat shocked and relieved at the quiet, I proceeded to read to them for a while. I always had to try to balance my attentions and be fair, but the push to be close to me as an adult would at times necessarily lead to competition.

ATTENTION-SEEKING BEHAVIORS

As the children grew comfortable with the relationship, they would ask adults to watch them or sit with them as they played, built with toys, or worked a puzzle. I knew that Vicki wanted me near her one day when she was working on a fruit and vegetable puzzle. Normally she was good at puzzles and rather fast, but this day she seemed to be angling for my attention, as she could not seem to find which vegetables and fruits fit in which molds. "Could you help me do this?" she asked me a couple of times as I stood nearby interacting with several children. I sat down with her. "Where does this go?" she would ask me about each piece in what would normally have been a simple puzzle for her. With nearly twenty children often seeking my attention, I could not blame her for finding a fairly sophisticated (for a four-year-old) way to keep my attention.

I gradually mastered what almost came to seem like an art as I tried to balance children's bids for time and attention from me. I would move from building a puzzle with Nick, to building bristle block boxes with Tracie, to hearing Kenny asking, "Mr. John, let's go in the block area."

"OK," I said, as I finished up with some blocks for Tracie.

"Come on, Mr. John, come play with me in the block area," insisted Kenny.

"I'll come in a minute, Kenny," I told him, wanting to get some closure playing with Tracie first. The art was balancing the urge to go spend time with a child who wanted me without precipitously abandoning the child I was with at the moment. After spending some time with Tracie at the table, I joined Kenny, joined by Lance and Nick, building a racetrack out of blocks.

My presence provided a golden opportunity for children needing reassurance or an adult relationship. With most children, I could spend some time playing with or reading to them, and they appreciated it; then they would get distracted with something else and I could move on to another area. At times, they would try to keep me with them, and I would try to stay by them until they or the whole class changed activities. For other children, seeking attention from me was a daily pattern. Jill was a girl who, after getting to know me over a couple of weeks, wanted me to go everywhere she went. Almost every time she saw me, she said, "Come over here" and pulled me by the hand. I would try to spend time with her, but she was never satisfied and always wanted more. One day I finally told her, "I need to see what the other kids are doing, too," and I added, "I like you wherever I go, Jill. You don't have to worry about that." This seemed to help, at least in the short term. But the next day the four-year-olds moved to another playground while I was interacting with some three-year-olds. Jill noticed that I was not immediately following her class and started crying. Ms. Lisa, an assistant teacher, walked with her to the other playground. We all knew that I could not instantly return to Jill simply because she cried. Once we got inside, she got to sit near me, as I did want to reassure her that I liked to spend time with her. It was sometimes tough to show affection while promoting independence and individual choice.

UNCERTAINTY AND SEPARATION ANXIETY

One day, Mark was sitting on the monkey bars outside looking very sad. I came near and asked how he was, and he said his mom had left him, so he was sad. "Does your mom usually stay with you all day at school?" I asked, trying to take a logical approach.

"No, last night she left," he said.

"Oh. Did she come back?" I asked.

"Yes," he said hesitantly, but still seemed very worried and possessed with separation anxiety, which I had never observed in him over many weeks. Once he started playing outside, he enjoyed himself, but he wanted me to stay with him and catch him coming down the slide for a while. When another class started to go inside, he said, "Are you staying out here with me?"

"Yes, I am," I said, "because I like you." I did not want to be his "extra mommy" or let him get dependent on me, but I also wanted to give him more attention on a day he really seemed to need it.

A few days later, Mark said to me, "I want you to sit by me." I noticed that he had been saying that to me a lot recently. I did not want to get too involved with Mark, as he seemed to be causing me to lose sight of the reasons I was there in their classroom. He had started assuming that I would stay with him the whole time I was there, yet I needed to observe all and give other children some attention, too. I sought a way to distance myself from him while showing Mark I was still his friend.

One act that prompted these thoughts came when Benjamin told Mark one day in the classroom, "Hey, you're my friend. Play with me."

"No, I'm not playing with you anymore," said Mark.

Alarmed at Mark's attention to me at the expense of his peers, I chimed in, "You should play with Benjamin; he's your friend."

"No, I don't want to play with him; I want to play with you," said Mark, and he pulled me away.

He had been pulling me around a lot lately. I often went with him, but I thought I might need to get more forceful about doing what I wanted or needed to do. Later that same day, he even verbalized that sense of control. When I would not push him on a swing fast enough, he said, "I won't be your friend anymore." I decided I would have to call that bluff, and say, "Even when you are mad at me, I'm still your friend." Sure enough, he stayed mad a little while, but soon he would be my best buddy again, and I felt less controlled by him.

Strong reactions to being "left out" of adult company or support involved tears. I observed separation anxiety many times, through the years, but almost always the children overcame it after a few days or weeks of attending the center. On one of my early days of volunteering, I noticed Amy crying in the classroom even after making a turtle for herself at the art table. I was never sure whether to leave such sad children alone and give them time, or try to comfort them and risk making them feel worse. I eventually felt compelled on that day to say something to her, so I went over and told Amy I was sorry she was sad. She told me tearfully that she had wanted another hug from her daddy. I told her to ask for an extra one the next time she saw him, and he would be happy to because he loved her. (Luckily, I knew both her parents, which helped me give such comfort!) This seemed to help, and Amy joined Sarah and me to read a book that Sarah had found. I was glad I could make her feel better, and overcome that uncertainty and risk that overshadowed some interactions between adults and children.

The worst case of separation anxiety that I observed involved David, who never seemed to feel confident and comfortable with adult support at the center. He would continue to cry for nearly an hour, at intervals, after his mother or father left him. "I want my Daddy!" he would say, again and again. Ms. Stephanie discovered that if he was kept busy, he did much better, and as I interacted with him I found him to be a perceptive, intelligent, and creative four-year-old. Outside, he spurred other children on to build different kinds of dinosaurs out of some large building blocks with him. But for a long time in the mornings, and again at naptime, he would start crying and saying, "I want my Daddy." One morning, his father had stayed for a while, but Ms. Stephanie told me that David then was even more upset when he left. David was one child who quickly sought a closer relationship with me, and would follow me or sit with me, even if he was still crying some. A few days after he started attending, I said, "Hi, David," when I came in the room, even though he was crying and saying, "I want my Daddy." I gave him a very brief hug, and then continued to respond to other children as they showed me things they had done. I sat at a table with Ryan and Vicki, and David followed and took a chair next to me, but continued crying for a while. "I want my Daddy," he would say at intervals, and Ms. Stephanie and Ms. Lisa would say, "He is at school," or "He'll be back after he has been to class."

"You have to have a fun day at school, first," I told him at one point.

"I don't wanna be at school," sobbed David at this. "I don't wanna be happy. I wanna be very sad."

"OK," I told him. "You be sad; that's OK." In a way, acknowledging this feeling seemed to help him gradually calm down. As Ryan and I built with blocks and Vicki and I looked for alphabet letters on the blocks, David gradually started finding blocks for himself and even stopped crying and started to enjoy himself.

He could even be objective about his own emotion. A few days later, I came in late and he was already there. "When my Daddy left I was crying," he told me. Ms. Stephanie told me that he had been crying, but she got him busy helping her with the bulletin board. "He perked right up when you came in," she told me. Sure enough, David soon said to me, "Wanna help me play this game?" So I played with him a while at the table. "Where are you going?" he asked when I got up a while later.

"I'm going to get a drink of water," I said, as the class got ready to go outside.

"Are you coming with us?" he asked.

"Yes," I said. Apparently I was becoming an adult he could trust in place of his parents when they left him at the center. Still, his crying and anxiety went on for so many mornings that his parents decided to pull him out of the center; this was the only time I observed separation anxiety so serious that a family gave up on the center.

A FOCUS ON ME: BECOMING A KEY ADULT

I could see that I became an important adult to relate to for many of the children. I often knew when a child was ready to seek closer interaction with me by his or her questions. "Are you staying in this room?" one girl suddenly asked me one day. Another asked, "Will you be here till rest time?" A boy asked me, "Will you be back?" when he saw that it was time for me to leave. These questions made it clear that they were interested in relating and wanted me around. At times, children showed a stronger seeking of connection with me by suggesting that I come to their house or, alternately, that they come home with me. One day, I was holding a pair of sunglasses Jill had given me to hold, and I walked to the high shelf. Alex happened to be standing nearby. "I'd better put these sunglasses on the shelf so I don't take them home with me," I said in a friendly tone.

"I want to go home with you," said Alex, out of the blue.

"You *do?*" I asked, surprised.

"Yes. Take me home with you. . . . Can I go home with you, 'cause you're my friend?"

"Well, I think you belong at school," I said, a little uncertain. I was flattered, but knew that him coming home with me was out of the question.

He understood. "Hey, my mommy might wonder where I went to," Alex said.

"Yeah, she wouldn't know where you were. She'd say, 'Where's Alex?'" Hearing my agreement, he went off to lunch, satisfied that he could not really go with me.

During my second year of volunteering at the center, Kenny made a relationship with me a high priority. After a few weeks, I would hear from the teachers that on days I was not there Kenny would ask about me. Ms. Kim quoted him as saying, "Where's Mr. John? He's not my friend. He won't play with me anymore?" in his anger at my not being there. When I did get to the classroom, Kenny would very quickly run over, give me a hug, and want to stay with me. He began to insist we do things together, and clearly wanted our relationship to extend beyond his school setting. One day he said we should walk to Kmart. "That would be fun," I said, but Kenny always wanted to do these things immediately, not at some future date, and he was serious about them. "But your mom or the teachers would wonder where you were," I explained.

"We could sneak out like babies," he said. "You could take me. The cops wouldn't find us."

I was not sure where the latter reference came from, but taking up that theme, I said, "I couldn't do that. I don't want to steal you. If you haven't done anything wrong, you don't have to worry about the police."

"We haven't done anything wrong," said Kenny.

"That's right," I said.

"You won't steal me; you could just *borrow* me," Kenny persisted.

"*Borrow* you?" I said, taken aback and laughing inwardly. Kenny was determined to have me go shopping with him, and stayed near me a lot that day.

Kenny remembered our discussions, too, over many days, which was another indicator to me of how determined he was to have a close relationship with me. Several days later he came over to me and said, "I'm ready for you

to borrow me now. I'm going to Junior Mart." I could distract him for a while
as long as I spent time with him, but he would soon return to that idea: "We
can sneak out of the yard. Open the gate and get out of the yard. We can tell
the police you're just borrowing me."

"You think the police would believe that?" I asked.

He did not seem sure about that. But Kenny had it all figured out, and he
was persistent in trying to get the two of us out on a "field trip" together. One
day, he asked which car was mine, and I pointed it out to him sitting over in
the parking lot. A few days later, I happened to be in the observation room
when Kenny arrived at school, and I noticed him walking ahead of his
mother, looking intently over at the parking lot where my car was. After he
was in the classroom for a little while, I was still in the observation room
when I heard my name mentioned. When I finally did go into Kenny's classroom, after stopping in the three-year-olds' classroom for a few minutes, Ms.
Kim told me, "Someone's been *looking* for you!" And Kenny came over and
sat on my lap to talk for a while. He told me he had seen my car, and then
seen me in the three-year-olds' classroom. I felt although it was nice to be
wanted, Kenny's centering on a relationship with me was almost intimidating. I was glad he could connect interpersonally with me, but I worried that
he would expect too much of me or be heartbroken in some way when
things did not go his way. I must admit, though, that when a child took to
me so strongly, it was soon reciprocated. I would start to think about him or
her on days I was not volunteering, and would have to work harder to not
be totally monopolized by those children when I was at the center.

Perhaps as a result of having to share my attention, or generally not getting what he wanted, Kenny did have his "angry" days, toward me and
everyone else. Noting Kenny coming in and using a hostile tone with everyone one morning, Ms. Stephanie explained, "His parents were mean this
morning, and now he's acting toward others the way he's been treated." He
kept calling me "chicken," and when he got frustrated coloring on some paper, he insisted that "Mr. John made me mess up," though I had not been
near him during that time. As the day went on, he warmed up to me and began acting "normal" once again. But children who were fixated on a close relationship could exhibit frustration or anger at things not going their way. On
the whole, I think such relationships were beneficial, as the connection we
made seemed special. Kenny, for instance, headed off to kindergarten a few
months later, wanting me to visit him there even after his fixation on spending time with me had receded somewhat.

Near the end of my fourth year of spending time at the center, I walked into
the four-year-olds' classroom and found all the children busy with activities. I
made a point to greet the teacher, Ms. Stacey, and two of the children who were
near to me, and decided to sit at an empty table by myself and "play" with some
building toys. Usually, almost immediately, *at least* one child wanted attention

from me. But that morning, I had several minutes of sitting quietly alone and observing. Eventually, Timothy saw me, came over, and gave me a hug before going back to the block area. Then Alice came and sat across from me at the table after she was finished doing her art. Mary came over and sat next to me after Ms. Lisa had finished reading her a story. Evan then came by to tell me something, and stayed standing next to me, building. "I wanna sit in your lap since I don't have a chair," he said. Charla and Alexa had also joined us at the table. Ms. Lisa remarked to me, "Mr. John, you have a table *full*." I thought of the comment the center's director, Ms. Debra, had made during my first months at the center: "Children congregate around you." At times like this, when I backed off, the children in the end would pull me back into relationships with them as they sought a new round of adult attention.

Clearly, anyone working with preschool children must expect varying levels of support seeking. I found that ignoring or rejecting such support seeking made the child more distracted and feel worse. Responding to the child's need for affection often went far toward satisfying it, and the child could then be naturally or strategically distracted by another activity. I was often tempted to resist such a "needy" child, thinking he or she would monopolize my time for hours if I yielded. I found the opposite to be true—spending a little time met that affection need, and both parties could then focus on the next activity. Whether a child sought to understand the real power differences between children and adults, reduce uncertainty about how to interact with each adult, or develop a closer relationship with an adult, he or she often showed a sense of urgency that may be traced back to infant attachment-seeking behaviors. Anxiety over separation from parents or other events at home could lead to positive and negative attention-seeking behaviors at the child-development center. Such attention seeking was a constant reminder that the child-care center was only a part of each child's life. For some, it was just another set of fun activities, for some a daily distraction, yet for others it was clearly their major source of adult attention and affection. Diplomatic responses to children needing high levels of adult support were crucial for maintaining a supportive communication climate at the center, as well as for providing necessary relational sustenance in young children's lives.

9

Children Expressing and Controlling Feelings: Tragedy or Comedy?

Children at ages four and five were still learning how to express feelings in controlled verbal ways. They were still not far removed from the age when some version of crying or screaming was their only available avenue for expressing strong feelings. Several of the children I observed returned to this method fairly readily. Other children the same age, however, showed some surprising sophistication in naming or describing their feelings. Around ages four and five, children first gain a limited ability to enact voluntary, convincing facial displays (Philippot, Feldman, and McGee 1992). They remain highly likely to display negative faces reflecting their true feelings, however. Thus, with preschoolers, "what you see is what you get," in terms of emotional displays; they tend toward blunt honesty in emotional expression. The children I observed did, however, pursue a variety of communication strategies based on the emotions they felt. Those more able to read and respond to the emotions of others generally proved to be more popular (Philippot, Feldman, and McGee 1992), and all were developing and improving their ability to understand others' emotions and manage their own. Some children at preschool age had clearly mastered some ability *not* to express all feelings experienced (Saarni and Weber 1999), while others often seemed to be ruled by their emotions. Some began to show concern with controlling emotional displays in order to "fit in" with peers, as becomes highly important in later years of childhood (Fine 1987). Being called a "crybaby," for instance, was resented and undesired by the four- and five-year-olds. Clearly, one major item on children's social negotiation agenda was the nature and duration of emotional displays to be permitted. Both adults and peers consistently reinforced norms of feeling expression.

MANAGING FEELING EXPRESSION

One four-year-old, Blake, had found that when he cried or hollered he got more attention He would do this often at the center, and his teachers were continually telling him to *talk*, or "use words," not to yell or cry. At four, he was viewed by the staff members as acting like a baby by expressing feelings too readily in that way. Yet any child, at times, would express feelings suddenly or violently. One day, Kenny was frustrated because he could not find a toy he had built (someone else had probably taken it apart). He tried to build it again, but wasn't satisfied by his attempts. Suddenly he threw the pieces down and went to the other side of the classroom. A few minutes later I tried to show him a square lollipop Michael had made. "Yeah, right," he said impatiently. After a time, he recovered his equilibrium, but he was venting his feelings on the edge of acceptable ways for a time.

A few days later, Carl and Brian were having trouble playing when things did not go their way. It looked like Carl had learned at home that crying gets attention—because at any poke, shove, or light hit, he would start crying. As he played ball with several other children, if *he* did not get the ball, he would start to cry and say, "I *never* get it," and wander away or sit down where he was. He could not, on that day, pick up on the pattern of several children scrambling for the ball, though he enjoyed having just me or another teacher play ball with him. Brian, on the other hand, kept saying, "I'm telling on you," if he felt slighted in some way, or if he noticed something he believed was against the rules. He overused this strategy to the point that at the start of circle time Ms. Stacey said, "No telling on anyone; we're sitting on carpet squares," before Brian had even said anything! He, too, would grab a ball and walk away from a game if he believed that another child would not throw it back to him. He *had* made a sort of progress from hitting or pushing a lot to telling the teacher a lot.

Some children vented more feelings by putting others down or crankily refusing to follow directions, making them seem moody. Two months later, David saw me on the playground as he was getting out of his car with his father. "Hi, Mr. John!" he said happily. One never knew how David would be when he arrived in the morning. Sometimes he was quiet, grumpy, or both, and sat in his cubby for a while, but at other times he was happy enough and just began playing. On this day, he and Timothy were buddies, and David seemed to be in a good mood. Inside, during circle time, David made sure to sit beside Timothy. Ms. Stacey began calling names of the children to put a picture on the board before their snack; she eventually called Timothy, and then Madeline.

"You didn't call *me*. . . . You didn't call me," said David, first plaintive and then growing grumpy.

"I will call you, David . . . listen for your name," said Ms. Stacey, as she continued to call other children's names. "Things won't always go your way, David, but you still need to wait and listen for your name." Then, when she *did* call David's name, he would not move from his carpet square. "Your name has been called, David; you need to go to snack," said Ms. Stacey. "I'm not going to do it again." David was still sitting there when all the other children had gone to their snack. "I need this carpet square," said Ms. Stacey soon after that, and she swiped it out from under him. "You know if you try this in kindergarten, you know what your teacher will say? She'll say, 'You can sit in the office.'" David continued to sit there, crying angrily. He never did eat his snack. In this temper tantrum he hurt only himself, as later he did ask Ms. Stacey for his snack, but it had already been thrown away. Not all children would go from seeming happy and well adjusted to pouting and angry as fast or as often as David, but many would seem moody to greater or lesser degrees. I could tell, from observing, that children's natural tendency to respond openly and outwardly to their emotions pushed them to the edge of acceptable expression of those feelings more often than adults. This was refreshing in that it was fairly clear how a child felt about people or events, but disconcerting in that these feelings would be so strongly displayed. Clearly, the children in the child-development center setting were being guided by their teachers toward socially acceptable ways of expressing their feelings.

Micah was a four-year-old child who, on his first day at the center, was enjoying playing around the classroom. When circle time was starting, and the children were told to sit down on carpet squares, Micah kept saying "No!" and then when a teacher eased him onto a carpet square he began to cry. Starting with an "I want my mommy," he kept on howling through Ms. Stacey's talking. "Some kids when they are new aren't used to circle time yet," she told the children. "Micah will get used to it." And indeed, he *was* listening, because when Ms. Stacey mentioned Mickey Mouse shoes, he interrupted his crying to say, "I saw Mickey Mouse at Disney World." Shortly thereafter he resumed his wailing. But then after circle time was over, he was happily playing around the room again. As the days passed, he learned to sit quietly in circle time and keep his feelings to himself. I never found out why he was so afraid or vexed by circle time at first.

A more serious case was Brian, who was noted for having violent tantrums and having to be removed from the classroom at intervals. While I could see some sadness and anger in him, he seemed, overall, fairly even tempered to me. In all my hours spending time at the center, I had never seen one of his tantrums. But teachers would certainly talk about them, and they would affect the teachers' later interactions with him. One day, Brian was swinging on the tire swing, and a teacher was telling him his turn was over. She suddenly became very forceful toward a recalcitrant Brian: "Brian, *you are* going to get off and let Jessica have a turn." Seeing me nearby, perhaps looking curious, she said as an aside to me, "We've been having troubles," and pointed at Brian.

"What has been going on?" I asked. "I noticed something seemed to be going on about him when I got here."

"He has been having violent episodes—violent tantrums that he needed to be removed from the classroom. He has so much anger inside," explained Ms. Teresa.

"Yeah, that's sad," I responded, thinking of my own observations of him. "He's such a nice kid when he's in the right mood."

"Yeah, we're working with his mom to get some help; he needs it," said Ms. Teresa. Judging by the center staff people's normal love and tolerance for children, their lack of equanimity in Brian's case convinced me that he did indeed have a problem with expressing anger in an explosive, violent way.

Some children expressed strong feelings the opposite way—they withdrew into a quiet, morose mood and did not want to play with anyone or even participate in the class circle time. I noticed Sam in this kind of mood one day. Once we went outside, he seemed to perk up and play and communicate more again, acting his normal happy self. Both methods of changing verbal expression communicated strong feelings, but the quiet child was harder to notice than the hollering or screaming child was. Unfortunately, the loud children, almost by necessity, received more attention from the adults at the center, but the adults often would reassure one another that such outbursts were primarily to get attention and would try to avoid overreacting or yielding to children who were simply yelling or "acting out" their feelings. Teachers encouraged the children to express their feelings by using words.

Indeed, children this young still were working on how to label their feelings, as well as only beginning to understand their feelings' sources or causes (Denham 1998). Children sought to respond to and express emotions felt in some way, though the way chosen might not be rational, well considered, or even directed at the person who engendered those feelings. I had been at the center many months and had gotten to know Kenny very well when he came in irritable one morning. Any time Ms. Stacey or I asked him a question, he would answer in a put-out tone. "Such a tone," said Ms. Stacey, partly as an aside to me.

"Why are you so angry?" I asked him, to try to get him to pinpoint his feelings.

"Because, I want to be at home," he replied.

"At home! You just got here, you know," said Ms. Stacey, in a teasing tone.

"Yeah," I said, "You just got here."

"Well, I wanna be at home," he said.

"So, you'd rather be at home, huh," I tried to say empathetically, since I could at least relate to that feeling. Who has not had such a day?

Evan came over to a table nearby.

"We're mad, aren't we?" Kenny said to Evan.

"What?" said Evan.

Kenny repeated himself.

"Why are you mad?" asked Evan.

"Because he's irritating me; Mr. John is irritating me," said Kenny.

Evan looked uncertain.

"I don't mean to irritate you," I said.

"Yes, you do!" said Kenny.

Then I repeated myself.

"Yes, he does, right Evan?" said Kenny. "He is, right Evan?"

"Yes," said Evan.

"See?" asked Kenny.

Evan laughed.

"Tell him it's not funny," said Kenny.

"It's not funny to you; it may be to him," I said, growing irritated myself at these accusations. "I don't know why I'm irritating you; I'm only doing what I normally do," I said.

Kenny gradually warmed up to me again, but he did remain rather distant on that particular day. Kenny was fairly sophisticated in expressing his feelings, and was able to talk about them rather than throw a tantrum, but he seemed uncertain of their source, projecting his irritation at whoever was nearby.

The center staff clearly valued feelings and the children's rights to them. But staff members insisted that feelings be channeled through words or through moving away from others and being alone for a while. Yelling, screaming, or any type of negative physical contact was immediately discouraged. The children, in turn, seemed to recognize the need to channel feelings in socially acceptable ways. For instance, none of them wanted to be called "crybaby," which name other children would not hesitate to invoke if they perceived a child crying a lot or crying for what seemed to them like "trivial" reasons. But even as children learned to control the expression of their emotions, others observing knew where they stood. Anger, irritation, or sadness on the part of a child were often on display for all to see. So were positive emotions—love, happiness, and delight would lead to happy faces, gleeful laughter, eye contact, and running over to give a hug. Children's refreshing honesty about their emotions, combined with their learning to explain and understand their feelings, led to some of the most rewarding and challenging interactions I observed and participated in at the center.

LISTENING FOR RELATIONSHIPS

Key to managing one's own communication of feelings was to be still and open to others' communication. Listening was a key communication skill that the teachers at the child-development center treasured and continually sought to elicit from the children. Any listening that indicated learning was prized by the teachers, even if the results were sometimes humorous, as in one incident I observed after several months at the center. Ms. Teresa, the teacher aide, had put up on the bulletin board play money, much of which looked real except for size and color. Hannah and Beth were looking at it. Hannah pointed to the picture on a $1 bill. "That's George Washington, the first president of our country," said Hannah.

"Well, *good,* Hannah! That's right; you're right," said a surprised Ms. Teresa.

"Who is *that?*" Hannah asked, pointing to a $20 bill.

"Well, . . . you *would* ask me that," said Ms. Teresa. "Ask Mr. John . . . maybe he knows."

"That's Andrew Jackson," I said.

"Andrew Jackson?" Hannah repeated. "Who is that?"

"*That's* Abraham Lincoln," said Ms. Teresa, indicating the $5 bill Hannah had pointed to.

"Emmerham Lincoln?" Hannah repeated. "This is Mister Ham Lincoln," Hannah then told Beth. Ms. Teresa and I laughed. We heard her again, later, saying of a $5 bill, "That's Mister Ham Lincoln." Her listening was not perfect, but Ms. Teresa and I were impressed with the interest it indicated.

Children wanted to be listened to at times, just as the teachers did. They were learning that if they desired to be listened to, they must at times be still and listen. Listening could help friendships, as Allan and Mary experienced one day. Allan and Mary approached the table where snacks were laid out. They saw cut-up oranges at each seat. "I don't like this snack," said Mary.

"Please eat it," said Allan earnestly. Apparently, he wanted to sit down to snack, and he was afraid Mary might not join him.

"I don't wanna eat it," said Mary.

"I want you to," said Allan.

"I know; if I won't eat it this time, I will eat it the next time. The next time we have this I will eat it," said Mary, deferring the unpleasant act. Allan accepted this, and sat down and sucked on his oranges. Mary did sit next to Allan, but she threw her orange slices away. Her response to Allan though, showing she was listening, seemed to strengthen their relationship.

Being listened to was viewed as rewarding by children, as I found within the first few days of being with them in the classroom. I noticed that Nick came and told an adult every time another child was mean to him, whether it was hitting, calling names, or laughing at him. He did not necessarily expect any further action—just telling an adult about it seemed to make him feel better. After "telling," he would move back to playing without waiting for the adult to confront the child he was complaining about. On another of my first days at the center, Dale came over to me as soon as I walked into the four-year-olds' classroom and told me about his new boots; they had been scuffed and would have to be polished black again. "How were they scuffed?" I asked.

"On the sidewalk," he said. "And on a root in front of my house. I broke a root in front of my house." He then wanted me to converse with him a little while. Clearly, having someone to talk to was desirable, and Dale trusted me after knowing me for several days. One way I could get children to listen was to tell them a story. Before naptime one day I started telling Neil and Wesley the story of the three little pigs, and soon six or seven more children, and then half the class, had come over near me to listen. I tried to be a good listener to the children, and they seemed to appreciate it, and this enhanced the closeness of my relationship with many of them.

At times, just being listened to could provide a child with a sense of security and belonging. Dale had been out of school for two weeks with chicken pox when one day I found him sitting on the playhouse steps outside. "Dale!" I said. "I didn't know you were here. When did you get here?" I asked, sitting down beside him, since he was sitting alone and didn't look very happy.

"I just got here," Dale said.

I sat with him for a while, and when a teacher, Ms. Gwen, came by, I said, "Ms. Gwen! Look who I found. Dale's here. I haven't seen him in so long. I've missed him."

"Yes, he was missed," responded Ms. Gwen. All this was for the benefit of Dale, of course. Soon, he opened up to me and told me all about being sick and about things that had happened at home. He seemed to like sitting with just me at first, and then he wanted me to go with him around the playground. Eventually, he found some other children he decided he wanted to play with. Clearly, listening to Dale with my undivided attention strengthened our relationship and boosted his spirits.

Just as listening could indicate regard, respect, or friendship, not listening could indicate a lack of desire for a relationship. One morning, I was sitting at a table near where Blake and Ken were playing with some toys.

"Blake! . . . Blake! . . . Blake!" called Timothy across the room. Blake showed no evidence of hearing him, busily working with some blocks. The room was not very noisy and the call was quite clear. Blake was ignoring Timothy.

I interjected, "Timothy is calling you, Blake." Still no response.

"Kenny! . . . . Kenny!" Timothy tried calling across the room from the block area again.

"I don't wanna come over!" responded Kenny forcefully.

"I don't wanna come over!" echoed Blake. Kenny and Blake continued playing with toys at the table. Clearly, they did not want to leave their toys or table for Timothy, and Blake communicated this by ignoring Timothy. Once he heard Kenny refuse verbally, Blake adopted his approach and answered the same way. His communication attempts rebuffed, Timothy called a teacher, Ms. Norma, over to play with him. She did so. For Blake, not listening to Timothy seemed quite a natural way to communicate a lack of desire to interact or play.

Several months later, for several days, some of the girls would tell each other secrets, whispering in one another's ear. They clearly liked the exclusivity of the information they got to share and listen to, indicating their friendship. Then they started telling me, whispering in my ear and not wanting me to tell anyone what they said (I was not always very sure what was said, but I responded as if I appreciated being told the information!). Listening—or being allowed to listen—was a clear indicator of a closer, and exclusive, relationship.

The fact that children listen for and expect certain types of messages was humorously illustrated for me one day when Neil began telling some of his friends the story of the three little pigs. His friends politely (for children) listened, but had comments about anything they heard as wrong or inconsistent:

"And I'll *huff* and *puff* and *blow* your house down. And his house was made of twigs," explained Neil.

"Sticks. It's made of sticks," corrected Wesley.

"The book says twigs," insisted Neil.

"Well, OK," said Wesley.

"And the wolf went to the next house made of brick. 'I'll *puff* and I'll *huff* and *blow* your house down,'" said Neil.

"'I'll huff and I'll puff," corrected Ali.

"Listen, I can't remember every bit—every little thing every time, all right?" responded an irritated Neil. He then proceeded with the story, and the other boys continued to listen. It was an indicator of their regard for Neil that they did so, even if they corrected or clarified his story at times.

The children took refusals of other children to listen personally, as I noted one day at lunch. Blake and Matt were sitting next to each other, and Matt asked Blake casually, "Is that a monster on your shirt?"

"It's my shirt, don't worry about it," said Blake crisply.

"Is that a monster?" pursued Matt.

"It's my shirt, don't worry about it," said Blake again.

"But that's a good T-shirt," said Matt encouragingly.

Blake put his hands over his ears and insisted, "You're hurting my ears!"

"Fine," responded a totally frustrated Matt. "Fine. I'm not gonna be your friend *anymore.*"

"I don't want to be your friend," concluded Blake, and this was followed by eating in silence for a while. I did not observe what had put Blake in a bad mood or made him angry at Matt, but he clearly was not going to be friendly to Matt and indicated this by refusing to listen to him or answer his question. A few days later, out on the playground, Hannah tried to tell Mia something she clearly did not want to hear, as she plugged her ears and moved away.

"I just want to tell you one thing," insisted Hannah, following. Mia shook her head, kept her hands over her ears, and kept walking away to play elsewhere. Hannah went off and cried for a while after this. Later, they did play together, but over where *Mia* had wanted to go! Three weeks later, I saw Dale trying to tell Neil, Lem, and Timothy something, but the three boys plugged their ears and sang while Dale kept trying to talk to them. Soon, Dale gave up and moved away. A refusal to listen was clearly an indicator of anger, conflict, or a less important or deteriorating relationship.

Children also had to work on taking turns listening. I was sitting next to Hannah at the lunch table the next month, and she said, "Know what? This is very sad. Know what? This is very sad, Mr. John. Mr. John, this is very sad. This is very sad."

"Would you get on with what you're gonna say?" chimed in an impatient Allison, sitting on the other side of Hannah at the table.

"OK," said Hannah. "One time we had a bobcat kitten that was nice but it jumped on Mr. Carl and it jumped on Mr. Smith, and it jumped on my dad, so my dad had to have it killed. He was afraid it would jump on me, so he had to have it killed."

"Oh, that *is* sad," I said. "It was acting too wild, huh?"

"It was a nice kitten, though," said Hannah. Then Carl, on the other side of me, tried to say something as Hannah started to say something else.

"It's my turn!" said Carl. When Hannah would not stop talking, Carl started making singsong noises.

"Stop it!" said Hannah, and when Carl persisted she started to cry.

"I'm gonna tell on you if you don't stop, Carl," said Mike, sitting further down the table. But Carl proceeded to tell about his dog jumping on his head and then running away, which got the children's attention, while Hannah kept her head in her hands. Children found being listened to very rewarding, but sometimes had trouble changing roles and listening as effectively, especially when they were involved and enthusiastic about what they wanted to say. Often the children worked on balancing being a good listener with getting attention and being listened to at intervals. Those who never talked, or always tried to talk, had more relational difficulties than did those who had found a more comfortable balance.

HUMOR USE AND EMOTIONAL SOPHISTICATION

Invoking and understanding humor indicated an ability to take multiple perspectives and at least some development of reasoning patterns. Humor use was highly valued and encouraged at the center. The children seemed to provide most of the center's workers with amusement on a daily basis, and laughing "at" and "with" the children was generally consistent with their love for the children and desire to work with them. Humor was also evident in staff member conversations, as they would often joke with one another and laugh together. Humor served as a social facilitator, helping staff members get along even in stressful situations by eliciting a sense of shared meaning (Meyer 2000). While humor can unite those who share it, division and disaffection result for those who consider the humor as occurring at their expense, causing them to lose face (Cupach and Metts 1994). Children at the center almost always took adult humor as indicating affection, but humor among peers was

as likely as not to be perceived as an attack. Ongoing action and previous relational contexts would influence whether humor united or divided children
(Meyer 2000). Children who were often close or trusted one another were likely
to treat laughter as an invitation to join in further interaction, while less close
children were likely to see in laughter a verbal attack.

For the children, laughing could serve to unify parties in relationships.
Some kind of joke or incident that they perceived as funny would cause one
to laugh and others to follow suit. Usually, this clearly indicated to the participating parties that the relationship was sound or growing closer. But the
difference was crucial, for the children, between laughing "with" others and
laughing "at" others. Being laughed "at" was taken as a type of insult and
indicator of a clear social division. One morning about a month after I began
observing at the center, Alex, Will, and Michael were playing together at a
table. As he built with LEGOs, Alex said, "Ours is going to be a pirate ship."

"Mine is going to be a pirate ship, *too*," said Will.

"Your hair is sticking up," observed Alex.

"No, it isn't," said Will.

"Yes, it is. You just can't see it. It's sticking up from sleeping on it," explained Alex. No humor was evident yet in Alex's comments.

"That's not nice," put in Michael.

"Well, don't laugh at it," said Will.

"I'm not going to laugh at it; it's just sticking up," finished Alex. They all
continued to build with LEGOs, and their relationships for the moment
stayed sound. Humor or laughter was viewed by the four-year-old boys as a
potential threat to the relationship, or "not nice," as Michael had said. Alex
agreed not to laugh so as not to create a rift between them.

At times, an attempt at humor by one child was not taken as such by another. One day when the children were sitting in the circle area, Nathan put
his thumb in his mouth (which was very unusual), took it out, and saying,
"Slobber, slobber, slobber," put it on Timothy's face.

Timothy cringed away, saying, "Stop it! I'm not gonna be your friend anymore!"

Nathan tried it once more, seeing Timothy get even more frustrated. Then,
all the children settled down to listen, and the two boys followed suit,
remaining where they were. Nathan had tried something he thought would
be amusing, but Timothy did not find it so. After circle time that day, Nathan
played with Timothy as usual; the attempt at humor seemed to be forgotten.

The age of the laugher often made a huge difference in how the laughter
was interpreted to affect the relationship. Peers, unless highly trusted, were
seen as opponents if they laughed at a child. Yet, adults could laugh, and
usually the children would look delighted and take it as a sign of approval.
The four- and five-year-olds took adult laughter as laughter "with" them, and
accepted it; but other children's laughter was often viewed as laughter "at"

them, and was viewed as an insult. This was evident in Nathan's reaction one day when he was playing with some LEGOs on the floor next to the box full of them. He came over briefly to glance at a book I was reading to Hannah, and as he walked back over to the LEGOs, he accidentally knocked the box upward. LEGOs flew out and it fell back down with a loud crash.

"Nathan!" I said in surprise.

"Are you all right, Nathan?" asked Ms. Stephanie, who was sitting nearby.

Looking shocked, Nathan nodded, and started putting nearby LEGOs back in the box. Soon, he started to smile, and I said something like, "That was loud," and began again to read to Hannah. I heard a slight laugh from Nathan and began to laugh with him a little. He suddenly looked upset, though, when he heard the nearby Brandon and Sam laughing.

"It's not funny!" Nathan said hotly. "They're laughing at me."

I paused again, and said, "*Are* you OK, Nathan?"

He said "Yes," and continued to build with LEGOs.

I said, "Good," and again went back to reading.

"It's not nice that you're laughing at me," said Nathan to the other two boys, and then all continued to build individually. Nathan was much more upset by his peers' reaction of laughing than by mine or even by the surprising event itself. I was a trusted adult; Brandon and Sam were peers whose friendship could be changing and uncertain.

Children did, however, successfully use humor with one another to strengthen their relationships. Such humor between children was often nearly undecipherable to adults. One day at lunch I heard the children invoke the *form* of telling jokes, but did not see the humor in them.

"Wanna hear a joke? Wanna hear a joke?" asked Lem. "Why did the chicken cross the road?"

"Why?" asked Sarah.

"Because it wanted to swim!"

"Why did the pig cross the road?" put in Will.

"I don't know," said Sarah.

"Because it wanted to swim," said Will.

Then Thelma tried one: "Why did the elephant cross the road? . . . Because it wanted to get wet."

Thelma's friend Yolanda then said, "Knock knock."

"Who's there?" said Thelma.

"Chicken," said Yolanda.

"Chicken who?"

"Buck-buck-buck," said Yolanda.

Then Lem joined back in: "Knock knock."

"Who's there?" said Yolanda.

"Pig."

"Pig who?"

"Oink-oink-oink," finished Lem.

Will made the final entry: "Why did the elephant cross the road? . . . Because it wanted to see its children!" The children laughed hilariously at these jokes. I could see how each answer given was incongruous or unexpected in some way, just as in adult humor. The children patterned their humor after adult joke telling, even if the content left some sophistication to be desired.

Once in a while, though, children would joke with each other in a way that adults could see humor in, also. One morning, Alex and Carl were sitting together at a table. Alex had made a big pointed gun out of blocks. "I'm gonna turn you into the blue Power Ranger," he said.

"There is no blue one," responded Carl.

"I'm the black Power Ranger," said Alex.

"I want to be the black one; I'm the black Power Ranger, too," said Carl.

Alex got a dramatic look of surprise on his face and put his hands on his cheeks. "Aaaaaahhh!" he mock screamed.

Carl laughed heartily.

"Do this, too!" encouraged Alex.

So, Carl put *his* hands on his cheeks, and mock screamed, "Aaaaahhhhh!"

"Aaaaaaahhhhh!" echoed Alex.

"I'll be the black Power Ranger," said Carl, returning to the subject.

"*I* have a Power Ranger sword," stressed Alex.

"I have one, too," said Carl.

"I got it for Easter. It's a black one."

"Mine is, too!" said Carl emphatically.

Alex got a dramatic look of surprise on his face again, and this time the look alone was enough to start Carl laughing. Alex laughed, too, and suddenly grabbed Carl in a hug. "I love you, Carl," he said.

Carl, still laughing, seemed a little embarrassed, and said, "No, I don't love you," in a teasing tone.

"Yes," said Alex, and Carl did stay close to Alex for a while as they continued to play. Endearingly, the two four-year-olds found common ground and common regard for each other through humor. Their sharing of humor dramatically enhanced their friendship that day.

Sometimes, a child would tell a great joke, at least from an adult point of view, almost without meaning to. One day, some maintenance workers came and removed the small carpets from the classroom as the four-year-olds ate lunch. I went around jokingly asking the children where their food had gone—"Where's your spaghetti?" I would ask.

"It disappeared," most would tell me.

"Mr. John! Mr. John, my milk disappeared," Neil told me from his spot at a table. Soon, he told me, "Mr. John, my milk appeared back," after he was given more. Then I moved near Daniel.

"Where did the carpets go?" Daniel asked me with one of his wide-eyed looks.

"They disappeared, didn't they?" I said to him.

"They went on vacation," said Daniel, seemingly out of the blue. This so tickled me that I repeated his comment to Ms. Stacey, and Daniel, overhearing me, looked delighted. His comment, so fitting and unexpected, actually did have some background. Earlier that day, Daniel had asked me to play with him in the dramatic play area, and there he kept telling me about going on vacation. Sharing the humor of his neat incongruity later that day brought us all into a closer relationship with one another. Daniel felt like an appreciated member of the class, and we adults shared the joy of seeing children learn and grow comfortable enough to joke around.

Children would also purposely "clown" for adults as well as one another, using it as a way to get attention and reinforce or strengthen relationships. One memorable instance of such humor came as school was ending before the Christmas holidays. Ms. Stephanie busily took decorations off the walls in the morning. Ms. Teresa, helping her, soon started on the class Christmas tree, removing decorations and putting them in children's cubbies or in the big box where the tree was stored. At one point, she had to ask the children to move away because they were crowding in and trying to help remove decorations. Soon, Ms. Teresa removed the top half of the tree. "It's kind of sad, taking down a Christmas tree," I said conversationally. "Now we only have half a tree."

"Awwwwww," said Michelle dramatically. Hannah and Christy helped Ms. Teresa remove the lower branches of the artificial tree.

"We get checks?!" said Ms. Teresa suddenly, and moved toward Ms. Judy, who had appeared in the hallway with them.

While Ms. Teresa was distracted, Hannah, Christy, Amy, and Michelle all continued taking off branches and putting them in their box, until they were all off. Then they even tried to put the tree stand in the box, but it seemed too big.

"This needs to stay out; Ms. Teresa will have to place this one. It's too big," I said, taking the stand off the box. "All we have left is the stump."

"Oh, no more Christmas tree," Michelle said, and started to pretend to cry. Soon, all four girls started to "cry," and very dramatically went over to the carpeted block area and flopped down on the floor, still crying. I moved off, chuckling outwardly. All this finally attracted the attention of Ms. Stephanie, who was in the doorway talking with another adult. I told her they were crying about losing the Christmas tree.

Ms. Teresa chimed in, "It's not *me*, it's Ms. Stephanie!"

Ms. Stephanie, smiling, turned off the lights to get attention and said, "I'm sorry. . . . I'm sorry, but we needed to take it down since we're all leaving school, and when we come back it will be after Christmas. It's all right— you'll still have Christmas at your own house! It's all right."

All of us adults were smiling or laughing by now. The four girls looked at each other, grinning, and moved on to play something else. All involved—adults and children alike—seemed to enjoy this incident, and it lightened and kept open the communication climate in the classroom.

Sometimes, children would trick others for the fun of it, and the acceptance or rejection of the humor could build a relationship or prevent one from developing. One warm spring day, out on the playground, Kayla found a worm, and was showing it to all the children who congregated around her. She got braver and picked it up, but "Eeeeew!" she said, and when she flinched the worm fell onto Hannah's hand. Hannah laughed and started moving around the playground with it cupped in her hands, followed by other interested children. Finally, Ms. Stephanie asked them to leave the worm on the ground. Then Evan pretended to have a worm in his hands, and let Brandon chase him around the playground, saying, "I wanna see it."

After running from Brandon for a while, Evan came near me and showed us both his empty hands. "Trickster," Evan said. He enjoyed playing a joke on us, counting on me to laugh and having found a humorous way to get his peers to play with him.

Probably the most frequent form of humor at the center, for adults, was sparked by children acting in an adult way or clearly mimicking adult communication. Usually the staff member would laugh at this or joke with the child in response, and later would often share the event with another staff member. Almost never was a humorous reaction from an adult taken as divisive by a child. Seven weeks after I started my time at the center, Michael was walking around the classroom looking very businesslike, holding a sheet of paper. Then he approached me.

"Mr. John," he said, "Write everyone's name on this."

"OK; why?" I asked.

"Because, if their name is on here they can go to Jamaica."

Ms. Donna, sitting nearby, put in lightly, "But maybe some people don't want to go to Jamaica."

"Well, this is just a first thing, to see if they want to go. If they want to go, I can, I can check them off," explained Michael. I was laughing inwardly, as I knew that his father was a geography professor and often went on trips of this sort.

"OK; everyone's name. Just at this table?" I questioned.

"No, everyone in the whole classroom."

"OK." I wrote everyone's name down.

Then Michael went around the room, asking all the children if their names were on "the contract," as he called it. "Is your name on here? Did you sign this contract?" He approached one boy and said, "Jim, if you have a few minutes, I'd like to talk to you." This was serious play for Michael, and he was not joking at all. The other children would generally listen to and answer him just as seriously, some going along with the game, and some saying "No."

The idea of getting lists of names stuck with Michael for awhile, as two days later he was once again asking people to sign a piece of paper. He and Jim were moving around the classroom together, and Jim came over and asked me, "Write your name on here."

"My name?" I asked.

"Yes," said Jim.

"OK," said I, and wrote it.

Michael explained, "Now, everyone who signs their name here has to help us."

"Wait a minute!" I said, in a mock outraged tone. "You didn't tell me that!"

Ms. Donna, who had signed just before me, said, "Yeah, I signed a blank contract; he'll have me over a barrel."

"Yeah, you didn't tell me I'd have to do something," I told Michael and Jim.

Apparently because we were playing along with their game, neither boy seemed upset by our questioning them.

"You'll have to help us protect Will," explained Michael, as he and Jim moved on around the classroom. I never did find out from *what* we were to protect Will, but Ms. Donna and I shared a chuckle.

I observed this tendency for the children to unwittingly initiate humor with incongruous adult behavior several times. After snack time one day, Jim asked Ms. Stacey, "Can we watch a movie today?"

"We'll think about it," replied Ms. Stacey.

"Can we watch a movie today," repeated Jim, "'cause we're going to have a few showers?"

All the adults nearby laughed at this, since Jim, who knew that the children often watched a tape on rainy days, sounded like a weatherman.

Nonplussed, Jim explained, "That's what I heard; we're gonna have a few showers."

Lem, finishing up his snack, then parroted Jim: "We're gonna have a few showers."

Once in a while, humor would come from an adult (usually me) being treated as a child by another child. Ms. Debra and I were laughing one day when I told her that I did not often get invitations to birthday parties. "Oh," she said laughing, "you are now part of the *in* crowd." In the classroom earlier that day, Kayla had walked over to me with an envelope after she and her mother had distributed invitations to the other children's cubbies. "Here's an invitation to my birthday party," she said. I was moved, but also found it humorous that she considered me enough of a friend to invite me, too.

In a similar way, much humor stemmed from adults playing along with children in their pretending. One Friday afternoon, it was funny for all three adults to see Carl start getting out carpet squares for his friends to sit on. "I'm going to play circle time," he announced.

"You only need five carpet squares, for five kids in the class," Hannah told him.

He put out five carpet squares. "OK, sit down on a carpet square," Carl demanded. Amazingly enough, most of the children played along. "If you don't sit on a carpet square and be quiet, you'll have to leave the circle," Carl said, just like a teacher would.

Then, Mr. Stan said he would be Carl. He wandered over and crashed into a wall, while Carl demanded he sit in the circle. Finally, Carl dragged Mr. Stan over to the circle of carpet squares.

"Face me," said Carl. "No, face the front of the circle," he said, as Mr. Stan sat sideways. "You said to face you," said Mr. Stan.

"No, turn around," said Carl. Mr. Stan then turned backwards. "No," said Carl, and on it went. It was hilarious for the other adults to observe this reversal of roles. Suddenly, Billy grabbed Mr. Stan around the neck.

"Teacher, teacher, he's choking me," complained Mr. Stan plaintively. Carl went over to try to break them up.

"Being the teacher is frustrating, isn't it?" said Ms. Stephanie, looking on.

Then Timothy sat in the chair and said, "I'm gonna be the teacher." The game degenerated at that point into a wrestling match with Mr. Stan, Billy, and Carl. It was a fun, unifying, humorous interlude for all present on that Friday afternoon.

Another day, during the spring, I was sitting at a table playing with numbers and number books, when Khari told us that he had a witch at home.

"*Eh*, heh, heh, heh," I laughed like a witch. "Did you bring that witch to school, Khari?"

Khari ran to the door, saying, "I'll take her back home," and then rushed over to his cubby, and then back to the table. "Do it again," he said to me. Twice more he cajoled me into laughing like a witch, and he would then rush over to his cubby to hide her behind his coat. Khari finally said, "I took the witch back home."

Nathan, who had been watching all this, said, "Good. Witches turn people into frogs; she might turn us into a frog. I don't want to turn into a frog."

After Khari had put "the witch" behind his coat, he told us he would keep her there.

"I want to get *away* from here," said Nathan, from where he was playing. This made me laugh, and Ms. Stephanie wanted to know what he had said, so I repeated it. Then I mentioned to Nathan that all one has to do is throw water on a witch, and she will melt.

"I'm not afraid of a wicked old witch," said Nathan confidently. "Monsters aren't real," he added, reassuring himself and us, too, it seemed. Then the conversation moved to other topics.

A similar situation developed, again with Nathan, a few weeks later. He was sitting near me at the table, building a rocket ship, while Amy played next to me with a bus she had made out of big bristle blocks. She also had made a house and a garage for the driver. Their interaction provided me with some comedy. "Oh, there's a rocket on the road," was one of Amy's reactions to Nathan's building and playing. Amy also told him, "Give me my bus back," in a mocking but friendly tone that made me laugh out loud. Nathan and Amy both got an excited look when I laughed with them, and soon after, Nathan said, "Give me my bus back, Amy," to see how I would react. I seldom saw more excited, loving looks on children's faces than when another adult or I laughed with them. Laughing together seemed to indicate for all of us a strong sense of trust and closeness, and was crucial to making the children feel loved and wanted. Thus, I found myself ever seeking a child's smile or laugh, knowing that it could help us work through a conflict, rough day, or shaky relationship. Rare interludes of poorer climate at the center were noteworthy for their lack of humor, whether between staff members or between adults and children. As with adults, I found a sense of humor or fun crucial to a positive climate for working, learning, and living in a child-development center.

Since acting on great anger or frustration was unacceptable, children could deal with those feelings through play or humor. At times, with preschoolers, it helped to let them vent their emotion for a time before talking with them about a label for the emotion, what events caused the feeling, and ways it could be expressed. If a child was sad, for instance, we could acknowledge that, and label it: "I'm sorry you're sad," or "You look sad." Discussion could follow or the child could be given some time alone or aside, without pressure. Once they could symbolically and verbally express feelings, children learned flexibility and reason in emotional expression. Acceptable expression of emotion is one of the key teachings of any child-development center, so centers naturally channel children's emotions in adult-directed ways. Such channeling to the point of denying children's emotions, however, could lead to trouble later when children do not know how to explain or express the emotions felt (Leavitt and Power 1989). Yet guidance by adults, and increasingly by peers, teaches acceptable and useful feeling expression strategies. Listening to children, acknowledging their feelings, and modeling desired ways of expressing feelings are crucial ways child-care centers help grow civilized adults.

10

Initiating Roles and Play: Growing Relationships along the Way

One key question that drove my research when I began was "How do children initiate and improve relationships with their peers?" Many studies had documented *that* it happens, and even extensively documented *who* it happens to; and it was known that more relationships are initiated by and with children who are more socially skilled and who use more "prosocial" strategies, like cooperating, sharing, or caring (Burleson and Waltman 1987; Haslett and Samter 1997; Rubin and Ross 1982). But I wanted to know *how* children did it. Did they ask to be friends? Did they just become friends with whomever was nearby? Did they fight with each other first? As my other chapters indicate, at times they would do all of the above. Often, a child would hover near another child or group of children, seeking to act like them in hopes of being drawn into interaction (Rawlins 1992). But I found the most common strategy for initiating and strengthening relationships for the four- and five-year-old children was simply proposing or taking roles in games. My observations of this demonstrated the seriousness with which children pursue their games and pretend lives. It is easy for adults to laugh at or take lightly children's games as "just play," but my experience showed that most of children's time each day was spent in role-playing or other kinds of games. They truly were "practicing" for life in the world in their own imaginary lives. By interacting with each other during the course of this play, they enacted their most common method of forming and growing relationships with other children. Often, their interactions began with an assignment of roles for a game, or one child would simply enact a role or character and others would play along with no explicit negotiation of roles.

I noted this tendency in my journal during my first month of observations:

> When the children play, they just take up roles and drop them. If there is a group playing, one child may just ease quietly into it. If it is one or two playing, the child might ask, "Will you play with me?" or "Wanna play this?" or "Can I play?" Joining a group, especially if an adult is part of it, seems to be no big deal (less threatening). Yet joining one, two, or even three kids often requires some explicit negotiation. This may be simple, however, as one appoints himself or another to a role: "I'm Batman; you're the Joker," or "You're the dad and I'm the son." This is often all it takes for children to agree to start playing together.

The practice of role-playing allowed the children a great deal of creativity in managing relationships, along with the creativity of their games. They might initiate a cooperative relationship (playing house, for instance), or a competitive one (playing good versus bad) during the course of their interaction. Sometimes competing roles led to *real* conflict, which would then be a test of the relationship. Cooperative roles would strengthen the idea that the children could trust one another, leading to a longer-term relationship. I was impressed by how their play life was a natural and crucial extension of their formal, rule-following school life.

TAKING AND ASSIGNING ROLES

Shortly after I started spending time at the center, I observed a conversation about rather abstract roles among three four-year-old boys. They were under the steps of the raised playhouse outside, and somehow the conversation turned to who was smart. "I'm smart because my mom said I was smart," noted Michael.

"I'm smart," added Alex.

"Yeah, everyone's smart; everyone in the whole *universe* is smart," said Will.

"I know more; I'm smart," said Michael, growing competitive.

"I know more about tree things than you," said Will.

"Mr. John is smarter because he's a lot older than us," said Michael.

"No, I'm smarter than Mr. John," said Will.

At this, since I was standing nearby and they obviously knew it, I could not resist putting in a humorous, "You think so?"

"I'm smart; my mommy said I was smart," added Michael, and then the conversation moved to other topics. The boys played together for quite a while after this, so apparently their initial conversation about smartness set the groundwork for their continued interaction.

I noted the reinforcement of the friendship of a pair of girls one day a few weeks later. They had come in to wash their hands, and Janice was about to turn the water on while Terri stood at the sink. "Hey, don't turn it on!" insisted Terri.

"If you're my friend, you'll let me turn it on for you," said Janice.

"I'm not ready yet," said Terri, as she soaped up her hands. "Turn it on when I say. I'm washing with the soap right now."

"Oh, you should have told me," said Janice. She got in front of the sink next to Terri, and told her, "You can turn it on for me."

"OK," said Terri. "Turn it on." Janice did so, and both girls laughed when the soap fell into the sink and splashed the water. "Turn it off," said Terri. "Now I'll turn it on for you."

"Not yet, I'm not ready," responded Janice. "OK."

"I'll turn on the hot," suggested Terri. "It won't turn on."

"Someone locked it down here so it won't turn on," explained Janice. "I can get a paper towel!" They both fought for a paper towel, and Terri got one first. Janice got the next one, dried her hands, and threw the wad at Terri. Terri threw it back, but by this time they were finally heading back outside, where they played together for much of the morning. This sophisticated turn taking and cooperative effort was undertaken with lots of merriment by the two girls. The surface appearance was of two silly four-year-old girls playing about while washing their hands, but closer observation revealed very much testing and developing of the relationship, as each girl offered help to and channeled help from the other.

Often, friends were made quite spontaneously. Usually, there had been some prior interaction between the children involved, but it may have been days earlier. A child would say, as Matt did one day, "I'm a frostbite lion," and growl menacingly. Other nearby children would then become frostbite lions or similar creatures, as Matt, Carl, and Will did that day. A combination of trust and imitation seemed to lead to a sense of commonality or shared meaning, as demonstrated through the children's cooperation in creating a play reality. Sometimes, several boys or girls would build cooperatively without much being said at all. I once noted four boys working together on a "hotel" of blocks for quite some time, with very little verbal communication. Occasionally, one would correct another as to where certain rooms were. But for the most part, each accepted what the others built onto the structure without much comment.

At other times, the children would invoke adult concepts and roles in a "childish," playful way, but the relationship implications were still serious. On another day during my first months at the center, on the playground, I heard Will ask Terri, "Will you marry me?"

"No, I want to marry Matt," said Terri matter-of-factly.

"I'll marry you," said Yolanda. Then, she added, "I'm gonna marry Justin."

Hearing this, Justin moved closer and tapped Yolanda on the shoulder. "You're going to marry me?" he asked, in a tone of some amazement.

Yolanda nodded, and said, "Yes."

A thrilled Justin responded, "Oh, thank you for marrying me!"

"I want to marry Justin," said Terri then. "We can *both* marry Justin."

This got Alex interested, and he quickly put in, "Girls, no; girls don't marry girls!" They moved on about their play, and I never heard the final marriage arrangements, but several of these children did continue to play with one another throughout that day. The incident was humorous for an adult listening in, but the children pursued such role conversations with so much earnestness that the conversations clearly mattered to them. Children did not attach to the concept of marriage the eternal seriousness that an adult would, but discussing it was a clear indicator of liking for and acceptance of another, as Justin's strong reaction indicated.

The children at the center seemed to go through phases of discussing who would marry whom. After I had noted children saying "I'm gonna marry Gina" or some such phrase for several days, Lem told me, "Mr. John, ya know who I'm gonna marry?"

"Who?" I asked.

"Carrie," he said, grinning. Just to see his reaction, I started to stalk over toward her, as if to tell her, and he said, "Don't tell her." I looked at him, and he said again, "Don't tell her."

"OK," I said, and walked away. Soon, the class had gone outside, and sure enough, Lem and Carrie played together much of the morning. I saw Jimmy go over and talk to the couple briefly, but soon he was alone again. I walked by him as he stood alone.

"I don't know about all this talk about marriage," said Jimmy in a skeptical tone that made me laugh inwardly.

"Who's getting married?" I asked.

"Lem . . . Lem told Carrie he's gonna marry her," he said.

"And what did she say?" I asked.

"Yes," said Jimmy. "She said yes. I'm gonna jump Lem," he added. "I'm gonna marry Carrie." And sure enough, Lem later came over and told me that Jimmy and Ray were kicking him and Carrie. I went to talk to Jimmy, and he said, "I told you I was gonna jump him." I talked to him about real and pretend; yet I was struck by the intensity with which these obviously pretend roles were played out by these five-year-olds. I felt like I was caught in the middle of a soap opera that day.

ROLE-TAKING FAILURES

Asking to participate could lead to failure, as well. Lem was playing with a toy airplane one morning that he had brought to school that day. Michael approached him and said, "Can I play with that airplane?"

"No," said Lem.

Michael simply walked off to another area of the classroom to do something else.

Then, Carl asked Lem, "Can I play with that airplane?"

"Yes," said Lem, and he let him. Carl was clearly more of a friend to Lem than Michael was, as Carl got to play with the airplane several times during the morning, while I never observed Michael playing with it. Sometimes, though, persistence with such appeals would pay off. Two weeks later, another child approached Lem as he was playing with a group of toy animals.

"Can I play with you?" asked Alex.

"No!" said Lem firmly.

"*Please?*" said Alex plaintively.

"No," said Lem again.

"I'll be your friend," said Alex.

"No," repeated Lem.

Alex picked up a nearby car anyway and began to play with it.

Apparently acquiescing, Lem told him, "You can play with that and be the zookeeper." Lem seemingly was willing to share the cars, but not the animals.

"OK," Alex responded, and I noted that the two boys played together off and on throughout that day. Persistence in the face of initial refusal also paid off for Thelma, the next week. Thelma sat at a table where several children were already building with blocks.

"I don't have anyone to play with," she said, and paused. "No one will play with me."

The bid for sympathy elicited little response.

"Play with yourself!" said Michael sharply, continuing to play with blocks.

"Yeah, play with yourself!" echoed Yolanda, sitting next to him.

"No one will play with me," repeated Thelma.

"I don't care. Good, no one will play with you," said Michael.

"Michael, can I play with you?" tested Yolanda.

After a brief pause, Michael said, "*Yes.*"

"Because I'm helping you, right?" prompted Yolanda.

"Yes," agreed Michael.

"Here," said Yolanda, and handed him a little block.

In the face of the team aligned against her, refusing to be sympathetic, Thelma simply stayed at the table and began building with blocks, too. She built objects similar to those Michael and Yolanda were building; soon she was building the same things they were, and interacting with them as well. Rather than taking Michael and Yolanda's refusals at face value and leaving, she took them as a temporary setback and remained ready for interaction with them. As time went on and they shared an activity, the usual friendship between Thelma and Yolanda reasserted itself, and all three interacted together for quite a while.

An assertion by a child that she or he would play was often enough to spark a relationship. Ivan and Neil were kicking a soccer ball to one another one day outside. "Throw it to me," insisted Ivan. "Don't kick it. Throw it to me."

Neil was working on picking up the ball, and he finally did it. "OK, I'll throw it," he said, and he did.

Ivan got the ball, but Billy ran up to try to get it also.

"I'm not playing with you!" exclaimed Ivan.

"I'll play with you," said Billy in response.

Almost without missing a beat, Ivan replied, "OK," and they threw the ball back and forth for a little while. Ivan and Billy accepted each other and played together for a while based on the spark of that brief initial encounter. While the boys knew each other as classmates, they had not been playing together at all recently beforehand.

Sometimes, the announcement that the class was going outside would prompt instant negotiations of roles. One day, Ms. Stacey made such an announcement and told the children, "Please walk to your cubby and stand there."

"Yay! Buddy!" exclaimed Ivan. He grabbed Timothy's arm. "I'm Batman."

"I'm Robin," replied Timothy.

"I want to be your *dog*," stressed Alex.

The roles apparently negotiated, they joined the other children as they filed outside to play. At times, such role negotiations were not successful, and children would have to try to take up with new friends. About a year after starting at the center, I heard children talking about playing and roles as we walked out to the playground. "Timothy, you're my buddy," Ivan told him, as he walked alongside him. "Will you play Power Ranger with me?"

"No," Timothy replied quietly.

"Don't you wanna play Power Ranger with me?" asked a surprised Ivan.

"No," said Timothy. "I'm gonna play with Erin."

"With who?" asked a still disbelieving Ivan.

"Erin," said Timothy.

"I'm not gonna be your friend," said Ivan.

"Next time I'll play with you," said Timothy reassuringly.

"I'm not gonna be your friend now," repeated Ivan.

"I'm gonna play with Erin. Tomorrow I'll play with you, OK?"

"No, I'm not—"

"I'll play with you tomorrow," insisted Timothy. When they reached the playground, Timothy did play away from Ivan, which was unusual as the boys were regular friends. Later that day, though, they played together some. I was not sure if Timothy was just testing Ivan's friendship, or had a crush on Erin. I decided maybe both. A few days later, Carrie went over to Hannah and said determinedly, "Hannah, I just want you to play with me."

"No," said Hannah.

"Yes!" said Carrie.

"No."

"Yes."

After a few rounds of this, Hannah walked away to play somewhere else. This was one of the most direct approaches I ever observed to initiating play together, and in this case it failed. The girls played separately as long as I was there observing that day. I realized that the vicissitudes of young children's relationships could set a precedent that even consistent and lengthy observations could miss. Perhaps Hannah was just not in the mood to play with Carrie, which she usually would do at least a little, or perhaps there was an earlier conflict I missed that had damaged their trust.

CHOOSING ROLES

As the months went by, I watched with interest how children decided what to "be" or do. The decision usually seemed to be very spontaneous—it resembled a process of individual or group brainstorming. There was little criticism of ideas; children usually followed along or moved off elsewhere. "I'm a cat," one boy would say, and then another boy and girl who were nearby would become cats along with him. Another might say, "I'm a saber-tooth tiger," following the play pattern but differentiating an individual role. Such activities seemed to last, on average, twenty to forty minutes, before most if not all children would move on to a different game or activity. Usually, by then, something had distracted the children, or a new idea for play had occurred to them. When they were playing their roles, though, they fully enacted them and might belittle or reject a child who tried to join in or just wandered by. This interloper would be "tested"—attacked by tigers, called a monster or a robber, or whatever fit in the game. If the child played along with the role, or insisted on an alternative role that fit the game somehow, he or she would usually be admitted to the game. At other times, though, a "tested" child's rejection might lead to hurt feelings ("She won't be my friend," I might hear), or even a fight.

Sometimes, if the children were playing competitively, they would seek reassurance that the competition did not extend into their "real" relationships. I noted this once when two boys were playing with dinosaurs they had built out of blocks. They were making them fight and clash violently. After a few rounds of this, one boy said to the other, "Pretend we're friends," and they maneuvered their dinosaurs around the table together for a while. The closer or more long-term the relationship, the more readily agreement would be reached about subjects discussed and actions being planned. On another morning, Ivan built a road out of blocks with a bridge over it. He was putting up some toy signs when Neil came over with his truck.

"Hey, watch this," said Neil, and he flung his truck under the bridge, knocking it sideways.

"Don't do that," said Ivan, fixing the bridge.

"No, it should be like this," said Neil, and he sent his truck more slowly under the bridge, so that it stayed still. Ivan went back to putting up signs, while Neil sent his truck under the bridge again, but again it was knocked askew.

"Quit it!" said Ivan. "Just get off my bridge. Just get off my bridge." Neil then moved over and started putting more toy signs by Ivan's road. "No," said Ivan, but then he relented. "OK—Put them on the side like this," he directed. They built together for a while, apparently having found some shared meaning in their play.

Children expected a certain cooperation in role-playing even from peers who were not directly playing with them. One morning, Mary, Alex, Carl, and Jenny were playing with cards containing pictures of opposites. They then took them around the room delivering them to other children, to teachers, and to me as if they were mail. As I was handed some "mail," another teacher joked, "I hope they're not all bills." The children kept these delivery rounds going for quite a while, delivering and also collecting cards in their roles as mail carriers. The other children either did not seem to care, if they were involved doing other things, or would play along, gladly accepting the "mail." A few children wanted to join in being mail carriers and gathered up cards on their own. As Mary tried to get some cards back from Shaun, he refused to yield them.

"I need two more," Mary told him. "Two more." So Shaun gave two to her, one at a time, and he was left with a set of his own to play with as "mail." This game had expanded to involve nearly half the children in the classroom; and almost all of them cooperated in it.

AMBIVALENT ROLE-TAKING

Not all attempts at cooperation were completely successful, of course. Early one morning, Jawon walked up to a table where Alex, Shaun, and Paul were playing with large LEGOs and toy dinosaurs. He initiated interaction with a statement about a dinosaur: "This dinosaur likes to eat that one." The other children accepted his presence at the table and his cooperation in play with them. Yet, later the same day, Alex walked over to where Carl and Shaun were again playing with the dinosaurs, and made a similar statement about dinosaurs he was carrying. Carl did not respond, so Alex moved closer.

"Leave me alone; stop bothering me," said Carl, and went on playing with Shaun.

"I'm not bothering you," said a somewhat puzzled Alex, who then played at the same table for a little while by himself. Children would often initiate interaction with a simple play-related comment, but the acceptance or rejection of such comments could greatly affect relationship development.

The level of trust felt between those interacting, based on past interactions, seemed to play a part in determining whether a bid to join in play would be accepted or rejected.

At times, a child would try too hard to join another in play, to the point where his or her actions were resented as interference. Timothy went over to the counter one day to play with some big pegs in holes. Ryan, who often played with Timothy, followed him. "No, leave me alone," said Timothy, as it became clear that Ryan would try to play with him.

"You have to share," said Ryan, grabbing some pegs, too.

"Stop," said Timothy, getting the pegs back from him.

"Teacher!" said Timothy. "Ryan won't leave me alone."

"Ryan," said Ms. Stephanie. "Timothy is playing with those."

Ryan refrained for a moment, and then asked, "Are you still my friend?"

"Yes," said Timothy.

Satisfied, Ryan tried a new strategy. "Here, Timothy," he said, handing him a peg to put in the board. Timothy accepted it and then tolerated Ryan as a helper.

One morning about two weeks later, I noted a stronger rejection of a bid to join in a game. Michelle and Rachel were playing around a kitchen table that Rachel had made out of blocks. Michelle picked up a block and pretended it was a phone. She gave another block like it to Rachel. "This is my phone; that's your phone," said Michelle. "Your phone's dirty."

"Yeah," said Rachel, looking at it.

"My phone's nice and clean," said Michelle. "Let's call each other, OK; let's call each other," she added. Then she made dial tone noises as she dialed. "Hello?"

"Hello," Rachel answered, and they continued to talk.

Carl came over to them and said, "Want me to be your guys' little dog?"

Rachel and Michelle looked at each other, not sure, and Michelle whispered in Rachel's ear. When Carl asked it again, they plugged their ears, and Carl sat on their "table."

"Get off the table."

"Get off, Carl," they said, and Carl got up and crawled away like a dog. His offer to join their play rejected, he still adopted the role he wanted to and found somewhere else to play.

I also was subject to these relationship-managing strategies on the part of the children. When trying to start or improve a relationship with me, the children would at times ask me "teacher things" like to tie a shoe or to help them get or do something. Other times, seeing how I would play and talk with them, they would try to initiate play with me much as they would with a peer. One day, Terri came over to me and said, "Pretend you're my daddy, OK?" When I agreed, she said, "Daddy, look at my snake," holding a long chain of plastic pieces. For her, saying, "Pretend you're my daddy" became a very common pattern. It seemed like with many of the children, especially the boys, getting me involved with a chasing game, or hide-and-go-seek, would later lead to more role-playing games. Once the children found a fun pattern that got me playing or interacting with them, they would want to repeat it nearly every day I was there. One time out on the playground, Matt kept coming up with ideas for role-playing games, like: "Grownups are the tyrannosaurus rex and kids are the triceratops and run from the tyrannosaurus." I noticed that day that all of Matt's creative ideas for games conveniently had me in the role of chaser!

The children also seemed to realize that once they got into a closer relationship with me, they could trust me more than other children. Once I was building towers out of blocks on the floor with David and Gina, and Brian would fly his "airplane" over us at intervals, to get attention. He at times would playfully knock over the little towers I built, apparently knowing I would not get really angry at him. He refrained from knocking over David's or Gina's towers, however, knowing that might have serious repercussions for his relationships with them.

One memorable incident showed how seriously the children took their role-playing games. David and Jimmy were playing with Sarah in the block area, and they began a pattern of saying, "It's gonna blow up!" and jumping out of the block area as fast as they could. They repeated this game several times, and Sarah, rather hesitantly, would leap out after them. After one of these times, Jimmy said, "It blew Sarah up." Sarah looked at him, nonplussed. But she kept on playing with them, with David now saying "It blew Sarah up" every time they all leaped out of the block area (Sarah, admittedly, always last). Each time Sarah looked sadder, and soon she became frustrated. She started to cry and walked off and sat down in another area, still crying.

"David," I said, disappointed in him and wanting to show it. "Now you're being mean. See, now she won't be your friend." He looked a bit remorseful. Ms. Stephanie noticed Sarah crying, and asked her to come over, and they talked together.

Soon, Sarah came back over to the boys and told David, "She wants you." David looked at Ms. Stephanie, and she beckoned to him with her finger. He reluctantly walked over to her, and then returned after she talked to him. Sarah had started building with some blocks again, but once David had returned he and Jimmy started the "It's gonna blow up!" alarms again.

This time, David said, "It didn't blow Sarah up." Then he looked hopefully at me. "Hey, I made her feel better," David told me.

"That's great," I said. I was glad to see David was developing a good conscience at four.

The way his earlier comments cut to Sarah's heart demonstrated how significant role-playing and creativity were in forming, building, and damaging children's relationships.

Taking, proposing, and negotiating roles in games were the most common and crucial strategies children used for managing relationships. The pretend roles of their play allowed children to learn such key skills as adapting communication strategies to others (Delia and O'Keefe 1979), emotional control (Sypher and Sypher 1988), understanding the needs of others (Parker and Asher 1993), and understanding reciprocal obligations to maintain shared meaning in activities (Bigelow, Tesson, and Lewko 1996). Through practicing communication in games, children prepared themselves for "real" interactions as they grew older. For preschoolers, of course, there was little actual distinction made between "real" and "pretend" communication—both could be crucially important relationally and psychologically. For any child-development center, playtime should not be seen as an unneeded break between adult-structured and adult-imposed activities, but as essential communication practice and relationship-management rehearsal time.

11

Children's Strategies for Expressing and Receiving Affection

As one who had studied public and organizational communication for years, I had become accustomed to a certain "professionalism" that pervades organizations in our society today. People in most adult organizations communicate for a purpose, and even get to know and like one another, but there are certain personal lines people do not cross. Expressing strong feelings is generally frowned upon, and certain affectionate behaviors like touch are almost never observed, fraught as they are with potential psychological threat. In the world of the child-development center, the norms of suppressing emotion and maintaining some "professional distance" were clearly thrown out the window. Children at ages three, four, and five were still learning how to act in organizations, and they had not yet formed consistent personal or "professional" barriers to the expression of their feelings of affection. Children, it has been shown, *must* be touched affectionately in the earliest years of their lives for them to thrive physically and psychologically (Vargas 1986). It follows, then, that preschool children would continue to be highly motivated to gain and show affection even as they moved into a more formal organization like a child-development center.

As children grow, the desired tokens of affection change. A smile, a look, or a shared phrase may replace touching and hugging as affection for a child growing older. While four- and five-year-olds have begun to add such varied strategies of affection to their repertoire, hugging and maintaining proximity remained as taken-for-granted and common strategies for most of them. Several levels of touch behavior have been categorized, including professional/functional, social/polite, friendship/warmth, love/intimacy, and sexual arousal (Heslin and Patterson 1982). Most North American adults are used to the polite handshake as a greeting or to functional touches when

163

getting a haircut, for example. More intense touching or affection episodes are quite restricted in terms of frequency and context. Preschool children, on the other hand, readily touched or sought touches to indicate liking or even at times merely potential friendship. These strategies became embedded in the culture of the child-development center as structured normative behavior, adding extra dimensions of expected nonverbal communication.

I should admit that I came into the situation of working with children as a rather "nonaffectionate" person. I tried to be warm and friendly most of the time, but I was naturally quiet and rather reticent when encountering new people or situations. I gradually learned that with most children, a pattern would emerge, starting with the child initiating talk with me, then often coming near me, then wanting to sit next to me or follow me a lot, and eventually to wanting to sit on my lap or get a back ride. I could track relationships by these indicators of closeness. How much to touch or hold the children was a question for me from the first; I sought to balance the promotion of learning and independence with providing comfort and allowing a close relationship to form. Clearly, proximity and touch were strong relational symbols for children (as they still are for adults in ways!), and they seemed to have more resonance or importance for children than for adults. Adults may be more used to being in proximity to strangers, for instance, while for a child, sitting near or playing near someone was a clear indication of a growing relationship. I was often moved by strong expressions of affection from children, and became more and more comfortable with both giving and receiving affection. I was reminded multiple times that love and belonging are basic human needs, and working with children served both to illustrate and fulfill these needs.

SUDDEN AFFECTION

For the children, expressing affection literally meant being close to another. I would thus be surprised when children suddenly enacted their affection. One day, early in my time at the center, Emily was pretending to be a cat, crawling around the classroom. "Meow," she said.

"Are you a kitty-cat? I like kitty-cats," I said, whereupon the "kitty cat" climbed into my lap for a few minutes. A little later I walked over to Chris, who had been saying, "Mr. John. Commere!" Emily followed me, and when I sat near Chris in the block area, Emily sat on my lap. "No," said Chris, trying to push her away. We sat while Chris built with blocks, and when Emily and I stood up, he said, "Mr. John, commere; come closer, come closer." He grabbed my arm and put it around him, and said, "Now stay like this." I sat down and he got in my lap and built for a while. When it was time for a story, he helped me clean up the block area and then said, "Mr. John, sit next to me." Emily said the same. I sat near them as they sat on their carpet squares. I believed in allowing and showing affection; but on the other hand I did not want to distract from learning or promoting independence. I even grew reluctant to sit on the floor near the children at such times, knowing that children would seek to sit in my lap. I hated to tell them "no" or push them out of my lap; it seemed too much like rejecting them. But at other times, if I sat at a table, or sat in a chair behind the group as they watched a movie, I often had a request like, "Could you sit down here so I could sit in your lap?" This type of request mostly came from children who had interacted with me for at least several weeks. I sought to appreciate and reciprocate children's affection, since for them it was a central relationship priority.

As my time at the center went on it became more and more common for children to rush over and give me a hug when I arrived at the class or as I was leaving. This too, surprised me at first, but I came to cherish it. At times, one child rushing to hug me would provoke a whole flock of them to come over for a hug. Some children would want hugs or to sit in my lap within a few weeks of my first regular arrival in their classroom, while others would take months to decide they wanted to get or express affection that way, too; others, of course, never sought or desired hugs or lap sitting. After about four months of volunteering, I was about to leave one day when Yolanda said, "I want a hug."

"OK," so I hugged her.

"Hug me," said Mitchell.

I did so.

"Hug me," said Michael.

"OK," I said, and hugged him too.

"Hug me!" said Mitchell again.

"I already did!" I said, surprised, but in a joking tone.

Ms. Stacey, laughing, said, "Well, hug him again, he'll be happy."

"*Two* hugs!" I said, going over to Mitchell again. "How many hugs do you want?"

Mitchell held up nine fingers.

Moved, I hugged him and left the classroom. The hug was usually the first indicator of this closer relationship in the perception of the child. I had been seeing Nick outside on the playground only for a couple of months when one day I said "Hi" to him, and he said "Hi" back and later played ball with me. He then kept returning to me and taking my hand. When it was time for his four-year-olds' class to go back inside, I told him, "I had fun playing with you today; have a good time inside," and patted his head.

"I'm gonna miss you," he said, hugging me.

"I'll miss you, too," I said, taken aback. I was surprised by such a sudden outburst of affection from a child I did not know very well. Two weeks later, I was even more surprised when I ran into Nick with his father and brother in the center hallway, preparing to leave. I had played "chasing the bear" with Nick and several other children outside that day, and now I noticed Nick pull a younger boy who resembled him toward me. "You wanna meet this man?" he asked his brother. "This is my little brother," Nick then said to me.

"Well, *hi,* little brother," I said in a friendly tone.

"His *name* is David," said Nick, insistently.

"Well, hi, David; thanks for telling me," I responded.

Suddenly, Nick threw himself over and hugged me. "And I love you," he said. Shocked and overwhelmed, I grabbed him in a hug and said, "I'm glad you came to school; that was fun playing outside." The incident was especially memorable in that it took place in front of his father and brother, and in that I did not know Nick very well. I told his father about how we had played chase that day, and told them all goodbye.

I gradually saw a pattern to the progression of ways children would express affection to me and seek affection from me. The "social layers" stripped away faster with children than with typical adults. Usually, at first they were quiet, obedient to all their teachers, and restrained. It was often hard to tell how they felt or what they were thinking. As time passed, they felt more comfortable in the child-care setting, and also with me. Then they would talk more, and respond with words or stay nearby when I initiated conversation. Eventually, the children would initiate conversation with me through a question or asking me to play with them. Then they would sit on my lap or ask me for a back ride out on the playground. They would show their distress when I had to leave for the day, and give me a hug. "Where are you going?" or "Stay over here," or "Don't go in the other classroom," I would hear, endearingly, when the children perceived it was time for me to go. At the end of my first year, several of the five-year-olds knew big changes were in store, as they would soon head for kindergarten. One boy, Alan, who had not usually wanted much physical affection, one day came over and grabbed me in a hug. He sat on my lap twice that day and did not want to get off for clean-up time. Before naptime, he got on my lap and started kissing me. Finally, I had to ask him about all this affection. "Why are you kissing me so much, Alan?" I said.

"Because I love you. I want to say goodbye to you because I'm going somewhere tomorrow."

"Well, you're a good buddy, Alan," I responded. "I'm glad you remembered to say goodbye," I added, hugging him. It was such forthright expressions of affection, which would come fairly often from children after they had become comfortable with me, that made me realize again and again how much influence I had in their lives—and how much influence they had in mine. Direct statements of love, however, were relatively rare even from children, and I was taken aback by them even as I was moved. The first time a three-year-old said he loved me, I was very shocked, and he moved on to something else so quickly that I had no chance to respond. I had walked into the three-year-old's classroom and begun to read a posted note. "Mr. John," said Thomas, a three-year-old I had known for several months. He had been too shy to talk to me at first, but by now he was clearly comfortable with me, often getting back rides from me outside.

"Yes, Thomas," I said absently, still half reading.

"I love you," Thomas said grinning, and moved away to play elsewhere.

I froze, startled, and the moment has stuck in my mind ever since. I resolved in the future to make sure to respond and tell the child how I really felt, by giving an "I love you" of some kind in response. I found the children were teaching me how to express affection myself! While such direct expressions of affection stood out, more often the children sought or expressed affection as part of their play.

GETTING AFFECTION THROUGH PLAY

One morning I walked into the three-year-olds' classroom and Chris came over, gave me a hug, and said, "Come over here, Mr. John! Let's see the animals." Chris had always been friendly and open, but had never seemed so interested in my companionship before. We went from poster to poster along the wall, and he was pointing out animals to me. "Come on," Chris kept saying. "There's more over here." When I pointed out a "toucan bird" he started seeing them and pointing them out to me on every poster. Then, he went into the block area and said, "Come on, there's a circus. Sit down." I sat with him in the block area for a while, and he took out toys, systematically saying, "This is a circus truck, this is a circus airplane, this is a circus horse." I realized that children would determinedly seek my attention and get me to play with them, and that they took that attention and time spent as evidence of affection.

Michael was a tough, quiet child who at times would step rather out of character and pretend he was a baby. He liked to pretend I was his daddy and cuddle like a baby in my lap. This seemed to let him get affection from me in game-playing fashion without being seen as a *real* baby. Sometimes, other children would call me "Daddy" playfully too, and want me to pick them up or play house with them. During my first few weeks at the center, Timothy was being extra affectionate and wanting me to sit near him. He kept saying, "Daddy, you're my daddy," and giving me hugs. Sometimes I wondered if such children did not have a father in the home. Timothy's father did live with him, but he was on a long trip away from home at the time, and so Timothy channeled some of his affection for his father to me. I was flattered that I was found worthy of such love, and I could not help but reciprocate it, "formal organizational researcher" or not.

The children were so affectionate at times that it was overwhelming. I was sitting in the block area one morning, watching Ross build a house. Nick came over and joined him, even after his "Can I build with you?" brought a half-hearted "No" from Ross. Ross did not really seem to mind, and they built together happily for a while. Soon, Ms. Stacey asked everyone to clean up, as it was time to sit in the circle area. I helped Ross and Nick put the blocks away. Suddenly, Ross jumped in my lap as I knelt in the block area and said, "Daddy!" Then Nick came over, fell on Ross and me, and also said, repeatedly and playfully, "Daddy." Often such cute incidents ended quickly, but on this day Jessica, and Trevor, and Elena, and Ivan—and perhaps a couple of other children—came over and piled onto me. Perhaps being at the bottom of a pile of football tacklers would feel similar, if heavier! I told the children to find carpet squares for circle time, and gave each a little hug, and they gradually all got off of me.

Some four-year-olds never grew comfortable with hugging adults or sitting in their laps in the child-care center setting. Some would be content with verbal interaction or proximity. A select few boys would express affection through hitting. Once when I came into the classroom, Travis came over, smiling and clearly happy to see me, and swatted me on the behind. I responded with a playful, "What was that for?" but I was rather surprised. Another time, Brent kept hitting me on the leg. I told him that I liked him and I was his friend, and asked, "Why are you hitting me?"

His response floored me. "For me, hitting means I love you," Brent said. He normally was quiet and nondemonstrative, but I could tell he was smart. His self-analysis helped me to realize that when boys would hit me playfully, they were not necessarily expressing anger or frustration. That took some getting used to for me, coming from a family in which touch was rare and hitting meant violence or punishment.

A measure of the children's desire for affection came the day a person dressed as Barney the dinosaur visited the center to take pictures with the children in each class. I noted reactions in that day's journal:

If there was any doubt that this dinosaur is a superstar among kids, it was dispelled by their reaction today. They could not have been more excited if Santa Claus himself were coming to visit. They were unable to stay still for long all morning until they saw him, and some would start chanting loudly: "Barney, Barney, Barney. . . ." They all wanted to hug him or talk to him, and as he was leaving they mobbed the fence like fans swooning over a rock superstar.

What is this hold he has over them? I guess being a huge, soft, cuddly dinosaur who sings about loving them makes him irresistible. Most kids have a seemingly bottomless desire to love (usually manifested by *proxemics*—closeness or cuddling) and be loved, which I keep discovering in my own interactions with them. They were so excited that they were out of control and tough to keep disciplined the rest of the morning after Barney left.

An icon of affection and love was the most popular character I ever saw visit the center. It certainly reinforced how important expressing affection is for children, especially through touching and hugging.

After several more months of my being around them, some children would color a picture for me. Sometimes this was the first major indicator of the child's desire for a closer relationship. Children I had known at the center who had gone on to kindergarten and first grade would give me gifts as tokens of their affection. I saw Timothy in his mother's car one day after she had dropped off his younger brother, and he waved and said, "Hi, Mr. John." He gave me a penny.

"What's this for?" I asked, rather moved.

"So you can buy a gum," he said.

"Well, thank you," I said, not wanting to take his penny from him. "Why don't you buy one for me, OK?" I asked him.

"OK," said Timothy, and his mom said farewell and drove him off to school. Especially around Christmastime, school-age children would typically find something to give me, whether a ball, or piece of candy, or a picture they had drawn. After several months of my presence, some new four-year-old children joined the class and did not seem sure how to react to me. They would see the other children hug me, sit on my lap, or get their backs rubbed at naptime. Their expressions told me that they wanted some of this affection, too, but they did not feel they knew me yet, so were uncertain. After some time of getting comfortable with me, they too would quickly move toward more touching or hugging. I remember two boys new to the class, who, after several weeks, would notice me kneeling or bending down for something and then would rush into my arms, throwing themselves on me like we were wrestling. I got the feeling they saw an opportunity for affectionate touch, and took it while it seemed appropriate for them to "hug" me playfully. When one or two children became fond of me and started to get hugs from or play games with me, several other children in the class would quickly move to that same level of relationship with me. At times I was stunned when a three-year-old I had only met a couple of weeks ago would run over to me, holding his arms up and wanting to be held.

Some children would seek more affection when they were quarreling with friends they normally played with, or when those friends were not present. One summer, I came back from vacation to encounter Kenny, who had talked with me at times beforehand, rushing over when he saw me to give me a big hug. "I missed you," Kenny told me several times that day. "I wanted you to come to school." He talked and talked about things he had done at home and things he wanted to do with me, like ride a motorcycle, buy a truck, or go hunting. "I'm gonna grow up right here so you can see me grow up. . . . I'm your brother and I'm *not* pretending."

Over the next several days and weeks, Kenny was often inseparable from me. He had not been this close to me before my vacation, so I was surprised by this sudden transition. He liked to sit and talk with me, and became very irritated when other children tried to interrupt what he perceived as his time with me. He told me he wanted me to come over to his house, "but you'll have to sneak," he said. He would not tell me why. He proposed a variety of trips with me. "Don't tell my mom and dad," he said. "They'll whip me." Again, he would not say why. It was clear that Kenny was encountering some kind of anger at home; he seemed desperate to maintain an affectionate connection with me. Another day, when some of the children were pretending to have a picnic with us, Kenny kept saying, "We're *not* pretending! Right? We're not pretending. Me and Mr. John are going on a *real* field trip." Most of the other four- and five-year-olds would launch readily into a play world with me, whether "driving around," having a "picnic," or going on a "spaceship." For several weeks that summer, Kenny was impatient with any pretend activity with me, and determined to establish a *real* relationship with me.

During my third year at the center, I would spend brief times in the afternoon visiting the after-school program there. Some of those children I had known since they were four years old; others I only met when they were six or seven. The older children were more reticent when it came to initiating relationships. They had to observe me longer and took longer to trust me. Even Timothy, whom I had known since age four, at age seven was more restrained in showing affection. A journal entry from that time explored my reasoning:

> Some days Timothy will hardly acknowledge my visit if he is busy playing; but on other days he wants me to play ball with him or chase him. Though last fall he wrote a poem to me to give it to me later, and has drawn me pictures—clear and moving expressions of affection. This suggests a longer-term commitment—less demonstrative of affection daily, but touching long-term demonstrations of affection persist. His younger brother, Thomas, is gradually following the same pattern: in kindergarten now, he no longer asks for a back ride every day I see him, and often stays away busy with play on days I visit, but he also wants a hug or will sit on my lap at intervals. For the older kids, playing with them is viewed as the key indicator of a growing or strong relationship. They have less desire for touch or straightforward statements of affection, feeling they are no longer appropriate. A desire to play games with me, or to greet me when they see me, are the biggest indicators of affection they typically show.

When the school-aged children did seek greater affection, they seemed to do so more surreptitiously, as part of a game of chase, or by standing or sitting close during other games. Most of us seem to abandon unabashed expressions of affection as we grow older, finding it too risky to express affection as we learn to enact peer-enforced or "grown-up" social roles. A clear appreciation for affection and its forthright expression was one of the joys for me of working with children.

"PICK ME UP"—HOLDING AND CARRYING

Quite often during my first two years of volunteering at the center, I would have a child approach me and say endearingly or commandingly (and sometimes both!), "Pick me up." I could seldom resist this appeal, feeling moved that the children would want and trust me to take care of them in such a way. In one such incident, Chris came over while we were outside and asked to be picked up.

"Why?" I asked.

"Because I want you to," Chris replied with simple childhood logic.

"I don't want to hit your head on this bar," I said. "Here you go," and I did pick him up.

Michael, standing nearby, saw this and said, "I want you to pick me up. Will you pick *me* up?"

"OK," I said, still holding Chris.

"I want you to carry me," added Michael.

"Carry you?" I said, responding skeptically to the babylike tone of the request.

"He hasn't carried anyone anywhere," chimed in Chris. Indeed, I was staying put with Chris. I tried to avoid carrying the children around the playground. These were four- and five-year-olds, after all.

"I'm not carrying kids anywhere," I said.

"I want you to hold me like Chris is," persisted Michael.

"OK. I will," I said reassuringly.

"Chris, it's my turn now. It's not your turn anymore. . . . Chris, come down." Michael pulled on Chris.

"OK, Chris, you've had a good turn; let's let Michael have a turn now." I let Chris down and picked Michael up and held him for a little. This satisfied both, and we all then moved to do other things on the playground. Usually, all I had to do was hold a child for a minute or two, and then he or she would happily move on to another activity. Most did not want such affection all the time. However, when one got such affection, often at least one or two more would want the same. After several months, the clamor for being picked up on some days got loud—outside, fortunately. One child cried when she was not first to be picked up, even though she had not asked first. Other children noticed, too, when children like Michael constantly wanted to be picked up. Alex had never indicated he wanted to be picked up, until many months into my volunteering time at the center. "You always—he always—you *always* pick him up," Alex said, referring to Michael. Alex rarely wanted to be picked up; touch as affection seemed to be a lower priority with him. But I wondered if the children who constantly asked to be picked up or to sit in laps made other children jealous, even if the other children never asked for the same.

After about a year at the center, I walked into the classroom one morning and Ross said, "Mr. John!" and ran over to give me a hug. "Pick me up!" he said. "Pick me up, please." Then he wanted me to stay with him whenever he or I wanted to move around the classroom. My strategy with children so desperate for affection had become to stay with them for a while. Then they would get started playing busily with something, so I could ease away from the scene. Usually that worked, but children like Ross were persistent and would soon follow me wherever I had gone off to in the classroom.

There were indeed days when the children seemed *too* affectionate, to the point of being clingy. Affection overkill could include climbing on me, crying for no apparent reason and wanting me to pick them up, or hanging on me and pulling me by the hand in too many different directions. Too much affection caused some children to forget my personal space, and assume it was theirs, too. I would not get too firm unless such children started knocking me over or making me step too close to other children nearby. Independence too was to be promoted at the center, so at times I would have to gently suggest we do something else, or I would see the child distracted and subtly move away myself. I tried to avoid directly rejecting a child seeking affection, but at times I needed to discourage it.

One day Michael had a difficult day in terms of trying to get affection. Many children liked for me to chase them around the playground, and then they would chase me. Michael had always been affectionate and liked to spend time with me, so I was quite surprised when he cried when I ran after some other children and away from him. After that, I tried to avoid "running away" from him, but I still made it clear that I could enjoy a game of tag, and he could, too. I let him catch me quickly, to reassure him that I was not really running away from him personally. Michael played along for a while, but quickly got upset when he did not catch me immediately. He told me that he was upset, that I was too fast, and he said, "I need all my energy back." He sat and pouted for a while, but later I played with him again and he was fine. I let him catch me quickly a couple of times as the game of tag ran out of steam, to show him he could catch me if he just tried a little. But the rest of the day he wanted to sit on my lap or have me carry him. Ms. Stacey, observing this, told him to go play for a while, which made him even more upset, and he started crying. She told me, "We need less holding, unless it's really necessary; it creates problems." She had a point, but I also felt a little blame falling on me for Michael's sadness. I wrote in my journal that day:

> The question is, when is it [holding] "really needed"? I probably should avoid carrying the kids around the playground. I haven't done that too much, but in the last few days this has increased. I need to do more "letting go" in that area. But I refuse to totally avoid affection for them. If it's disrupting the class or interfering with normal play activities, that's one thing, but I don't want to become cold and distant either. It's a tough fence to balance on, but we'll see if I can't let go a little over the next few days. I have to be careful not to overreact and become mean, taking my anger at Ms. Stacey, or really "the system," out on the kids. I need to go back next time with a fresh start, and a little more "detached" attitude.

Thus went one of my first wrestlings with the issue of how affectionate to be and how much touch and holding to allow the children to expect of me. I generally grew more reluctant to pick children up when we were inside than when we were outside. My view was that life is too short to refuse to give affection in service to some abstract concept like independence or classroom order. But I also wanted to respect the teachers and the classroom situation. "I suppose I will keep needing to balance on the edge of affection, but affection is better than disinterest," I wrote in my journal. On the whole, however, the teachers were quite supportive and even encouraging of the children being affectionate with adults as well as with one another, and facilitated relationship development effectively. After being at the center for some time, I was more demonstrative of affection with the children than I had been at first. I was more willing to give a quick hug or a pat on the back.

ALTERED AFFECTION NORMS

As my second year of spending time at the center began, I had developed certain norms about expressing affection. Hugs were always welcome. Any child was free to sit on my lap unless it was during times where there was an independent or group activity the children were expected to participate in. It also became clear to both the children and me that I was not comfortable picking them up for too long or carrying them around like babies. Back rides provided a compromise that allowed playful expression of affection through touch. One day, after I had given several back rides, Kyle was on my back and I decided to sit down and rest on a bank of pine straw near a climber.

"Are we taking a rest?" asked Kyle.

"Yeah, this'll be a rest," I said.

Lori and Brent came over and warned us, "You're in the fire! Look out!"

"There's no fire here," I said, in my tiredness choosing to take them literally rather than playfully. They started moving some pine straw to build a "fire" on the other side of the monkey bars.

"Will you hold this flower?" Lori asked me, handing me a tall blade of grass.

"OK," I said. "Pretty girls like pretty flowers."

"Lori isn't pretty," said Kyle.

"Sure she is," I said.

"Do you love her?" asked Kyle.

I found myself thinking, "How do I explain this? I'm not her father, I'm not really even her teacher. But I do love her. Can I make a five-year-old understand?"

So I said, "Well, you know, I *do* love her, but not as a girlfriend. More like a big brother loves a sister."

"Do you love me?" Kyle then asked, out of the blue.

More certain now, I said, "Yes I do, kind of like a big brother loves a little brother."

Kyle continued to sit beside me for a while, and seemed to enjoy just sitting together. I found myself thinking, "That turned into a rather deep conversation for a five-year-old." I also knew that Kyle's parents were splitting up at that time, so I could only imagine how Kyle might be reacting. I was glad to be there for him, at least for a moment. He was the type of child who would ask all kinds of questions, usually about the books we would read. We had several conversations as the months went on, but not about love or affection again—more about witches, sharks, and monsters.

As my third year began, one new boy, Brandon, had joined the four-year-old class. After only a couple of days of seeing me, he was comfortable enough to initiate interaction by saying, "Mr. John! Look what I made," or, "Mr. John! Come look what I'm building." He would often ask me to play with him or want me to sit beside him. As he observed other children interact with me who knew me well, he quickly progressed to expressing more affection. A few days later, he took my hand and led me to the book area to read to him. Outside, he often followed me and got me to chase him. After several days of seeing other children get back rides, he not only kept grabbing my hands, but told me, "I wanna be high up on your back." Usually it took children several weeks to get comfortable with the idea of getting a ride on my back. Even after years of working with children, I found myself a little stunned by how quickly a young child could become affectionate with me.

Long exposure to such affection cut through some of the rules and routines of the classroom for me and reminded me of why we were all *really* there: to learn how to relate to one another, especially in loving ways. The values of loving and nurturing children were modeled and communicated by the director and lead teachers in each classroom, transmitted by them to the part-time staff, and picked up and responded to by the children. Any culture seeks an equilibrium between affection and professional distance or objectivity (Saarni and Weber 1999). At the child-development center, I found a balance that cautioned children against showing too much affection, yet encouraged their basic strategies for meeting their need for it. As my months of being exposed to childish affection extended to years, I came to believe that we as adults are often too reluctant to give or receive affection. The stress children put on giving and receiving affection was a fine lesson for us all, I believed; it was of central importance to them, and ought to be more important for all of us in organizational relationships.

12

Children in Conflict

Whether confronting another child over a desired toy or attempting to manage a problem to please both parties, children would regularly engage in conflict. The inevitability of conflict in human affairs was demonstrated by the amount of space in my observation journals devoted to conflicts among the children. Children had a surprising repertoire of strategies in conflict, even at ages four and five. The staff at this child-development center took a fairly laissez-faire attitude toward conflict until it clearly endangered children or the overall peace of the classroom or playground. At times, however, some teachers would revert to the more familiar assertion of control in the face of conflict: they would say "Both of you move away," or take a disputed toy, or have both children sit in time-out. The recommended handling of conflict at the center was very communication focused: "Use words" was heard a lot. Children were expected to handle their own problems if possible.

A child who was hitting, kicking, scratching, or throwing things at others was most likely to be placed in time-out. Children were also told positively, "Keep your hands to yourself. If you don't like what she is doing, you tell her to stop or tell a teacher." The key value behind such advice was clear: "We need to talk about our disagreements." At one staff focus group meeting, the center director and other teachers noted their frustration at the near impossibility of enacting this value in the two-year-olds' classroom. "There, we can't tell them that 'you two need to sit down and discuss this,'" the center's director noted. Redirecting children to another activity was the typical fallback strategy, with time-out reserved for use only in response to dangerous or strongly defiant or mean actions.

Personally, even after teaching several college courses in mediating conflict, I found it difficult in the heat of a conflict to have both children involved discuss it with each other. Many times, teachers fell back on separating the conflicting children and asking them to go to another area. One of the benefits of an avoiding-conflict style was the time saved by not dealing with it, yet often the issues remained unresolved and returned to be dealt with later (Wilmot and Hocker 1998). The problem-solving or collaborative style was usually much more effective, but might require a teacher to disrupt ongoing classroom activities.

An additional difficulty in attempting to mediate disputes among young children was that there was often no clear issue to mediate—one child may simply have been "testing" another, or expressing anger at something else, which was difficult to explore with a four-year-old when one simply wanted to restore calm and order. Creative effort to come to a rationally discussed solution was at a premium when encountering child conflicts, but I knew their learning young would help them work out conflicts by mutual agreement at older ages. Teaching such creativity required extra energy and commitment even from me, who did not have the additional responsibilities in the classroom that teachers did. Still, one of the most rewarding feelings in my volunteer or research work came from helping children work out a dispute without an abrupt or artificial separation of the children or penalties for them.

I noted that even young children made choices about how to respond to conflict. In general, the younger the child, the more simple and restricted the responses to conflict were, and the more likely they were to be strictly competitive. This strategy did result in a clear, unambiguous outcome to the conflict (Wilmot and Hocker 1998). My own launching point for understanding the varied strategies I observed was categorizing conflicts based on regularly enacted conflict styles. First, conflicts with the competitive style stood out as dominant. Here, the child wanted to win or put another child down, perceiving some resource (use of a toy or time with an adult) as limited and seeking to get the most of it. As I continued to observe, children who yielded caught my attention. They did not want to yield, but they wanted the relationship more, and thus made the decision to give in during the conflict. A similar style, but one difficult to specifically observe, was the preference to avoid conflict entirely. Some children may have yielded not to preserve or promote a relationship, but simply to avoid being in a conflict. Third and finally, the most sophisticated strategy was seeking to solve the problem or compromise so that both parties could feel satisfied and happy. I saw this process more often than I expected to among four- and five-year-olds.

THE COMPETING CONFLICT STYLE

The first theme that emerged from observing conflicts at the center concerned pure competition—one child seeking something that must be yielded by or denied to another. During my third week, I observed a conflict that served as a model of many that I saw there over the next months. Dale came over and asked me to push him on a swing. When we got back to the swings, Brent had gotten onto "Dale's" swing. Dale asked Brent for it back, but Brent would not move. Dale said, "Brent won't move; get him off of the swing."

I told him it was mean of Brent to take that swing, but I would not make him get off of it. "What if someone took you off *your* swing; you wouldn't like that. Brent would be mad, like you feel now." For Brent, it seemed, had just found an empty swing and taken it. Too, there was a row of similar, un-occupied swings right next to the one Brent was in.

This did not assuage Dale's desire for that particular swing, though. He was now whining and starting to cry. Other children, seeing this dispute, made suggestions.

"I'm tired of hearing him cry; let's go somewhere else," Neil said to Brent. Brent would not budge.

"Here, you could use this one," said Ken, indicating a nearby swing.

"No, I don't want that one; I want the other one," said Dale, in tears.

"I'd really like to push you in this swing," I said, indicating an empty swing.

Dale shook his head no.

Finally, Teresa, who was in another swing near Brent, said that Dale could use her swing after she had swung in it once.

So I pushed her in the swing, and said to Dale, "After she's done, send Teresa to come get me and I'll push you."

Dale had calmed down, finally deciding that another swing might be better than none, after all. When Teresa came to get me, as I walked over to Dale in the swing, the teacher told everyone it was time to go inside. I felt a sense of frustration that Dale had been so busy arguing over a particular swing that he had missed having me push him in any swing. But this incident was a good indicator to me of how complex conflicts could be even for young children. Dale saw Brent's taking of "his" swing as a grievous territorial violation.

Another of the first conflict episodes I observed was more blunt and to the point, though just a little later the two girls involved were playing together happily, as often happened in children's competitive conflicts. On this day, Hannah and Brenda were in the home play area.

"Are you my friend?" Hannah asked Brenda.

"No," said Brenda, who then walked over to a toy phone and picked it up.

"I'm gonna call my mommy," Hannah stated, and grabbed the phone from Brenda.

"No!" said Brenda, holding on to the phone.

"I want to play, too!" insisted Hannah.

"No."

"Well, I'm gonna go in *my* dollhouse when I go outside," said Hannah.

"I've got a dollhouse," said Brenda.

"Not like mine," said Hannah.

"Go play somewhere else."

"No."

"Go play somewhere else!" insisted Brenda, and she pushed Hannah. Both moved away from each other at this point, and played separately for a while, but sure enough, the next hour they were both back in the home play area, happily having "lunch" together. Friendship had replaced the hostile attitudes I had observed earlier.

That friendships could be fickle was again demonstrated the next week, when I saw Dale putting pegs in a pegboard. A conflict ensued over sole possession of some toys in question.

"Hey," I said to Jason, "Dale has all purple pegs in there."

"Yep," said Dale.

"I'll help," said Jason.

"No, I don't want you to help," responded Dale.

"I'll be your friend," promised Jason.

"No," said Dale. Jason reached for the peg container. "No!" yelled Dale, and hit Jason. Jason then kicked Dale, so he kicked back.

"Dale and Jason! Stop it!" I said, moving in between them. After they were separated, Dale continued to work with the pegs, and Jason stood around nearby.

Michael then approached Dale and said, "I want to help."

"OK," said Dale, and Michael handed some pegs to him. But when Jason tried to help, Dale clawed at him. Jason clawed at Dale right back.

Once again, I exclaimed, "Dale! Stop that! You could hurt someone doing that."

Eventually, Dale got tired of the pegs and Michael and Jason played together with them. Then it was Michael saying, "I want to help."

Jason said, "No."

"I'll be your friend," said Michael, and I was thinking, "Here we go again." But Jason continued to play with the pegs, and as Michael handed more pegs to him, he accepted them peacefully. They continued to play together for a while. Apparently a friendship had survived a potential conflict. But Dale and Jason had competed fiercely for the pegs, and no friendship was soon in the offing for them.

Friendships could withstand such conflict and even strengthen after it, I noted, and one dramatic incident a few weeks later crystallized this finding: Dale and Brent were playing together that day, but their relationship seemed to go in phases day by day, rather like a bipolar superpower relationship in which neither side quite fully trusts the other. On this day their game of hitting and pushing one another got rough, and Dale hit Brent in the face, making him cry. Ms. Stephanie came over, and Brent insisted while crying, "*He started it!*"

"No, you started it; you punched me in the stomach!" insisted Dale.

"Well, you squeezed and twisted my arm!"

"You did it first!"

"No, you did," responded Brent.

"You started it!" insisted Dale.

"Liar, liar!" Brent said.

"I saw you *both* fighting each other. I hope you'll both be sorry and be friends, but if you can't play together, you *should* stay away from one another," Ms. Stephanie said.

"I do go, but everywhere I go he follows me," Dale explained.

"Well, he wants to be your friend," said Ms. Stephanie.

"But he always starts that rough stuff."

"Tell him to stop. Then move away. Keep your hands to yourself," finished Ms. Stephanie.

Dale went off by himself, and Brent sat by himself by a tree for a while. But sure enough, a half hour later, they were busy playing together again. Time seemed to overcome their competitive conflicts even though outright problem solving between them was absent.

Any simple thing could become an object of competition. One morning, Thelma was cutting hearts out of paper and putting them in a stack on the table. "They're for you," she told me. She kept adding to the pile of hearts on the table. Seeing this, Michael decided to cut some out for me, too. When Thelma saw the heart Michael had placed on top of the pile, she said, "That's not a right heart," and threw it off of the pile.

"I made it," said Michael.

"I make hearts better than you," said Thelma. They both kept cutting out several sizes of hearts for a little while, putting them in separate piles.

Another type of competition, strange from an adult's point of view, was over a scarce resource that was actually plentiful. One day a new boy in the class, Wentao, kept wanting to play "spaceship" outside. This had all started with Wentao playing with a spaceship Matt had built out of big blue blocks. Now, everything was a spaceship for Wentao. Wentao was with Matt playing up on a raised playhouse out on the playground and they began arguing over whose spaceship it was.

"It's *my spaceship.*"

"It's *mine.*"

"No, it's mine," they went back and forth, trying to push each other away from one spot along a long railing. Apparently that had been agreed to be the "driver's spot" for the spaceship. Competing instead of cooperating, they drifted apart for a while, but several hours later they would play spaceship again.

Girls, too, would test their friendships by competing over perceived scarce resources. Hannah was playing with Alison one day and both girls moved over to the coloring table. As they were talking, Alison said something Hannah did not like, so Hannah slapped a paper on Alison's face. "How's that?" Hannah asked.

Alison looked surprised, but did not say anything. They continued to interact, but soon Hannah grabbed the piece of paper Alison was coloring on. "Give that back!" yelled Alison as she grabbed for it. Hannah held on, and it ripped in half. "Now look what you did," said a crying Alison. They threw crayons at one another until Hannah moved away on her own. Alison put her head down on the table and cried until a teacher came over and asked what was wrong. It turned out that only two pieces of paper had been left in the pile; so when they first came over to the coloring table, Alison had been saying to Hannah, "You can't have both; we each can have one." Evidently Hannah had tried to take both, which damaged the trust in the friendship they had built with each other. Later, I noticed Alison trying to sit near Hannah, but Hannah kept moving away.

Some competitive incidents seemed to stem from children not knowing or understanding any other way to get what they wanted or even to get attention. One day, Evan came over to me and said, "Mr. John, nobody will ask me to be their friend." He moved off before I could think of an answer. Shortly after this, he headed over to a table where Julie was building a dinosaur and knocked it asunder. His violence seemed to stem from his frustration at not fitting in—but it unfortunately made his situation worse. The other children trusted him less and less, and therefore would avoid or tolerate him rather than letting him get close. A few days later, Evan seemed to be enjoying himself, coloring with Alex and playing with Julie. Then, all of a sudden, he walked up to Paul and broke a LEGO airplane that Paul had built and was flying. He and Paul, to my knowledge, had not had any interactions earlier. The violent act seemed completely arbitrary—but I wondered if it stemmed from continuing frustration at not having a "friend" or someone to consistently be close to or play with. The teachers at the center often cited home life as the source of the dissatisfaction and overreliance on competitive or violent strategies of children like Evan. The teachers tried to be consistent and loving in their discipline, but often felt they were on a losing campaign against the overall influence of such children's home lives.

Brian, as the youngest child in the four- and five-year-olds' class, was blatantly trying to develop friendships, and was having some troubles doing so. He was prone to hit or kick when he was angry and was the child most likely to be sat briefly in time-out. One of Brian's exploits for venting anger and frustration was spitting. This got him placed in time-out, but it also got him attention. Since he had trouble finding friends, he discovered he enjoyed the power he gained by spitting on other children, and continued for a time almost as if it were a game, laughing at the children's reactions. He had gone inside to get a drink of water, behind Neil and some others. As he walked back outside, he held water in his mouth, enjoying the scared or angry reactions of other children. He spat on Neil, and laughed. Neil was a gentle child, and prone to get picked on. So it figured that Brian would select him—Brian had characteristics of a bully in the making. Neil, on the other hand, was learning to argue back, and even to hit back when children like Brian attacked him. During Brian's spitting phase, Neil was even put in time-out once for spitting (while Brian was sat down at least three or four times). Brian was definitely a negative influence on peers, as other boys at times tried to test out Brian's common competitive tactics.

Brian's reputation got in the way when he tried to be nice and be friends with someone. At times, his merely going near another child or trying to join in a game would cause other children to quickly move away. They might say, "Let's go play over there," or "Get out of here!" or "You can't come in here!" or, most often, "I'm not your friend, Brian!" Thus, Brian was caught between his often-failed attempts to make friends and his reputation for hitting, kicking, and spitting. I heard him ask other children, "Are you my friend?" or "Will you be my friend?" almost every day. It reached the point where the other children would say "I'm not your friend," even before Brian had a chance to ask them. I saw Brian treasuring moments when his attempts to fit in succeeded. Once he lay on his stomach to watch a movie, and Timothy and David did the same. Brian scooted closer to them and said happily, "We're all doing the same."

When I found Brian hitting, kicking, or pushing, I tried to mention to him that doing those things might lose him friends. If he could learn that his tendency to violence prevented friendships, he might try harder with other strategies, especially if he enjoyed some success with them. However, it was a hard conflict pattern for him to escape. One day, Brian came into the classroom in the morning in a good mood, hugging his father goodbye. He built with bristle blocks at a table, and soon Timothy and Julian decided to sit at the same table.

"I want *all* the big ones," said Julian.

"That's fine," said Brian pleasantly. "I'll just build with these."

But still, for Julian, Brian could do no right. "We're *not* your friend," said Julian decisively as they continued to build at the table. Then Julian and Timothy took blocks from Brian and made him cry.

"Do you want me to tell the teacher on you again?" said Julian. "I will," and when he did Brian got chastised once again. Soon, they were all calling each other names, Brian yelled, and a teacher had them go to different areas. It was sad to see Brian so happy and cooperative, but have the other children force him into the same unhappy pattern. They all, even the teachers, seemed to have Brian negatively typecast. As time passed, however, and new children came into the classroom, Brian managed to "grow out of" his bad reputation and develop more friendships.

Competition could also be sparked by a developing relationship. Children would discover a commonality or enjoy playing with one another, but then the details of their interaction would become the basis for a dispute. One morning, Timothy was building with LEGOs at the table where I was sitting. Laura sat across from him and started building something else. After a while, she said, "Timothy, you wanna be friends?"

"Yes," said Timothy.

"Yeah, we can be friends together," said Laura. They built things together at the table for quite a while, and then it was time to go outside.

There, they wanted to play football with me. I would throw to one of them and that child would throw it back to me. There was no problem taking turns for a while, but then Laura got the ball when Timothy thought it was his turn.

"Give it!" said Timothy angrily. "It's my turn!"

"I will," Laura said as Timothy pulled at her. "I just want to tell you first . . ."

"Give it to me!" yelled Timothy.

"I will if you'll be friendly," said Laura.

"Give it!" said Timothy, in his stubborn, strong-willed way. Then their conflict escalated into a shoving war, and a nearby Ms. Teresa put a halt to it. Timothy told me he wanted to be on my team, and so Laura did, too. They pulled me two ways for a bit.

"Choose which one of us," said Laura.

"I like *both* of you," I said. "I'm not gonna choose between you." I knew enough to avoid provoking that kind of conflict. "I'll play with both of you," I said.

"Let's go play somewhere else, Mr. John," said Timothy.

"We're *all* friends here, come on," responded Laura, who followed as well. Further conflict was avoided when Laura decided to join in play with some other children, and Timothy and I went over to the slide.

Getting beyond the competitive desire to be first could be very difficult for some children. Joseph and Matt both wanted me to help them climb a pole one day. Matt had been there first, and then Joseph had joined him. After I walked over to them, I said, "Listen, I'll help both of you climb up the pole, if you can decide who will go first." They still both hung on to the pole, whining to each other, "I want a turn," and pushing each other's faces and arms. "Hey, I like both of you," I said reassuringly. "I want to help both of you up this pole." Since I had seen Matt at the pole first, I then said, "Will you let Matt have a turn, Joseph, and then I'll help you up?" Joseph reluctantly sat under the playhouse, and pouted. After helping Matt up, I asked Joseph if he wanted to climb up. He shook his head no and stayed seated under the playhouse. Then Thomas came running, saying "I want to," and suddenly Joseph did run over first to get his turn. Two weeks later, Ivan and Lem seemed to be developing a relationship based on competition. I was sitting at the puzzle table after Julie had asked me to come over there, and I was watching her do some puzzles. Soon Ivan came over and then Lem, and they each worked on a puzzle. "I beat you!" said Lem, after finishing his puzzle.

"So what?" said Ivan, who was working on a larger, harder puzzle. Then, after Lem had started another puzzle, Ivan finally finished his. "I beat you," said Ivan. This type of one-upmanship continued between them for a while at the table, and then later outside, when they began chasing and tackling each other. When I showed Lem how to play tic-tac-toe on a large board outside, he made all the rotating blocks *O*s.

"I want to play," said Ivan, and soon had them all *X*s.

"I won," each said in their turn. Their friendship seemed to develop and extend through their competition.

When things got violent, however, was the worst for all concerned. I remember feeling, as an adult, that violence simply must stop. It was difficult to entertain thoughts of mediation or talking out the conflict when one observed a boy hit or push down a girl, for example, or a smaller boy. Sometimes violence began as friendly pretend or wrestling games got too rough. Some days seemed uniquely violence prone: Evan and James would fight and begin to get violent, and I would have to separate them. Then Shaun would be poking and wrestling Paul, who then started crying and wanted adult comfort. Days like those were enough to make one sympathetic with those who have a low tolerance for being around children.

On one such day, I encountered an ongoing war pitting Ivan and Shaun against several other contingents. While still inside, Ivan and Shaun started running from Evan, who was playing some kind of wild wolf. This was dangerous and violated classroom rules, so Ms. Stacey asked them to sit at the tables. Later, outside, Ivan and Shaun turned mean, grabbing and pushing smaller children like Michael, Matt, Thomas, and some girls, Michelle and Rachel. Let it not be said that media do not influence children—the "Power Ranger" kicks and hits apparently proceeded that morning to *real* hits and pushing others down. Ivan and Shaun were not normally so violent, and were usually protective and affectionate toward Michael, Ivan's little brother. They seemed to be playing a team threatened by some "bad guys" and they took their game too far or too seriously. They nearly, but not quite, hurt Michael and Matt, who a couple of times that day ran over to me and said, "Don't let them get me," as they grabbed onto me. During the weeks when violent days like these became more common, the children received talks during circle time about how "fighting is out" and keeping their hands to themselves. Eventually, "Power Ranger" play was banned from the classroom and the playground, since it led to many of these violent episodes.

Sometimes I seemed to be the perceived limited commodity prompting competition. One day about a year after I started at the center, Brent and Timothy were fighting continually, it seemed. Brent had built a sand castle outside and asked me to come see it. Timothy preceded me to the castle and stepped on it. Brent yelled, and said, "He stepped on it!"

"Timothy," I said. "Why did you step on it? I wanted to see it!"

Timothy did not answer, and Brent built the castle back up.

I told him that it was "neat," and helped him by putting a flag on top in the form of a long blade of grass. Timothy took it off. "I don't like it there," he said.

"Give it back!" said Brent, and put his hands around Timothy's neck.

"Brent!" I said. "Remember what we said about choking?" Brent had been cautioned against this several times before over several days.

"You're choking me," said Timothy.

"Why won't you give that back?" asked Brent.

"Because I don't want it there," said Timothy.

"I'll choke ya," said Brent. Then Timothy moved away, and Brent looked for an alternative grass clipping for his castle. Brian came over and looked at Brent's creation.

"Step on it!" said a returning Timothy.

"No! Don't," said a panicked Brent. "Don't step on it!"

"I'm not; I won't," said Brian. "We can build like this." He started building a sand castle of his own. Thomas, Timothy's younger brother, came over and began helping Brent by pushing some sand over to him.

"Are you my friend?" asked Brent. "Will you be my friend?"

"Say no, Thomas," said Timothy.

"He doesn't have to mind you," said Brent assertively to Timothy.

"Oh yes, he does," said Timothy.

Timothy and Thomas soon moved elsewhere, while Brent and Brian continued to build. Eventually, Brian said, "I need more sand," as his castle was smaller than Brent's. Then he decided he could put his sand on Brent's castle. "Here; here's some more sand." He and Brent continued to build in the sand together for a while. Later, I noticed Brent and Timothy again exchanging harsh words. A conflict was clearly ongoing; some kind of competition had set in between them. I also noticed that both boys had wanted a lot of affection from me lately, and that within weeks both would be moving into kindergarten. I wondered if pressures in seeking affection and attention from adults in their familiar world and uncertainty about leaving it had factored into their longer-term competition with each other.

Days when fighting seemed to be more common were certainly more trying and tiring from the perspective of an adult. On such days competitive conflict seemed to be the only style in evidence. My journal entry on one of those days eighteen months after starting observations at the center reflected this:

Today was a day with lots of crying, pushing, and shoving—the kind of day one perceives those who dislike children must think of as typical. Early on, Brian started crying and pushing when Manolo and Michael told him they did not want to play with him. This put him in a bad mood for a while; and later I saw him approach a table where Manolo and Kayla were building a tower out of blocks, and Kayla held her hand defensively in front of the tower and said, "No!" clearly expecting the blocks to get knocked over by Brian. He refrained, however, and once he felt he had friends again, he was in a good mood again.

Outside, several of the children wanted me to build a house with them out of the big blocks. Michael began it by asking me to build him a "tent" out of two of the blocks, like I had for him on Monday. Then several more wanted one, but we only had enough blocks for one tent and one square "house." Many of the three- and four-year-olds tried to get in or on the house, and there was again crying and pushing at this point. It did grow to seem endless this morning. It seemed that when one child stopped crying from being pinched or pushed, another was starting. This is clearly a symptom of the move to a younger group of kids—they are more likely to scream, cry, hit, or push immediately upon encountering an offense to them. "Use words," I found myself saying a few times today.

In spite of the apparent pervasiveness of competition in conflict, alternative strategies for dealing with conflict also emerged.

THE ACCOMMODATING/YIELDING CONFLICT STYLE

Conflicts among the children did not always lead to mutual name-calling, physical violence, or intervention by a teacher. Sometimes, the children did manage the conflict themselves; often one child, deciding that the conflict was too disruptive or was endangering a valuable relationship, gave in to another. I viewed such a result as a step up from the uncontrolled competitive conflict that I more often observed, yet the children who yielded did not get their needs met, even if the relationship was preserved and further conflict avoided for a time.

One day about a month after I started at the center, I noticed a potential conflict brewing on the playground. Michael was walking around with an angry expression on his face. Soon I saw him talking to his younger, three-year-old brother, Roy, on the playground, demanding that he give him his hammer back. Roy had a toy hammer, apparently Michael's, that he had brought from home. Matthew followed Roy around the playground for a while, saying that if Roy did not give the hammer back he would kill him. Roy, in turn, looked more and more depressed, but would not yield the hammer. Finally, a few minutes later, after Michael had been distracted by playing something else, Roy suddenly gave Michael the hammer. "Here," he said, and happily walked away from his brother. Matthew seemed relieved and offered to give him something in return, but Roy had already walked away to play with others. The brothers had abruptly made up.

Another case of yielding to resolve conflict I noted three weeks later. Daniel was sitting at a table building with LEGO blocks. I sat down next to him for a while. "Look at my spaceship," said Daniel.

"Is that what that is?" I said. "I thought so. That's sure what it looks like."

Soon, Ivan came over to the table. "Y'know what I'm gonna build?" he asked.

"What?" I said.

"I'm gonna build an airplane."

"Good," I said.

"Where are all the big ones?" asked Ivan. Daniel had used all the long LEGOs in his spaceship. "I need some of those long ones," said Ivan.

"No, I used them," said Daniel.

"He used them right now for his spaceship," I explained to Ivan, hoping to defuse a potential conflict.

"I need some. He won't share," said Ivan. "Please, can I have one? I'll be your friend if you do."

Daniel paused a moment, and found that Ivan's persuasion was working. Daniel gave Ivan two long LEGOs, which was unusual for him, as Daniel was usually very possessive of whatever toys he was playing with.

Ivan said, "Thanks," and proceeded to build an airplane. Daniel remodeled his spaceship.

Then, Sam came over and said, "Can I have some of those?" No answer at first. "I want some of those," pursued Sam.

Daniel had evidently had enough. He broke his spaceship into the box of LEGOs and cheerfully moved away, letting Sam use those LEGOs. His yielding clearly had dissipated a potential conflict.

Friendships, as noted earlier, could be tested through competition, but there were times when certain children did not trust their relationship with another enough to take conflict too far; and thus they would, in the end, yield. Jason and Sam had developed an ongoing friendship one day as they played on the playground. Jason had a hula hoop, and somehow got Sam inside it and pulled him down to the ground. When Sam fell, he scraped his upper arm and went to Ms. Stephanie crying. Jason had an expression on his face seeming to indicate feeling remorse, but apologizing did not fit his image of himself. Jason moved off, saying, "He's just a little old crybaby."

Later, during circle time, Sam said to Jason, "Look what you did to me," pointing to his arm.

"I don't care what I did to you," said Jason abruptly.

"Why did you do this?" asked Sam meekly.

"It doesn't hurt me; it only hurts you," said Jason.

"You better not do this again," said Sam.

"I don't care what you say," said Jason.

"You better not," said Sam, but things seemed unresolved as the teacher shushed the children for circle time. Afterward, as they got up to go to lunch, Sam went over to Jason and suggested they sit together as they usually did. "Sit by me!"

The result was that Jason, who had started to sit next to Jawon, left him and did go to another table to sit with Sam. They interacted during lunch as usual. Jason had been mean and never apologized or shown remorse, but Sam seemed in the end to decide that continuing his good relationship with Jason was worth more than pushing the issue.

THE AVOIDING STYLE

It was difficult for children to adopt a competitive posture if they did not feel confident or secure enough. This could lead them to avoid conflict. Shaun was normally very quiet and easygoing, and seemed not to understand when other children were mean to him. After some weeks at the center, he learned to assert himself more, but he clearly was uncomfortable with it. One morning, I observed him say "No" or "Stop it" when another child started to break what he had been building out of LEGO blocks. Then, when he and Evan knocked their toys together, Evan broke apart Shaun's toy completely. Without tears, Shaun came around the table to me and said sadly, "Evan broke my airplane apart."

"Did you tell him you don't like that and get mad?" I asked him. He did not say anything, but got on my lap, still at the same table, and built something else. That seemed to make him feel better. He did not become competitive, but withdrew and worked on something else, getting some supportive affection from me at the same time. The original conflict issue was not faced or resolved, but for Shaun the alternative behavior he enacted made him happy.

Distraction was also used by staff members to try to defuse some child conflicts. One day, Matt tried to pick up some toy animals, and Brent began to holler loudly.

"What's the matter, Brent?" asked Ms. Michelle.

"He won't share."

"Please share, Matt," said Ms. Michelle.

"I was playing with those," insisted Matt, and I was not sure how long the conflict would go on. Then Ms. Stacey said, "It's time to clean up," and everyone began to do so. That conflict was defused for the moment, anyway.

I found, as an observer, that my own natural tendency to avoid conflict would have to be fought. When conflict arose, my inclination was to watch and observe, of course, and trust a teacher to intervene if things got too serious. However, teachers were not always around, and when competition for something was spiraling out of control, I felt inadequate just standing around observing. I forced myself to intervene when I thought I was needed or things were getting dangerous, but the avoiding style was always alluringly easy. One day, I was pushing three children in the tire swing, when two more decided they wanted to get on. Only three could swing on it at one time, and the children knew this. When the tire slowed down, the two started to clamber on anyway. "Push us!" said some of the children already on, as well as those climbing on.

"Wait; I can't push with more than three kids on there," I said, and started to move away. I was reminded that I had an affinity for an avoiding conflict strategy. When children would not do as I said or were in an unpleasant conflict, one of my preferred tactics was to say something like "I don't like to hear that" or "That's sad," and move away. Often this would distract them or defuse the conflict if it involved me. But other times it would not, and a teacher would have to intervene to correct or mediate. I knew I could not always rely on that strategy. In this case, as I moved off, Erin and Matt started hitting and clawing at each other's faces. Oddly, this was after all but three children had already given up and left the tire swing. Matt started crying, and Ms. Teresa asked them both to hop off. Erin resisted at first, but Hannah said, "I'll get off too, with you." In the end, avoiding conflict had made the situation worse, as nobody got what was wanted—a push on the tire swing.

THE COMPROMISE OR PROBLEM-SOLVING CONFLICT STYLE

The most rewarding conflict style to observe was a problem-solving style, where the children genuinely tried to make both parties happy. Sometimes they could do this with the encouraging intervention of an adult; but surprisingly often (to me), they managed some problem solving on their own.

It was often difficult, as an adult, not to intervene for the sake of ending ongoing conflicts among the children, but in my role as observer I did not want to become the arbitrator of all disputes. I found that children very often could resolve conflicts for themselves, even if not via the adult "ideal" of talking through a conflict and reaching an agreement. I also noted that the staff would refrain from intervening in conflicts whenever possible, and would discourage the overuse of tattling. Still, the urge to intervene, and the real danger of taking sides, was something the teachers and I had to watch out for. One day Jason and Matt were playing together on the playground when Jason accidentally hit Matt's arm with his foot. Jason had not even noticed.

"We'll be dogs," said Jason. "Let's get some food."

Matt stood still, looking tearful, and said, "Ow! You kicked me!"

"What?" Jason said.

"You kicked me!"

"I did not!" asserted Jason.

"You did too, on the arm," said Matt.

"Let's go get some food," repeated Jason.

"No, it hurts," said Matt, in a somewhat whiny tone.

A frustrated Jason then came back with "OK, if that's the way you're going to be," and he walked away.

I asked him, as he came near me, "What is Matt being?" figuring that he would fill in the blank.

Jason did. "A crybaby," he responded, and he moved away and pouted for a little while. Fortunately, Matt didn't seem to hear me. I probably should have stayed out of the disagreement, especially since I clearly empathized more with Jason. Jason, later, kept trying to go near Matt and play with him, but Matt kept rejecting him.

Other children would sometimes intervene to resolve a conflict. One day on the playground, Brent was crying because another child had pushed him. Neil came up to him and said, "Come on, let's go and play something." Brent moved off with him, clearly feeling better.

Adults at the center also tried to model problem-solving behavior for the children. Ms. Stacey, lead teacher in the four-year-olds' classroom, had gone to a conference one Friday. The next Monday, she had the children role-play during circle time. She had Jay and Thelma come up to the front of the group. She had Jay pretend to kick Thelma. "Now, Thelma, what are you supposed to say?" she asked.

"Tell them to stop it," said Thelma softly.

"That's right," said Ms. Stacey. She had all the children pretend to have such an incident with a partner, and then say what they were supposed to say. When a child approached a teacher to tattle, the teacher's most common responses were "Did you tell him/her to stop?" or "Tell them to stop," or "Tell them that hurts and you don't want them doing it anymore." Children were encouraged to resolve their problems themselves in this classroom exercise and through weeks and months of consistent teacher statements and behavior.

A couple of weeks later, Daniel saw Neil, Sam, and Jason bowling in the block area, and Daniel decided he wanted to bowl, too. "No," said Neil, Sam, and Jason, partly because they did not want him joining them, but also because only three children were allowed in the block area at a time. Daniel told Ms. Stephanie that they would not let him play, and she told Daniel that he could bowl when they were finished or at least one of them left the block area. When he did not get his way, Daniel cried and grabbed two of the bowling pins. Neil and Sam chased him, but he would not give them back. A teacher had Daniel put the pins back, but not much time passed before he grabbed another one and ran and hid under a table. Once again Sam and Ms. Stephanie routed him out. This pattern looked like it might continue, until Jason and Neil tried a new strategy. "Here," said Neil. "You can put up the pins, OK?"

Being talked to in this friendly way changed Daniel's attitude. "OK," he said, and placed the pins in their places. "I want a turn to do it!" he said, after Neil had knocked them over with the ball.

"No, first Sam and then you," said Neil. "I'm gonna teach you to bowl." This new strategy seemed to pay off, as the boys, including Daniel, took turns peacefully for quite a while. The teachers seemed content to bend the rules in this case and let all four of them continue, especially since it was a rainy day and we were not going outside.

Another instance of friends trying to manage conflict involved Brent and Neil. One morning when Neil came in, Brent was building a submarine out of LEGOs at a table. Neil told him that he wanted to show him something. Neil took him over to a window looking out at new playground equipment that was under construction.

"I *know* about that. I *already* know about that, Neil," said Brent, as if irritated at Neil for getting his hopes up. They went back to the table and built with LEGOs. Brent soon began taking LEGOs that Neil wanted to use.

"Mr. John," said Neil to me, sitting nearby. "Brent took my LEGOs."

"Brent, don't take his LEGOs," I said. "Build your own thing."

Brent dropped Neil's LEGOs on the floor.

"Don't break them!" Neil said. After a pause, with Brent still using the disputed LEGOs, Neil said, "I won't play with you if you keep taking my LEGOs."

"I don't care," said Brent.

"Then you won't have anyone to play with," said Neil.

"I'll just play . . . with one of the teachers," said Brent, apparently reassuring himself.

They did keep talking at intervals after this incident, and played together as friends several minutes later. This was an example of a testing process children would go through—they would fight, but then stay together and "be friends" with one another after the fight was resolved or moved past. Those friendships, forged in conflict, would last for a few hours, a few days, or even a week or two.

About two months later, I was sitting at a table where Cindy was playing with some big plastic snowflakes with little balls on all the ends. Hannah came over and sat near me. "Could you build a doggie?" she asked.

"Well, I think we can," I said. "Let's see what we can do." I started to put together what looked like a dog, and then Hannah made it bark and eat and drink. She started picking up other pieces to be food and drink.

Cindy, seeing this, started gathering up pieces and clutching them on the table under her arms. Hannah then started grabbing some more for herself and holding on to them. "I have more than *you*," said Hannah.

At this point, I interjected a distraction. "I think your dog is hungry," I told Hannah. She again started using some of her snowflakes as food, and Cindy began building a crown.

Soon, Hannah grabbed a green snowflake that Cindy had just set down. "Give it back," said Cindy.

"You have that one," said Hannah, shoving another toward her.

"I want the green one," said Cindy.

"No, because you didn't ask me for it nicely," said Hannah. "What do you say? What's the magic word?"

"Please," said Cindy, softly and reluctantly. Hannah gave her the piece.

Later, she gave her others, once saying, "Here's an orange, since we have *lots* of orange ones. . . . We both have two greens." Hannah had moved the interaction toward politeness and cooperation, and as it progressed Cindy was clearly happy with it, too, having found a friend.

During that same week, I successfully encouraged problem solving among the children by posing a negative consequence for competitive conflict. Out on the playground, two children asked me to push them on a swing. Then each was trying to push the other away from the swing. I walked away after saying, "I'm not gonna push kids who are fighting." A few minutes later, one of them ran over and told me I could push them now. They had stopped fighting.

At times, the children made creative problem-solving deals on their own. One day, Wentao took some wheels that Michael had been building with. "Hey, give those back!" Michael said. "Give them back to me! I was using those!" He started to cry a little. "Ms. Stephanie, Wentao took my wheels."

This drew no reaction from the teacher, so he tried another tack. "If you give me that wheel back, I'll give you a dollar."

Wentao was reluctant, but eventually he agreed to give the tires back "if I can have some of those square things." A deal was struck.

For several days after this incident, I heard Michael, every time he wanted something, say, "I'll give you a dollar. I'll bring it from home, I promise." Natalie was the first to get tired of that promise and say, "I don't want a dollar." Michael then had to think of something else to offer. But he had found a useful bartering strategy and he returned to try it again and again.

Another instance of trading for conflict resolution occurred when Matt, Timothy, and Ivan were in the block area, making up the three allowed in there at one time. Timothy left to play with one of the musical instruments set out in another area. Daniel came into the block area as Matt was building blocks up into a large "house." Daniel picked up two triangle blocks. "Where do these go?" he asked.

"Get out of here," said Matt. "Timothy is playing in here."

"Timothy went over to play an instrument," I said, overhearing.

"Where do these go?" repeated Daniel.

"I don't need them. You don't know how to build a house," said Matt.

At this point, Timothy came back toward the block area. "Hey, he got in there when I was just fixin' to come back," he said.

"You left to go play an instrument," I reminded him.

"But I was just fixin' to come back," persisted Timothy.

"Daniel couldn't know that," I noted.

Then Matt said to Daniel, "Hey, I'll give you some chips for a surprise if you leave the block area."

Daniel looked hopeful. "Really?"

"Yeah, I'll give you some chips, OK?" said Matt.

"OK," said Daniel, and he left the block area. I don't know whether he eventually got his chips, but the positive promise from Matt was enough to resolve the disagreement, and Timothy got to go back into the block area.

Once during my observations at the center, I was part of an extensive problem-solving negotiation that was fun to see. Out on the playground, Neil was being chased by a clearly angry David, and Michelle was running after them both. Neil ran up to me and said, "Save me! Save me!" David and Michelle followed.

"Why is David chasing you?" I asked Neil.

"I pushed him—" said Neil.

"He tried to push me off over there," said David. "He's trying to kill me!"

At this point, Neil decided to run again, and David took off after him. David was genuinely angry, but Neil and Michelle seemed to be enjoying the chase more as a game.

The chase continued for a while, but then David gave up and plopped himself down grumpily for an interval.

"Will you chase me again this afternoon?" I heard Neil ask him.

Meanwhile, Michelle came over to me and said she wanted to play basketball. We began to throw the basketball through squares in the monkey bars. David came over, still seeming tired and grumpy, but saying he wanted to play. "OK, you're on my team," said Michelle.

We continued to shoot "baskets," and soon Neil came over. "I wanna play. Can I play?" So Neil started shooting, too.

"I'm not on his team," said David. "I'm on your team," he said to Michelle.

"Yeah," she said.

"Will you be on my team? Who'll be on my team?" asked Neil.

No answer. "No one will be on your team, Neil; you've made everyone too angry," I half teased.

"Yeah," said Michelle. "Everyone is angry with Neil."

"He was trying to *kill* me," said David. "Everyone's mad at you, even Mr. John. Right?" he asked, moving from assertiveness to hoping for confirmation from me. Since I had appeared to take sides, I decided I had better explain more fully.

"I think I know what Neil is doing," I told David. "He doesn't want to hurt you; he wants to be your friend, but he wants you to chase him. That's why he's doing these things to you."

David acknowledged me with a grumpy grunt. "He's trying to kill me," he kept repeating at intervals.

Neil soon tried to placate David. "I'm *not* trying to kill you," exclaimed Neil.

"Yes, you *are*! Remember when you almost pushed me off over there? That's trying to *kill* me," David exclaimed forcefully.

"I *am* not," insisted Neil. "Are you wanting to *fight*?" he then asked, frustrated.

David seemed uncertain; he responded only with a dirty look. He was now under the monkey bars in the sand, building a mound. Neil and Michelle were leaning on the monkey bars near him. "You were trying to kill me," David grumped.

"No, I wasn't. Are you wanting to fight?" repeated Neil.

Another dirty look from David, and Neil moved away.

Then Michelle proceeded to talk to her friend David based on all she had heard. "He's not trying to kill you, David; he just wants to get you to play with him," she said, and then repeated it again to a morose David, trying to convince him. "See," she said, "now he won't play with you anymore . . . and I won't either because you're too grumpy."

"I am *not* too grumpy," said David.

At this point, Neil returned. "I'm sorry," he said. "I'm sorry I pushed you . . ." and he continued to talk to David in a low tone. Soon, they were sitting next to each other. A little later, when I casually walked nearer to them, Neil said to me, "I made David feel better."

"You did? How did you make him feel better?"

"Just by talking," said Neil. I told him that was terrific, and that I had heard him say "I'm sorry," and that it was good that he wanted to be friends with David. They both told me they were building a castle together, and later they sat next to each other at lunch.

Some attempted problem solving that did not end so nicely took place a couple of weeks later on the playground. Neil and David were playing soccer, kicking a ball back and forth, and Teresa wanted to play. David let her, but she was not good at kicking the ball. She would kick at it and nearly miss, and grab the ball and hold it. David quickly got very impatient. "Kick the ball!" he exclaimed loudly. "You can't hold it!" As soon as he could, David would kick it back to Neil. When Neil kicked it back, Teresa tried to get it. When David got it, Teresa sat down on the ground, crying. David, frustrated, slammed the ball down next to her and walked away. Neil just kept waiting on his side.

At this point, Ms. Lisa decided to get involved. "David, let her kick it," she said. "Come on, Teresa, and kick it." When the ball came back from Neil, Teresa tried to kick it, missed, and picked the ball up again.

"No!" said David. "You can't hold it. . . . Kick the *ball*!" he yelled.

Teresa, crying again, said, "Stop being *mean* to me."

Ms. Lisa encouraged her again, saying, "Come on, Teresa, you have to kick the ball. You can kick it."

Teresa tried again as the ball came back from Neil, but it came closest to David and he kicked it. Teresa started crying again.

"That was on my side," David explained. "That was on my side, so I had to kick it." Neil kicked the ball back again, this time near Teresa, but she was still crying a little and missed it. David moved off to get the ball, shaking his head. He returned to a still-crying Teresa and said, "That was on *your* side, you need to kick it," and he actually dropped the ball at her feet.

She kicked it a little way, tried to get it, and broke down in tears again. This time, Ms. Lisa said, "Come on, let's wash up your face," and led her inside the building. Teresa then got the privilege of being one of Ms. Lisa's lunch helpers. Neil and David continued kicking the ball for a while. This incident clearly demonstrated some problem-solving attempts by a concerned Ms. Lisa; a calm, patient accommodation by Neil; but also an apparently crippling impatience and control by David. The incident ended badly, but I did have a sense that the children involved had tried.

Indeed, the goal of the center staff, and even at times the children, was to progress to a point of at least trying to overcome conflicts through communication. If that did not work, then separation or distraction was acceptable, and being seated in time-out would result from dangerous hitting or kicking. The desired progression of handling conflict was from yelling, screaming, hitting, or kicking to at least being able to calm down and move away and then to ideally being able to talk about a disagreement and work out a solution. Both children and teachers, however, were often hard-pressed to seek this ideal during the stress of busy days. Separation was probably the most common response to major conflicts. The time and energy it took to encourage problem solving among the children were at a premium, but the results of improved communication skills and better-managed relationships were well worth the effort.

The communication culture at the center stressed a need for flexibility in conflict management. The ability to pick and choose among conflict styles is key to managing conflicts effectively (Wilmot and Hocker 1998). Trying different styles in different situations leads to better communication overall. Children progress from simple competitive styles in the form of shouting matches and physical tugs-of-war to disengaging and moving away, and then to actual verbal negotiations. Adults can model and guide children through such a process, but too much or too hasty interference may only temporarily end the conflict, leaving key issues unresolved. Such interference may also stifle children's creativity and learning about conflict styles. Adult intervention in child conflicts at the center occurred when major threats to safety or major breaches of center rules were observed. Flexibility and adaptability in managing conflicts are crucial, and child-care centers should be key venues for children to develop such skills.

13

Adults in Conflict: Research Pitfalls

Through my years of volunteering and then doing research in child-development centers, I found their staff members to be among the warmest, kindest, most pleasant people I had worked with. Inevitably, however, I observed conflicts between staff members and was involved in conflicts with them. Usually, in the centers where I had participated, the norm of politeness and getting along that the staff modeled for the children would permeate their work relationships. While getting along with coworkers was almost universally perceived as necessary to set a good example for the children at the center, at times this goodwill was forced, and underlying conflicts gradually emerged.

I don't mean to imply that the child-development centers I worked in were actually conflict-ridden or unpleasant places to be. On the contrary, they were some of the friendliest, most supportive places I've had the pleasure to work. But where people communicate, conflict will ensue, and perhaps such conflict stood out even more in what was typically a nurturing environment. During my research, I found myself for a time in the awkward position of being distracted from observing and communicating with the children by ongoing conflicts with two key staff members in one classroom. While tragic to me at the time, these conflicts were strong learning experiences, and telling of them will shed light on the rewards and pitfalls of doing ethnographic research "in the field" by actually becoming part of the society or workplace one is studying. As I organized my notes, I found that for almost three months there were almost as many on the adult conflicts observed as on the children's conflicts.

SETTING THE SCENE: THE CAST OF CHARACTERS

Let me "set the scene" by exploring how I typically interacted with the "cast of characters," the staff at the child-development center. I had approached Debra, the director of the center, with my interest in doing research in an organizational setting with children during summer. She was very supportive and encouraging, and suggested that I begin soon after the fall semester began, and I did so. While the center was equipped with observation rooms where students (and others) could sit and observe goings-on in the classroom, as I pondered my research and discussed it with Debra, I realized that I would gain the most understanding of communication patterns there by actually being in the classroom and interacting with the children. She agreed readily to this, and so I was introduced to Stacey, lead teacher for the four-year-olds. I remember walking into the classroom, being introduced to her, and then being introduced to the children: "This is Mr. John," she said, and "Mr. John" I remained through all of my months and years at the center. I soon met the lead teacher for the three-year-olds' classroom, Ms. Tanya, and the assistant teachers: for the four-year-olds, Ms. Stephanie, and for the three-year-olds, Ms. Wanda. Each classroom typically had one or two other staff members as teacher aides, and often there was also a student teacher or child-development lab student present in the classroom in the mornings.

I could fairly easily model my behavior after the staff members, but I was "second tier" and did not have as much influence over the children as the lead teachers did. Even some of the shorter-time staff members, the teacher aides, encountered this problem. Since they might work only a few hours per week (most were college students themselves), they too had difficulty developing full influence and credibility with the children. While for them it was awkward because as staff members they needed to have some control over the children, for me it was awkward because I hesitated to assume an authority position over the children. I did not *want* much control or influence in the classroom. For my purposes of observing and participating in communication with children at the center, I wanted them to feel free to communicate with me around, and not like I was an authority always ready to correct them or discipline them. I believed I was more an observer than an "extra teacher" in the classroom, yet my own interactions became so influential that it became easier for other staff members and even myself to explain my presence by calling me an "extra teacher." Sometimes, my opinion as a communication scholar was valued and a staff member would discuss events with me and ask my advice. About two weeks after I started at the center, Ms. Stacey started telling me about problems she was having with selected children and what she was trying to do about them. This was useful to me, and reinforced my role and sense of value at the center, as well as indicating our strengthening work relationship.

If I had hoped to become a quiet, "anonymous" presence in the classroom, events quickly prevented this. While I did not develop a lead teacher's authority over the children, I quickly did develop an affectionate and active relationship with most of them. Eventually, Ms. Stacey would ask me to read to the entire group of children during circle time once in a while, and then make the transition to snack or lunch. This was usually something a lead or assistant teacher would do, so it cemented my status as "extra teacher." I was more than a student observer, but less than a full-fledged child-development center teacher. As my "status" grew, other teachers and staff clearly expected my help in redirecting children or encouraging them to follow the rules, and I became comfortable providing that help. At times, too, I might be the only adult nearby, and simply could not refrain from preventing certain major violations or unsafe activities from occurring.

BEFORE "THE FALL": JOINING THE CHILD-DEVELOPMENT CENTER'S CULTURE

One way Ms. Stacey integrated me into her classroom was by treating me the same as an assistant teacher when the four-year-olds went to the zoo one morning. There were three groups of children, separated by Ms. Stacey by the shape of the children's name tags. Lions, bears, and ducks were the three groups, and I was in charge of watching the ducks. "Hold someone's hand. Get a partner," said Ms. Stacey as we entered the zoo. Carl and Amy joined hands, as did Mary and Michelle. Ryan took my hand, and I kept track of Brian, who stayed close. Those were my six "ducks." They were a good group, and behaved well on the trip. Ms. Stacey told me later that day that she was very glad I was "working" on that Friday; "Thank God for Mr. John," she said. "Otherwise it would have been just the two of us."

"How could you have done it with just the two of you?" I asked.

"I don't know," said Ms. Stacey. "The ratio, the ratio is I think fifteen to one."

"So you have your two," I said.

"Yeah, we're supposed to be able to handle them; I don't know . . ." said Ms. Stacey. I felt a useful part of the staff and helpful in the classroom, rather than a mere researcher/observer there.

Ms. Stacey also helped me appreciate the love the children showed. This could be quite disconcerting, especially during my first months at the center, when an outpouring of "Hi, Mr. John!" or the children's coming over to give me hugs seemed to disrupt classroom routine. Ms. Stacey would smile and welcome me as well. I admit that whatever good or bad was going on in my life, I could count on the staff and children at the center to truly value me, much more than my initial plan to observe communication at the center had prepared me for.

One day I was preparing to leave, and all the children were lying on their mats for naptime. As I reached for my backpack, one said, "Bye, Mr. John." A couple of other children then said, "Bye, Mr. John." The quiet of naptime was being broken. Then Evan came over to hug me, and before I knew it, it seemed like ten children had run over to hug me. I felt a little overwhelmed by this explosion of love. Ms. Stacey then came back into the room and said, "It was all quiet in here. . . . Listen, this is rest and quiet time," she told the children, and made sure they got back on their mats. I felt a bit guilty over disrupting the start of naptime so much, but just outside the classroom Ms. Stacey smiled at me and said, "Have a good weekend."

"I don't know where that came from," I said, pointing back to the classroom. "I thought they were all quiet."

"It shocked you, huh?" said Ms. Stacey. "It's a sign of the love, a good sign." Ms. Stacey's encouragement of the children's love went a long way toward helping me feel like I was an asset to her classroom, rather than an interference. Easy and encouraged affection was one of the main reasons that center was such a pleasant place to be.

Ms. Stacey was generally not very talkative or affectionate (except with the children), but at intervals she would laugh with me and other staff members and be very supportive. One such time came when Ms. Stacey returned after a week's absence. Shortly after I arrived, Robert had gone over to her to say hello. "Mr. John's here, too," I overheard him say. I looked over at Ms. Stacey on hearing my name.

"Hello, Mr. John," she said warmly.

"Hi, Ms. Stacey," I said. "Good to see you."

"Yes," Ms. Stacey said. "Robert came in this morning and asked if Mr. John was gonna be here today. I told him I hoped so."

"Good, that's nice," I said.

"I was early today," said Robert, who had come back over to me. I continued to talk to him for a while. It was quite rewarding to have love expressed to me in such ways by the children, and endorsed by the staff, in what had begun as a fairly typical "scholarly" research project.

BEFORE "THE FALL": HOLDING
AS AN INITIAL POINT OF CONFLICT

The first suggestion of conflict between myself and Ms. Stacey occurred in a fairly benign way. Some days a child would get onto my lap as I sat at a table and then would play with whatever was on the table. I was moved at first by the affection of these gestures, but otherwise did not think too much about them, as I observed other staff members or student observers act similarly in such situations. One day, Robert climbed onto my lap and began to cut "money" out of some paper. Alex soon came over and found that Carl had taken the last four sheets of paper. "Hey," he said. "He took the last paper."

"Are we out of paper?" I asked.

"He has too many!" Alex said, pointing to Carl.

"What are you doing with all that paper?" I asked Carl.

"I'm going to cut money," he said.

"You don't need all that to cut money. Here, give Alex two. Now you both have the same amount," I said. Then they both continued cutting out money.

"I want to sit in your lap and tell you numbers after Robert," said Carl.

"OK," I said, and wrote some more numbers for Robert.

"*I* want to sit there," said Carl. "Hey, I could sit on one leg and you could have the other. . . . Robert, you could have one leg and I'll have the other."

Robert moved over. So now I had two in my lap, but Ms. Stacey liked to encourage independence. "Robert, you need to sit on a chair to work. You boys sit on chairs. . . . Try to encourage them to sit on chairs," she added as an aside to me.

I always tried to follow Ms. Stacey's lead; she *was* the lead teacher, so I said, "Robert, sit on this chair here."

"Sit in the chair, Robert," Ms. Stacey said, and he moved. Carl had already stood up, but stayed in place. I remember thinking that they had not been bothering me or anyone else, and I was torn between interacting with the children in a relaxed way and distracting them so that I could ease him off of my lap. I never felt comfortable simply saying "no" to a child wanting affection, unless it was during a focused classroom activity. Certainly, too much "clinging" would be unhealthy, but *some* affection was needed at their age, too. I wondered how I could balance the competing values of independence and affection during my interactions.

The clearest indicator for me of the gap between my desire to allow for affection and Ms. Stacey's approval of it occurred about eight months after I began work at the center, when Michael was upset that he couldn't catch me while playing chase on the playground. For quite a while, he wanted to sit on my lap or have me carry him. Ms. Stacey told him to "go play" for a while, which made him even more upset and crying. She mentioned as an aside to me that "We need less holding, unless it's really needed; it creates problems."

A couple of weeks later, Ms. Stacey and I were more "on the same page" on this issue. Michael kept asking me to pick him up that day. I generally would, for a few seconds, and then we would go do something. This was endearing for a while, but, happening every half hour, it got old. Then Thelma asked to be picked up several times after we went outside. Ms. Stacey overheard Michael asking again and saw my reluctance (I had already picked him up once). "You need to stay on your own feet," she told him. "You can walk with Mr. John and stay around Mr. John, but you need to walk with your own feet." He did, for awhile.

Ms. Stacey and the other staff members reinforced the back rides that had become a playground ritual for me and the children. About a year after I came to the center, I was sitting outside on the playground alone, which was unusual; after months of chasing and back rides, I could hardly go outside without the children asking for one or the other. As I sat observing, Neil's mother came on the playground, bringing her son to the center, and she said, "Are you going to play all alone, Mr. John?"

"This is nice," I said. "It's rare."

"Yeah," said Ms. Stacey. "Let him rest, 'cause once they get started with him, they don't stop." Sure enough, one of the three-year-olds wanted a back ride a little while later.

After I had spent almost a year observing at the center, Ms. Stacey decided to leave her job there to work at her church for one year. Ms. Stephanie became the new lead teacher for the four-year-olds, and the year Ms. Stacey was not working at the center was noteworthy for the continued lack of conflict between adults. When Ms. Stacey returned the following year, Ms. Stephanie left to get married and move to another city. I knew I would miss her, as Ms. Stephanie combined warmth, affection, and assertive control in such a way as to make the children and those who worked in the classroom feel valued and important. I had felt similarly about Ms. Stacey, so I was very glad to hear that she was returning to the center, but Ms. Stephanie always conveyed an extra sense of friendship to me, along with kind guidance and cooperation with other staff members and children there.

AFTER "THE FALL": ADULT CONFLICTS MANIFEST

As my third year of observation at the center began, Ms. Stacey resumed her position as lead teacher in the four-year-olds' classroom. She and I greeted each other warmly, and I looked forward to another special year of work with her, the staff, and the children. Ms. Chaundra was new to the four-year-olds' classroom as assistant teacher, and Ms. Tracy had joined the three-year-olds' classroom as the new assistant teacher. It was a time of more transition in personnel than normal for the center, even given the common turnover at the start of a new school year, and this was when conflicts sparked between myself and staff members. I had established good working relationships, and in some cases friendships, with many on the staff, and I think that when conflict did emerge between some of us this made it seem more tragic and shocking to me. Several minor conflicts grew between myself and staff members who were new that fall, but the major conflict and the most difficult one to handle emerged between myself and Ms. Stacey. We had, through many months, established a warm working relationship, and this seemed to be damaged almost beyond repair for a time. The reasons always remained rather mysterious, but I did try to figure them out.

One day that fall, I saw an example of Ms. Stacey's "avoiding" conflict style. An assistant teacher in another classroom, Ms. Marilyn, opened our outside door to let two three-year-olds get a drink. "You're letting the cold air in!" Ms. Stacey said in a firm but joking tone. "You may stand inside, but keep the door closed," she added, as if she were talking to a child.

Perhaps thinking she was joking and distracted by another three-year-old still outside, Ms. Marilyn did nothing, and continued to stand in the doorway.

"Well, I guess I'm gonna get her; that must be why," said Ms. Stacey in a frustrated undertone. I could only hear this because I happened to be sitting at the same table. I wondered if it meant that Ms. Marilyn would be an assistant in the four-year-olds' room soon, and Ms. Stacey was not pleased. Sure enough, Ms. Marilyn soon came to work in the four-year-olds' room, and while I noted no open conflict between her and Ms. Stacey, there was no warm friendship, either. Ms. Stacey, I noted, tended to avoid conflicts, and tried to avoid contact with people she disagreed with. This made it hard to read her at times.

Our conflict first manifested itself as a small irritation during a day of otherwise normal interaction between myself, children, and the staff. Children would get their mats out and lay down for naptime much more quickly when Ms. Stacey was in the room. After she left, though, the noise level tended to rise as more children talked and more got off of their mats. On this particular day, Ms. Stacey came back into the room, and said, forcefully: "Excuse me; everyone should be on their mats. Stop calling Mr. John's name. It is rest time." While I had helped several children lay quietly by rubbing their backs at the start of naptime, I was verbally singled out as one more distraction. I resolved to spend briefer moments with the children and leave more quickly as naptime began.

Ms. Stacey was also more consistent in preventing lap sitting during any floor time, even when it was not the group circle time with the day's lesson. Her new assistant teacher, Ms. Chaundra, also enforced this strongly a few days later when the four-year-olds were watching a video before lunch. I sat behind them on the floor to watch with them as usual. Soon, Craig came over and sat on my lap. David, seeing this, also got on my lap, and after some mild pushing, both settled down and we watched the movie. Ms. Chaundra came into the classroom after being out for a while and said, "Craig and David, you need to sit on your bottom, on the floor. Everyone wants to sit on Mr. John's lap, so that's not fair." All had been calm and all were quietly watching the movie, so this remark surprised me. Ms. Stephanie, or even Ms. Stacey, in the past, with everyone calm and quiet, would not have said anything; indeed, many teachers during my time there sat with the children the same way. Mr. James, the other veteran assistant teacher, sitting in the room with me, certainly had not said anything. Still, I did not want to contradict a classroom teacher in front of the children. David got off, and I eased a reluctant Craig back onto the floor. I felt placed in an awkward position: I was expected to interact with the children, but was apparently expected to refuse all lap sitting or similar forms of affection when the children were together. If I could not point to a good reason like an important activity going on, I did not want to be a party to such rejection for an abstract sense of justice that I did not believe four-year-olds would understand. Later that day, I wrote in my journal: "I am loath to enforce Ms. Chaundra's fairness issue (i.e., no sitting on laps) and I don't plan to unless I understand this is a group decision by our staff. If all are quiet and content, allow for some affection, I say." This event also underscored for me the importance of consistency among adults in the expectations they placed on children. Yet, I must admit, my own desire to avoid conflict probably made this conflict worse. I never brought up the issue with Ms. Stacey and Ms. Chaundra; I merely tried to continue to balance showing affection with noninterference.

A few days later, Carl said, "Can I sit in your lap? Can I sit in your lap?" Did I reject him for the sake of fairness, or welcome him with affection? I chose affection; I nodded yes. He came over, but very quickly—and predictably, now—Ms. Stacey invoked the same rule that Ms. Chaundra had been enforcing: "I'm sorry Carl; you need to sit on the floor." I cooperated, maneuvering him to the floor in front of me and talking to him about the shapes he was playing with. I was troubled by these repeating incidents. The staff had apparently agreed on a new "rule" without mentioning it to me (if they even discussed it with each other). After a while, it seemed that any child getting on my lap would elicit a response from Ms. Stacey: "Everyone sit on the floor. Get out of Mr. John's lap." Now, unlike in the past, few staff members would sit with the children on the floor. I followed their lead, if reluctantly, and stopped sitting on the floor with the group of children at any time. I felt the fairness issue was being pressed too far, destroying spontaneity in communication and affection between the children and me.

It was during this fall, in October, that I assessed my conflicts with Ms. Stacey through the years. They had been few and far between, but I was trying to understand where things might have gone wrong. Ms. Stacey had been acting distant and less friendly to me for several weeks; but this fit with her quiet and humble nature, so that at first I did not notice. When I did notice I thought she might be preoccupied with her own life troubles, as so many of us often are. Yet, as time passed, I noted her laughing and joking at times with other staff members, but never with me as she used to. Neither did she make brief comments to me about the children as she once would. The incident that provoked me to start wondering about what was really going on occurred, once again, as naptime was beginning and I was getting ready to depart. On this particular Friday, I heard her say as I was leaving, "The lights are out. Talking is *finished*. This is *rest* time," to the children more insistently than usual.

I said, "Have a good nap, Da Juan," and patted him, and moved to do the same with Carl as he got on his mat near the doorway.

"Mr. John!" said Da Juan, wanting to say something more.

"Leave Mr. John alone," said Ms. Stacey abruptly. "Mr. John, I'm trying to get them to lie down quietly."

I finished patting Carl without responding, and waved to a still-beckoning Da Juan, and got out of the classroom. I felt chided and required to *reject* communication with a child for the sake of (seemingly unnecessary) rules and regimentation. This was actually one of very few direct statements Ms. Stacey had made to me over the past three weeks or so; I felt reprimanded much as a child must feel, and I must admit my own dominant conflict style took over. I avoided the conflict and simply left without a look at Ms. Stacey. I thought that this end result was probably what she wanted, but I left the center that day feeling devalued in a way I never had before. I had moved from being a helpful colleague to being an unwanted interference, it seemed.

I do think the rare conflicts I had at the center hit key issues for me in my own interactions with children: affection versus control or fairness, and correction versus benign observation and friendship. While rare, a typical conflict involved my performing an action followed by Ms. Stacey directly commenting on it in a way that suggested correction or command. I tended to choose accommodating responses to such conflicts, both because of my personal discomfort with confrontation (especially in a setting where I had always found relationships with adults to be warm and friendly) and because of my invited, nonstaff status at the center.

Around the same time, Ms. Stacey told me to "Encourage them to listen" as I sat behind some of the children at circle time—with the implication that I normally did not, or that I purposely distracted them in class. I found myself asking how things had come from such a warm collegial relationship to the point of almost no communication except when I was being chastised and told, though not in so many words, to get out of the classroom.

One day I was sitting at a table in the classroom, and Brandon came over and sat next to me drawing and cutting for a long time. "I wanna sit on your knee," he said cutely as he climbed onto my leg. Now hypersensitive to perceived classroom restrictions, I let him get on me but then distracted his attention by saying, "Well, if we sit at this table, we need to do art—to color or cut." So Brandon and Craig both went to get paper and scissors, and then sat beside me. I was thinking, "How sad." It never would have occurred to me in months past to try to maneuver Brandon off of me, even in a friendly way. From my perspective, it was yet another day of trying to give affection while promoting independence and active involvement in classroom activity. I was a firm believer that both were possible, but the balance point was clearly no longer the same for the classroom teachers as it was for me.

A few days later, as the children were washing up and sitting down for lunch, I brought in a few big cardboard letters from the three-year-olds' classroom. "*T* for Timothy," I said, and showed several children the letters that began their names. As I walked away, Ms. Chaundra remarked, "Mr. John, don't bring those letters in. Mr. John, it makes them loud; stop bringing those letters in," in a forceful but joking and friendly tone. The room had gotten louder as lunch was under way, and I chuckled in response, and said, "I won't bring more letters in." Ms. Chaundra verbalized this suggestion with a sense of fun even if there seemed to be a serious overtone, as ever for her, of keeping control. Ms. Stacey lacked the element of friendliness or humor in such situations. I wondered, though, why was such a fun little exercise a problem at all? Incidents like this did remind me to be a help and not too much of a disruption in the classroom; but on the other hand I refused to become *afraid* to communicate with the children. I wished the two teachers I worked with would stop treating me as if I was trying to disrupt their classroom. During these days, communication with the children seemed less important to the lead teachers than control of them.

Another incident occurred during November when I arrived at the door of the four-year-olds' classroom. I was arriving behind Da Juan and his mother when I heard "Yay!" and Brandon appeared and grabbed my leg. Timothy followed him and gave me a hug. I was still slightly outside the door, since Da Juan and his mother were still going in. Craig was coming over too, and at this point, Ms. Chaundra said, "You are to stay *inside* the doorway," and gently moved them back. As Craig grabbed my hands, she said, "Don't hang on him . . . move on," and pulled him away. There was no greeting or "good morning" for me, just a set of harsh reprimands for the children. This was yet another symptom of the cooler, less friendly climate at the center that fall. Fortunately, I had not noted it directly affecting the children—they seemed as happy and affectionate as ever. But I found myself, at this point, less comfortable trying to chat with Ms. Stacey, as she seemed distant and often unwilling to talk or include me in conversation, and Ms. Chaundra moved through phases of more distant and forceful responses to me, as well.

By now, communication-savvy readers must be asking, "Why on earth didn't you talk to them about these things?" Good question. In retrospect, I can point to three factors: First, it was difficult by this time to start even a casual conversation with Ms. Stacey, as she would act distracted or busy talking to a child when I made any friendly comment to her. I hesitated to further endanger the relationship by trying to confront someone so uncomfortable with any kind of sustained interaction with me. A second reason was that, during my normal observation hours, there was very little opportunity to "catch" Ms. Stacey when she was not in her classroom with children around. A third reason was the almost unexplainable feeling of shock and grief one feels when a good relationship seems to have collapsed for reasons unknown. Encountering mystery and tragedy, I found it difficult to initiate a conversation that could lay bare my feelings of frustration, sadness, alienation, and anger that had been building up for a month. I tried to be objective about the situation, wondering if I might be oversensitive or blowing these events out of proportion, and tried to observe and assess the situation further.

I did notice a change in the climates of both the three- and four-year-olds' classrooms that seemed unconnected to me, and seemed to result from the new personnel in each room. Ms. Chaundra, the new assistant teacher in the four-year-olds' room, and Ms. Tracy, the new assistant teacher in the three-year-olds' room, both acted more authoritarian and less tolerant toward the children, contributing to a less friendly climate. Still, at intervals Ms. Stacey would include me when she was talking to the children, or make a conversational remark that made me wonder yet again if I was overreacting to the changed climate and taking things too personally. Ms. Tanya, the lead teacher in the three-year-olds' room, and Ms. Marilyn and Ms. Melissa, teacher aides in each classroom, were typically warm and friendly, and I had developed good working relationships with them. Those friendly relations served as a contrast to my deteriorating relationships with Ms. Stacey and Ms. Chaundra. I resolved to let Ms. Stacey confront me, since I felt she would do that if needed, and I made sure to be friendly and open to communication with all. Yet Ms. Chaundra with the four-year-olds and especially Ms. Tracy with the three-year-olds had adopted a much more controlling, commanding tone. It made the center feel at times more like an institution than the extended family it had felt like in the past.

Another small incident convinced me I was not being thin skinned and that something would have to give eventually. As I talked with four-year-old Mary in the classroom one morning, the children were gathering in the circle area at the request of Ms. Stacey. Mary and I walked over to the circle area as well, and Mary kept holding on to me. As I prepared to move behind the circle area, "Turn around, Mary," said Ms. Stacey. "Mr. John, if you don't mind, let them interact," she added. Once again, this was one of the few things she had said to me all week, and I was chastised much as a child would be for disrupting a classroom activity. I was simply behaving normally, from my perspective.

CONFRONTATION AND SHOCK

The confrontation came, sparked by a standard routine that I seldom thought about anymore, and it was actually initiated by Ms. Chaundra rather than Ms. Stacey. When we went outside with the four-year-olds, some of the children, as usual, asked for a back ride immediately on getting to the playground. On some days, I was reluctant to start right out with back rides for everyone; so on this day, I said, kiddingly, "No, thank you," and let them chase me, laughing. Sometimes this would distract them and back rides would be forgotten for a while. But Carl came over and persisted in grabbing me and asking for a back ride, so I gave him one. Ms. Chaundra suddenly said, "Carl, get down from Mr. John's back; we're not having back rides today. Those other kids could not have a back ride, so we're not having back rides today." This was out of the blue, and she had certainly said nothing about this to me, so I asked Ms. Chaundra if the rules had changed. She said no, but if some children could not have back rides, none would have them that day.

"Who can't have a back ride?" I asked, in some confusion but trying to remain calm. I had never experienced such a dramatic interference by a staff member in my interactions with the children before.

"I don't know," Ms. Chaundra replied abruptly.

"Why can't they have a back ride?" I pursued.

"Well, *you* tell *me*," Ms. Chaundra exclaimed.

"I don't know what you're talking about," I said, growing genuinely angry. We drifted apart on the playground, and, a few minutes after this, I approached her again and apologized for being abrupt. I explained why I had delayed back rides that day, and she explained that her concern was with equal treatment of all the children. Our disagreements about back rides and lap sitting seemed to boil down to equal treatment. *All* could not get to sit in my lap, and if *all* could not have a back ride, none could. I had not meant to show favorites in giving back rides—though it must have seemed that way, since I first said "no" to several children, but later said "yes" to one of them. I did wonder if this issue had been brewing with Ms. Chaundra to lead to her sudden interference on this day. It was the most dramatic conflict I had ever had with any of the assistant teachers, but it was resolved amicably that day, as we both explained our positions and went on with our normal interactions with the children and with each other.

This incident prompted me to spark a long-overdue discussion with Ms. Stacey. After she had done a "1-2-3" exercise with the children as they went to lunch, I told her, "That was cute," and went on to tell her that I admired her teaching methods and had learned from them. After a now typical initial reluctance to respond to me, she seemed quite appreciative. I had made sure to give Ms. Stacey a friendly greeting each morning, even if that was our only interaction, to try to keep the stage set for positive relationship managing. After complimenting her teaching, I said I was sorry (a fine way to get people comfortable with talking, I found on this day) if I had seemed distant or distracted lately. I noted that she had seemed distant, too. She then broached the issue: "I only have a problem when you don't respond the way you always used to to the children when they come to you." She brought up the back ride issue, saying, "I have a problem with giving back rides."

"Oh, Ms. Chaundra told you about that," I said, though it hardly seemed possible that Ms. Chaundra had had time to discuss that day's clash with her.

Ms. Stacey shook her head, saying, "I have observed a real difference in the way you respond to the children this semester." I practiced my listening skills, nodding and maintaining eye contact. "They come to *you*, and they don't understand why you can't do something with them, because they are four. You would just push a child aside and say 'no.'" She also noted that in the book area, "a child might come near you, and you would move away or move them away." She suggested that a four-year-old needed some explanation of such "rejection." I kept asking questions, prompting a list of several perceived rejecting incidents spaced out over time, none of which I remembered specifically. "I'm glad we talked about this," she said. "You might find a different room to observe in, since you have been here so long." That was probably the most heartbreaking thing that she said.

I chose to avoid that particular statement, however, and feeling overwhelmed, said, "I had no idea that you didn't like back rides."

"Oh, I have no problem with back rides," she said. Now I felt like I was getting mixed messages, but I was feeling even more shocked by this sudden unloading of pent-up discontent, and since the children were beginning their lunch, our window of communication opportunity was closing.

"I have always felt welcome here," I said determinedly.

"You are welcome here," she said. "I'd prefer you let them know that Ms. Stacey stopped the back riding, because it creates problems," a familiar Ms. Stacey phrase.

The bottom line was that she believed I was being less affectionate with certain children. When I asked, "Which children?" she would not tell me.

"You know which children, Mr. John. I'm not gonna go there, for now," she said.

I truly did not know. "Back rides are a tired old ritual; they do need to stop," I said as she moved away to assist children with hand washing and beginning lunch. I said this strongly, but there was no inner conviction behind the words. Back rides had become a ritual of affection with the children, and having it pulled out from under me so suddenly was a shock. I had thought too much affection was an issue, but our conversation made it sound like there had been too much rejection. I stayed in the classroom through lunch as usual, and interacted with several children, but I felt like I was in a haze. I had considered ending back rides over the summer, as they at times became tiresome, and now I felt some regret at not having done that on my own. But what about all the other instances of rejection Ms. Stacey had alluded to? I honestly had no recollection of them. Perhaps my playful avoidance of giving back rides on some days had been misinterpreted. I had to start facing the fact of racial diversity, however, an issue that had not impacted my daily interactions until that fall. Several staff members and children in each classroom were African American, and since Ms. Stacey and Ms. Chaundra were both African American, I suspected I unwittingly had refused or seemed to selectively reject some of the African American boys and girls.

I came back to the center the next week with the realization that I *had* gotten careless about refusing back rides at times, and so back rides were indeed out. I also continued to discourage sitting on my lap in the circle area. But now I faced the additional challenge of not seeming to reject the children at the same time. On this day, as I was sitting at a table, first Brandon and then Jawon—who was African American—wanted to get in my lap. So, I thought, do I ease them out of it for the sake of fairness? Or do I keep them there to avoid not responding to them? First, Brandon said to me, "I wanna sit in your lap." I diverted him with, "Do you wanna build with these?" and got up and gave him my chair. I did stay, kneeling next to him and playing with him for a bit. Shortly after, though, Jawon simply got on my lap. I left him on me for a while, and it seemed like Brandon got shortchanged on affection this time. Now I was apparently overreacting and "reverse discriminating." I decided that I must do what I believed was right in the situation. If Jawon could be in my lap for a time, then so could Brandon or any other child who approached me while all were busy in different areas of the classroom. This ongoing conflict and its final confrontation had shaken my self-confidence in interacting with both children and staff, and forced me to rethink many daily behaviors.

Yet, after this confrontation, my relationships with both Ms. Stacey and Ms. Chaundra got better. I realized that all I could really do was to be myself and communicate and play with the children in the most effective ways I knew. I made a point to greet Ms. Stacey and Ms. Chaundra warmly each morning; and Ms. Stacey did seem friendlier. Outside, to my surprise, I only had to tell Timothy and Carl (separately), "my back gets too sore putting all the kids on my back, so I can't give any back rides today. I can play something else with you, though." (I refused to let Ms. Stacey be given credit or blame for that, taking it on myself.) Carl was disappointed, but eventually he said, "Chase me." Timothy also suggested a different game. I would miss giving back rides, but there were plenty of other ways to spend time with the children. As time went on, my conviction grew stronger that someone should have mentioned the issue to me *sooner*. Yet I, too, should have asked questions before things became so strained between Ms. Stacey and me. Both our "avoiding" styles had let the issue fester.

The conversation with Ms. Stacey also made me think about why I was spending time doing research and volunteering at the center and how I behaved with the children. I admit, I had come to take them somewhat for granted and had likely been careless about rejecting them at times. I found myself refocused, and remembered to simply enjoy being around the children, and tried to be as responsive and friendly to them as I could. What I regretted most about the entire conflict was that Ms. Stacey, after having been friendly for years and clearly comfortable talking with me, began treating me like an unwanted stranger. I wished she could have asked me about the issue, and let me know what she observed about my behavior. I left the confrontation feeling a bit betrayed, having been suddenly and inexplicably demoted from friendly helper to hindrance. It galled me, but the children and other staff members all reacted to me in the same friendly or affectionate ways as always. Perhaps I expected more from Ms. Stacey than she could give.

After what I thought of as "the great back ride controversy," I had some sense that the rift between myself and Ms. Stacey was healed, but there was still a communication gap between us, and I felt a more distant part of the four-year-olds' classroom. During fleeting moments things felt like "the old days," and Ms. Stacey would make a comment or a joke to me, but they were so rare as to seem like gems. My sense of loss and sadness continued. The day before Christmas vacation I decided to spread a little Christmas spirit by bringing teachers a wrapped present of candy and a candy cane for all the children. There really were many good spirits all that day. Ms. Chaundra joked with me, and Ms. Stacey spoke to me at intervals as "of old." After we sat in circle time singing Christmas carols, Ms. Stacey told me, "We'll have you read this book to them before lunch, Mr. John."

"OK," I agreed readily. That had not occurred for over three months, and I took it as a sign that our relationship was on the mend. I then got a "mass hug" after I read to the four-year-olds and Ms. Stacey asked them to thank me. While there was lots of good feeling to end the year, I still sensed that the relationship between Ms. Stacey and me would likely remain fractured. I had to try to remember to accept the change in the relationship and focus on the *children*. On many mornings, Ms. Stacey responded to my "Hello, Ms. Stacey, how are you doing?" only with a brief "Hello." It once again got to the point where she would barely acknowledge the comments I made to her. I noticed that she was fairly quiet toward everyone, and it occurred to me that perhaps she was having difficulties in her life outside the center. I resolved to continue "in spite of Ms. Stacey," but volunteering and being friendly and consistent with the children was made much more difficult without the support and encouragement of the lead teacher in the classroom. I found myself wanting to flee to Ms. Tanya's three-year-olds' classroom, where I felt much more friendly support from the adults. At lunchtime, I would often eat in the three-year-olds' classroom with Ms. Marilyn, since Ms. Stacey no longer invited me to eat lunch as she used to.

The climate in Ms. Stacey's classroom had become so closed to me that I found I could not proceed without some additional discussion with her. The next Monday I looked for an opportunity to talk to her, making sure to greet her soon after I arrived and getting (once again) a perfunctory greeting. I waited for a time when we were not directly involved with some children or other staff. Finally, as the children were eating lunch, Ms. Stacey was washing her hands, and I stepped up beside her. "I have to do that, too," I said.

"I thought you'd left," Ms. Stacey said.

"Not quite. It's almost time," I said. There was a brief pause, and then I seized the moment. "Ms. Stacey, I wanted to let you know; I miss very much the way things used to be between us."

Ms. Stacey shook her head, and said, "There's nothing . . ."

"I'm very sorry to see this distance between us," I tried to clarify.

Then she said, "There's nothing wrong. I've just been keeping quiet, keeping to myself," in a warm tone of voice. We proceeded to have a very friendly chat, in which I expressed my concern about our conflict having prevented us from communicating. She explained that she had been meditating and thinking about things. I got the clear impression that events in her life outside the center were preoccupying her. She asked if I was still teaching Sunday school, and about my son, and noted, "You've been here a long time; you know how things go. I have to talk and work more with the student teachers, since they're new." She mentioned being a Christian, invoking a commonality between us, saying that as such we are to "spread love and giving." I was thrilled to have a glimpse of the warm and friendly, yet humble, Ms. Stacey I had known. But I knew that I would have to take my reassurance from her, give her space for her silence, and continue my own tasks with the children at the center. The "mystery" of Ms. Stacey would continue.

As the spring semester at the center proceeded, there were no more conflicts, and the climate became more friendly again. The controlling assistant teacher in the three-year-olds' room left over the Christmas holidays, and Ms. Chaundra moved away that following summer. Early in the spring, however, I observed Ms. Stacey handle a potential conflict with Ms. Melissa, her assistant teacher. The four-year-olds' classroom Valentine's Day party had been announced in notes to parents as starting at 3:15 P.M. Ms. Melissa, I heard, let the children eat their special snacks after several were stirring out of their nap at 2:30 without waiting for parents to arrive. Ms. Anna, who was substituting that day for Ms. Stacey, said she tried to correct Ms. Melissa, "but Melissa wouldn't accept it." The next day Ms. Stacey talked to Ms. Melissa about it, presenting the issue in a friendly but direct way, and in the end provided suggestions for "the next time it happens." She was so supportive, and she *could* confront issues in a practical and efficient way while maintaining a good relationship. I could not help but wonder, "Why could she not have had such a conversation with me back when our troubles began?"

There *were*, however, indicators in the spring that conflict was no longer dominating my relationship with the teachers in the four-year-olds' room. One Friday in March, I came in and actually received a warm response from Ms. Stacey after my "Good morning," and a little later she told the children to clean up and get ready for snack and a field trip. They then started cheering loudly, and she had to hush them. Shortly after that she said, "Mr. John, it's like that commercial"—then she paused as Michael was telling her something—"that telephone commercial where the man is talking to the class . . . "

I imitated the little boy in the commercial—"Field Trip!"—as we laughed. This little effort at interaction stood out as so different at that time, but such interactions had once been common between us. I went along on the field trip to a pet shop with the children, Ms. Melissa, Ms. Chaundra, and Ms. Stacey. I mentioned to Ms. Chaundra that I had not realized it was a field trip day, and she said, "We were counting on you coming in. . . . I knew you wouldn't come in on Wednesday, but would be here on Friday." It had been a long time since I had heard sentiments like that from any adult in the four-year-olds' room! One day in April, Ms. Stacey greeted me warmly, chatted with me a couple of times with side comments and late in the morning, for the first time in months, asked, "Mr. John, have you had any lunch?"

As the school year wound down, I resolved to ask the director and each lead teacher I worked with for an assessment of me, to allow for any clearing of the air needed at the end of the most conflict-filled year of volunteering with children I had known. So I pulled Ms. Stacey and Ms. Tanya, as the lead teachers, aside to "get their advice" as I put it. I asked if each could tell me things I did at the center that she appreciated, and then things that I could do more or do less of. Ms. Tanya did not have much to say, only that she enjoyed the way I interacted with the children. Our relationship was so friendly that she seemed hard-pressed to offer me any objective feedback.

Ms. Stacey I found most talkative and friendly that day, and after she had finished a long chat with a parent, she sat right down at the table next to me. Though I tried to ask for the positives in the first question, she moved quickly to the issue that had stood between us over the past few months. "Well, one thing I notice has improved is that you respond well to *all* of the children." She moved on to negatives: one thing I could do, she noted, was to more forcefully correct children who were hitting one another or doing something unsafe. "Tell them, 'Be careful, hang on,' if they are on the monkey bars, or 'Keep hands to yourself' if they are hitting one another. Doing that will make you feel more confident in that," she said. Other than that, Ms. Stacey said, I was most welcome; "You're fine; you're all right," and she could think of no other negatives. She then brought up quite a list of positives for me to consider: "They look to you as a staff member; I look to you as a staff member." When she would take some of the children inside, she felt fine, she said, "because Mr. John is out there." She said that it was good to have a male influence in the classroom, as some of the children did not have fathers around—"they like to be next to you or sit in your lap 'cause they miss that." She pointed out that she liked how positive I was with the children: "You answer their questions; you talk with them. You are a smart man, Mr. John. When that book gets published, I sure want to see one." She had said that last line several times through the years; I sometimes felt she knew before I did that this book would be written, and it was an indicator of our positive ongoing working relationship.

Later that same day, she also noted that, "Mr. John doesn't eat lunch in our room anymore," when she saw Ms. Debra and me eating with some of the three-year-olds. I remember thinking, "After those months of icy silence, what did you expect?" But I said nothing, and appreciated the warm wishes returning. Ms. Stacey did say one other moving thing: "I'm glad you want to be in my class. I must be doing something right to keep you coming back." She said, "I love the Lord, and it just naturally spreads around [to the children]." She also pointed out that children need to be touched, possibly hinting that she *did* approve of such affectionate contact as hugs and pats. She noted that she would correct and be somewhat harsh with the children to prepare them for the world, but then would tell them she loves them. I told her I saw that as one of her strengths. She was consistent and always loving when interacting with the children.

The conflicts, uncertainties, and sadness—as well as the love and acceptance—I found in my interactions at the center showed me that communication could win out in the end for meeting the basic interpersonal needs of inclusion, affection, and control for the adults who worked there as well as for the children who learned there. When one becomes a part of any community through communication, whether as a researcher, student, or staff member, one seeks to meet those needs and gets into conflict when they are not being met. As a researcher, I found that I could not maintain "objective observations" in the face of either the strong love shown me by the children or troubling conflicts with staff members. Yet through becoming part of the culture, and getting into conflicts with others within it, I learned more about the culture and its values than any other method would have allowed. I also came away with the "finding" that a reluctance to communicate, or a desire to avoid confrontation while experiencing conflict, caused the most distress in my relationships there. This was a true learning experience, and through this chapter I seek to communicate about it to others.

14

The Emotional Impact of Working with Children

As my time observing and interacting with the children continued, I clearly was more involved than just as a "researcher" or "observer." I was becoming part of the children's lives, and they were becoming part of mine. I could see that my gathering of data was not the "dispassionate" scientific procedure we often think of in connection with research. Writing and reading my journal entries were emotional experiences. Reading the record of my growing relationships with the children was rewarding, and I would feel some moderate grief as they passed on out of my life. Emotional highs would be followed by lows, and times of questioning why I was there with the children. More often, however, I felt that I was gaining more from my time with the children than knowledge to write about. Part of life in any organization is emotion management. We all feel emotions, but from childhood, we learn to refrain from expressing them fully in many situations (Saarni and Weber 1999). Active display of certain emotions may be required regardless of current individual mood, as well. At the center, teachers and staff members were expected to be kind and considerate at all times, especially toward the children. Many emotions I experienced were new to me in a workplace setting. To continue my research, I had to learn the emotional expression norms of the child-development center culture and understand and manage my own emotional reactions to children and staff members.

COUNTERING NEGATIVITY

All emotions and the expression of them were respected at the center, but only within limits. Displays of great anger or major disruptions of the class-

213

room were not tolerated. In the weeks after Brent, a child notorious among the staff members for his angry displays, had left the center, he was remembered and missed. "He was so troubled, and had so much anger. It was hard to realize that all that anger wasn't really all directed at us, but we knew that," said Ms. Stacey. She felt she and the other teachers had been successful in emotionally integrating Brent into life at the center, despite his anger. Almost every semester, there would be one or two children in the classroom who would express strong negative emotions through tantrums or meanness. Much of the teachers' work then would be redirecting those children toward more positive behaviors.

As semesters progressed, I certainly found that the emotions I felt as I interacted with the children were not uniformly positive. Some days a child would be in a bad mood, misbehaving, or simply rejecting. We all had our moments. I recorded one such day in my journal during my second year of observing, when I was more comfortable with my role at the center but found myself overreaching a bit in developing relationships:

> When you pick up a three-year-old and he seems surprised, taken aback, and says, "Put me down," . . . When you go over to see what two of the three-year-olds are doing, and they say, "Get out of my house," . . . When you count "five friends" at one table, and one of the three-year-olds asserts, "I'm not your friend," . . . When the kids hit or bite when playing "chase" with me . . . When a couple of boys continue to walk through the water after I suggest they don't and then ask them not to . . . I wonder if I'm losing my "touch" and understand why day-care work can at times be tedious, stressful, and unrewarding. Yet they are all lessons—I tend to "cling" too tightly emotionally at times, and I relearn how to "*let go.*" We all have days where we need our space.
>
> And it also makes it too easy to forget the bright eyes and happy greetings of kids when they first saw me, kids wanting me to stand by them, play with them, or chase them, and wanting to get close or in my lap—all of which happened on the same, supposedly bad, day.

Some days the negative feelings dominated, and I would question my purpose in being in the classroom and my conduct. But children naturally wear their emotions on their sleeves, and as an adult involved with them it was difficult not to reflect and take to heart some of those emotions. Some children would express both positive and negative emotions within the span of a few minutes, putting our relationship on an emotional roller-coaster. Even "stepping back" and invoking some adult researcher objectivity could not eliminate the sense of distrust and betrayal that emerged after a quick change from affection to hitting and kicking. I had to remind myself that those children were seeking love and attention like all the others, just not in appropriate ways.

At the end of a week, I noted the clash of positive and negative days, and the dramatically different ways each made me feel:

The last two days of volunteering have seen "the best of times and the worst of times." In spite of having to leave in mid-morning for a meeting (after which I returned), much seemed to go well. Matt was happy to see me and wanted me to read to him. I had been angry with him on Monday for throwing pine cones at people (including me). But today he was clearly happy and well behaved, and wanted to spend some time with me, so I could not refuse. I read to him, and to Paul, and to Shaun. Ms. Judy spent some time vacuuming up beans that kids had gotten on the floor (they were hard beans for playing with). Shaun shrank away from the vacuum cleaner as it got close. "She's trying to vacuum you up, Shaun," I said jokingly. He laughed. Gary ran over and sat in my lap, and I said, "Ms. Judy's trying to vacuum Shaun up." He laughed, too. Later, the kids sat down to watch a movie. "I want to sit in your lap," said Jim as I sat down. Soon Julie and James were on either side, and after Jim got tired and moved, Kenny came over. The whole class got into watching the cartoons, and it was one of those days that (though a little squished) I left with a warm fuzzy feeling.

Today, however, was a different story. So many kids wanted me to read to them today that I read some books twice and felt a bit confined after a while (I usually try to circulate around some to different parts of the room). Shortly after I arrived, Julie came over and crawled on my legs while I was kneeling beside another child, and then Gary tried climbing on my back. When these behaviors are relatively rare and mostly affectionate, I don't get upset by this; I merely try to stand up and extricate myself gently. Today, after I had stood up, propped Julie up affectionately, and let go, Jim came barreling over and knocked Julie down. Her head hit the counter and it was bleeding. "Jim!" I said sternly. (Though I felt terrible myself.)

"I'm sorry!" he said, several times, clearly scared.

After helping Julie until Ms. Christina came with an ice block and took her to get a bandage, I told Jim, "I'm glad you're sorry for hurting Julie. That's why we don't push other kids." I hope it was a lesson well learned for him. Later, Evan and Alex were refusing to clean up the block area. Evan had to be taken out after he threw a block at Ms. Christina's head. Outside, several boys were wrestling with Michael, in spite of my asking them to stop. Alex jumped on Michael and split his lip. Jim made Gary cry by pulling his hair as they fought over a football. And the whole three-year-old class was running around and yelling before they were taken outside. It felt like the center was coming unglued. It was a day full of negative events that caused me to reevaluate my role.

I eventually concluded that negative emotions go hand-in-hand with the positive ones, and should be expected in work with children. I sought to make sure I was engendering more positive emotions than negative ones. I know I felt more positive, on the whole, from working with children than negative. As long as that was true, I felt rewarded for my volunteering and research direction. Learning about and participating in relationships with the children and the staff had some impact, both for me professionally, adding to our knowledge of communication, and for the children and staff in that particular classroom.

While I would feel the positive and negative emotions of growing relationships with the children, I knew I could not get *too* involved, or too much on their level. I was still an adult, with a research purpose for being with them that transcended what they or I might want from one another at any particular moment. I reflected on this need for balance one day in my journal:

> Today was a day of lots of demands on my time from the kids, which always turns out to be gratifying. I have found that in interacting with kids, one must balance one's involvement and direction with a "letting go." (On a larger scale, parents must do the same. We love kids, but as much as we love them, we must let them go to experiment, grow, and become their own person.) I have always gotten wrapped up in the lives and activities of the children I've worked with, but I've found it can go too far if I lose all distance and objectivity when it comes to ensuring a child's safety, health, or good behavior. I need to maintain some distance from the kids, as I am only a small part of their lives, and must not disrupt too much the classroom environment, even as I get close to them. Maintaining this balance is an ongoing concern. Even on days when I go to the center resolving to "let go," lay back, and give some distance, the kids draw me back in. They know what kind of interaction and affection they want from me, and they purposely repeat patterns they like, whether of games or types of interaction. So closer I get, interacting and playing with them. Then I need to work to *step back*, and let things be and develop for a while.

SUCKED INTO THE EMOTIONAL WHIRLPOOL

When a new semester started after a break, I was as glad to see the children as they seemed to be to see me. One day, I returned to the child-development center after a two-and-a-half-week vacation. The welcome was nice—almost overwhelming. William wanted to be picked up, Thelma wanted to color sitting on my lap, and Brent wanted to sit next to me during circle time. I was sitting at a table when Chris came in, and he came right over and leaned against me and got on my lap. Everywhere I went that day, a group of children would congregate.

I had grown attached to many of the children, reciprocating the loving emotions they expressed to me. I found myself torn between how much to remain an observer and how much to accept my own emotions about these relationships. I felt a sense of melancholy and nostalgia as the first set of children I had worked with at the center prepared to move on to kindergarten. Their move would lead to major changes in the classroom where I observed and would end several relationships I had developed with the children. A couple of weeks later, I noted in my journal: "Next week the school year starts with a new group. It will be fun but I'll miss Michael, who always wanted so much affection, and Nick, and Alex with his controlling intelligence; Yolanda and Thelma, the 'little women'; Terri and Sarah, such sweethearts. . . . 'The road turns' again." Many children I knew at the center changed classrooms at the end of a semester, and there would also be several new children added. It was always an adjustment to continue participating in the classrooms after such transitions; it seemed like I was beginning my observations and relationships with the children anew. But after a few months, those new relationships became comfortable and rewarding, until it was time for the next semester to end.

I knew that if I was to understand children's relationship management, I would have to be involved in communication with them. And indeed, I was highly involved, in terms of time and emotional commitment. Many of the children reciprocated this feeling. As I recorded one day, in stunned but loving amazement: "A touching moment for me as Evan arrived. 'Mr. John's here!' I heard him say excitedly to his mother as they opened the door. He came over as I was sitting on the floor during circle time and gave me a hug from behind." At intervals, my journal became a place where I could try to express the emotions I felt as my relationships with children grew and then ended due to life transitions.

I could also experience genuine empathy and concern for the children. One day, I noted in my journal my observation of Randy, whom I had gotten to know well and who expressed a great deal of affection for me. The previous year, his brother Michael had also developed a close relationship to me. One day, I wondered what was going on with Randy and noted my own attachment to him and his absent brother:

> Today Randy got into kind of a quiet, morose mood and did not want to play with anything or participate in group time. One always wonders—was it just a setback with events in the classroom or is there more going on at home? He seemed to come out of it after we went outside. I have to watch it—I have slipped and called Randy "Michael" a couple of times—in his affection and some mannerisms he really reminds me of his older brother!

I was also moved emotionally, and thereby moved to write, by events that I heard about or overheard that demonstrated what were to me amazing levels of affection for me from certain children. One day I recorded such an event:

> On Friday, we were outside along with the three-year-olds. One of them, Matt, saw me chasing some of the four-year-olds, and he wanted to be chased also. So on Friday I chased him a lot, and he was included in some of our games. He also had learned my name, which takes kids that young a little while. Imitating the four-year-olds, Matt would say, "Mr. John! Get me!" when he wanted to be chased. Today, as I was coming inside, Ms. Michelle, who works with the three-year-olds, asked me if I knew Matt. Yes, I said, the kid in her class. "Well, his mother came in this morning asking who John was, and I told her it was probably Mr. John. She said all weekend he had talked about John."
>
> "Yeah," I said. "He likes for me to chase him around the playground." "Well, then," said Ms. Michelle, as she headed back into the threes' room, "you're the

one that he loves." Quite ego boosting. It's nice to make such a positive impression after interacting with a kid. It reminds me of Alex's mom last summer, telling me I had made quite an impression on Alex as she always heard about how "Mr. John came today."

I had clearly become more than just another person who happened to be in their classroom for these children, and they also became more than just another child to me. New semesters would begin with some sense of loss because of the children who had left, but a sense of beginning with children new to the classroom. As one new era began, I wrote:

> A new semester begins with the kids. Lots of new kids and new assistant teachers give the center a different "feel" as fall semester begins. Yet I feel marvelously well accepted by staff who know me, and have quickly become friendly with new staff members. Child development seems to be a field for friendly people. When I first came in, a few of the kids knew me. "Mr. John!" a couple said when they saw me. Chris came over and started to climb up me. "I've been on vacation," I said.
> "Well, I missed you," he said.
> "You missed me, huh," I said.
> "Are you his dad?" asked a new boy, Evan.
> "No, I'm not his dad; I'm just an extra teacher for this class," I explained. Chris hugged my leg and went off to play.

It was exciting and fun to observe and get to know new children, as well as "old" children in a new setting. This tended to counterbalance my feelings of loss and emptiness as I missed some of the children who had moved on to kindergarten or other locations.

TIME PASSAGES: EMOTIONAL
MARKERS AND THE ROAD TURNING

Holiday time would draw out positive emotions from adults and children. I often was reminded of my strong feelings for the children at such times. Here is what I wrote as one Christmas break began:

> Today was the last day of school for the year before the Christmas holidays. Time to remember endearing acts and qualities of children who come to mind, today and recently.
> The three-year-olds opened a "class present" today. Each kid had a level of wrapping paper to take off. Inside was a box of candy canes, and each kid got one. "You can't have mine," said Ryan to me.
> "I don't want *your* candy cane, Ryan," I said.
> "You can have a piece of mine," said Michael. Later, after snack, they were eating their candy canes and Michael remembered. "Mr. John!" he said. "Here's a piece!"

I went over and told him, "Thank you," and how nice he was to offer me a piece, but that I would get a candy cane later, and he could eat the whole thing.

"OK," he said. Later, outside, he wanted a ride on my back and chased around with me for a while. Gary enjoyed getting some attention from me today. He got a back ride, and I told him, "By the way, Gary."

"What?"

"Merry Christmas!"

"Thank you." It's often amazing how polite kids are when I say that to them. Shaun brought candy canes for his teachers today. He gave one to me. "They're not for kids," he would say to kids who asked for one. He tended to grab my hand and hug it, and he loved getting chased outside today. Mary and Hannah wanted me to tuck them in for naptime today. "Hey Mr. John! Merry Christmas!" Laura said to me when she heard me saying it to Mary and Hannah.

The holidays gave us all an excuse to show more positive feelings toward one another, and I was struck by how the children picked up on this mood and were even more loving toward all of their teachers, including me.

Returning from a break was also a time for emotional demonstrations of relationships. When school resumed after Christmas break, I noted

warm greetings from Ms. Melissa, and the kids looked happy to see me. When I arrived today, Paul came over and gave me a hug. "I missed you," he said. Shaun and Evan came over for hugs. After that, it was a normal day. I was struck, though, by some extra affection displayed by some of the kids today. Nasser, Michael, and Alex climbed into my lap at intervals. Alex told me he was having a birthday party tonight. He's turning five. Then he wanted me to build with him and come with him somewhere else in the class. For Alex, that was a lot of closeness with an adult—he is usually more peer centered.

Such expressions of emotion strengthened my sense of belonging and relationship with the children in the classroom.

Another emotional time was the aftermath of the terrorist bombing of the federal building in Oklahoma City. This took place while I was spending time at the center, and I was unable to resist commenting about it in my journal:

I walked into the four-year-olds' classroom this morning wondering how anyone could try to blow up a building with a day-care center in it—I felt a little scarred by the Oklahoma City catastrophe. Evan came running over when he saw me. "Mr. John!" He hugged me. Jim followed him. "You got a haircut!" Jim said. "I got a haircut too."

"That looks like a good haircut," I told him. Jim stayed near me for much of the morning, wanting to sit next to me and then on my lap as he played with blocks on the table. . . . Today was surely a day for loving kids—in the aftermath of the Oklahoma City bombing, people are literally and figuratively holding their kids tighter, and I found that in myself as I spent extra time on a picture-perfect day. . . .

The day was so beautiful that I fled the office and wound up back at the center in the afternoon, observing the elementary school kids. I played catch with one boy, Joe, for some time—he clearly relished the attention, and I could not help but think—here I was, a college professor, outside playing and spending time with a cute kid who was certainly not my own, on a beautiful day. What a weird—but this evening also wonderful—world.

I certainly found comfort in my work with the children in the sad days following the Oklahoma City bombing. This served as a reminder to me that the relationships we grow serve as key support during emotionally trying times, especially relationships in which we are giving of our time or energy to others.

One summer, returning to the center after a long vacation, I sought to record in my journal my mixed feelings about "the road turning" and a new semester beginning. I titled this entry, "Images Today upon Returning":

> Finding Evan still there, to my surprise, and then my distress at thinking of him as a problem when I walked in the classroom and he greeted me with a big hug and told me he had gone to the beach, too. He wanted a story read to him, and asked me if I would rub his back at naptime hours beforehand. He kept wanting me outside with him for a back ride. "After today I'll be at Early Learning," he said. "Yeah, I'll miss you," said Ms. Stephanie. "I'll miss you, too," I said. "They should be nice there." "They don't give back rides at Early Learning," said Evan. "They don't, huh?" I asked. "No . . . maybe sometime when I'm at Early Learning you could come and see me there." "That would be fun," I said. I find myself sad that it actually probably will never happen.
>
> Sadness at finding out that Michael, my "backpack buddy," and Julie (such a little sweetheart) will not be returning. Even after so many years of this, my mind dwells on it and I am sad. "The road turns," again—though this year, the road has been turning often, as Gary, Jim, and Paul left . . . then Matt, and now Michael and Julie.

It had been a summer for pondering the impermanence of life and its relationships and learning to treasure the ones we have in the *now*. Even as I was saddened by the loss of some of the children from my life, I was intrigued and excited about what the "new group" would be like. The road went ever on, but it was always exciting, intriguing, and, in the end, full of love.

I noted this hope in my journal also:

> While the road *is* turning again, there is also continuity. There is Tricia and her creative play, cooking for me and taking roles (usually sister and brother) with me. There is Nick, bouncing around the classroom to me, and wanting his back rub and back ride (Jim passes that tradition on). And there is Timothy, who as I stood in the three-year-olds' classroom one day, said, "Mr. John."
>
> "Yes?"
>
> "You know what?"
>
> "What?"

"I love you."

"You *do*, huh?" I was not sure I had heard correctly, I was so stunned. Timothy moved away before I could say anything more.

I knew the rewards of my work with the children would always, in the end, outweigh the costs.

The passage of time gradually became emotionally relevant during my years of research with the children. Occasionally, events would dramatize my feelings of love and loss as children came into and out of my life. After two years of volunteering, I recorded such a moment in a journal entry labeled "A Moment of Tragedy":

> Running around the playground, I heard a yell: "Mr. John!" Something seemed a little different about it, and suddenly one of the kids near me, Nick, halted and said, "Jim." I stopped and looked in that direction, and sure enough, there was my old friend Jim [from last year] standing at the fence. He had said, "Hi, Mr. John," I realized, as I understood why his voice and what he said sounded different from the children I am now used to. I started moving toward the fence where Jim was standing. Then I noticed the open car door that Jim had obviously gotten out of, and his mom came out of the center's front door glowering at him and saying, "Get back in that car!" Jim reluctantly did so, slowly. Nick, noticing him suddenly, said, "Hi, Jim," only a few seconds after I did. All this happened so fast. I was hoping things would not be left like that, so saying, "You remember Jim, huh?" to Nick ("Yes," he said), I walked over near the fence where Jim had been. Jim, now sitting in the back seat of the car, turned and waved, but now he had his sad/mad face on. His mom, not realizing (I assume) the reunion that he tried to have take place there, drove off. (Jim's little brother Ryan soon joined us on the playground.)
>
> This incident is memorable for me because I felt so many emotions so fast. I was delighted that Jim remembered me and had made an effort (perhaps risking getting in trouble) to say "hi" to me and see me. I was thrilled to see Jim again. I was worried that he was getting in trouble. I was sad for him that his effort at reunion was so abruptly thwarted. And finally, I was a bit perturbed at his mom for seeming so oblivious to the reasons behind his actions and jumping right to being angry with him (I had seen *that* before). I'm sympathetic that Jim can be a willful boy and a handful, and that he needs to be chastised for doing something unsafe, but it seemed like he was "slapped down" yet again for simply trying to maintain a relationship. I hope he doesn't get into more trouble because he got out of the car. Yet part of me is cheering: "Way to go, Jim, it was sure great to see you again. Yes, I remember you!"

Seeing a child after months or years, and especially having that child recognize me, was a most moving experience. The incident above stuck in my mind because Jim, even at the risk of getting in trouble, made the effort to say hello to me. I thought how much a part of my life he had been, and now life events had made us estranged.

New semesters also gave me a strong sense of the passing of time. Especially in August, as the new fall semester began, many of the previous year's three-year-olds would be in the four-year-olds' classroom, and it would seem like the little children had taken over the bigger children's class. But, of course, they *were* the bigger children's class now. One such day I wrote:

> Today I am noticing the "newness" of this group of kids more. There is the sense that a "new" generation is truly in the four-year-olds' classroom. I come in the room, and now it is Chris who tells me what he is building, and Derek said "Hi there," this morning. Chris ran over to grab me to see an insect they had found and a bird's nest they thought they saw. Now, the repeated outside ritual is building a dinosaur out of big building blocks, which Derek usually initiates. Only Natalie tried to chase me today—no kids asked me to chase them or for a back ride for the first time in months of being here, which *really* makes me feel like the "next generation" has arrived.

It would take me several weeks to adjust to a new routine with the new set of children; an emotional time, in both negative and positive ways—and always rejuvenating.

I gradually got used to the cycles of children passing through the center. Besides the calendar-imposed relationship cycles, however, I did notice more ambiguous relational transitions. Times of reaching out and entering into interactions with the children would be followed by my maintaining more of an observer's distance. Some days were good days for "letting go"— mellow days where I might, for the first time in a while, walk into the four-year-olds' classroom to no greeting, because everyone was busy. That could set the tone for the day. Other days I could come in feeling quite dispassionate, and the children would greet me effusively and insist on drawing me into interaction with them, causing a "getting closer" tone for the day. This cycle was not planned, but seemed to happen naturally.

As the years I spent with the children at the center went by, I began to notice that, as the school year began, the relationship "slate" was in large part washed clean. The children I had gotten to know in the three-year-olds' class would move up to the four-year-olds', but most of the children in most classrooms were "new," and relationships began to bud and flower. It seemed to take several weeks for the children to grow closer to me. By spring and summer, though, relationships were more settled; the children were more comfortable in their roles and with me.

After the children moved on, I would wonder how they were doing and what they were like as the years went on. I had to doubt that they would remember me if I saw them, yet I was sometimes proven wrong. One day at an outside campus party, I noticed six-year-old Michael from the past year in the crowd listening to music with his mother. As one song ended Michael pointed at me and waved. I waved back. After this I saw him trying to pull his mother toward me. "This way," he insisted. But she did not realize what he wanted and moved the other way. I went over to talk with them soon after. Michael gave me a hug as I walked up and gave me several more as I stood talking to his mother and father. "Wanna see inside where my mom works?" he asked me, pulling my hand. This strong demonstration of affection from a child I hadn't seen for over a year moved me, demonstrating the mysterious power of love in relationships with children. I realized that sometimes we do not know how much influence we have over children until later.

EMOTIONAL CLOSINGS

As my mornings spending time with the children at the center came to an end, I could not help but reflect on the emotional impact the children all had on me. Pondering my future volunteering with children, I asked Ms. Debra, the center director, who had welcomed me at first and gotten to know me over several years, what she believed the benefits of my volunteering had been. She noted that having some male influence around was good, as some of the children did not have that at home. She said, "You take time for them; when you're here, your time is *theirs*, and they sense that." She pointed out that children noticed when I was with other classes—"Why isn't Mr. John here? When is Mr. John coming to our room?" They also noticed on days I was supposed to be there but was not. "Where's Mr. John? Isn't this a day for Mr. John to be here?" she quoted. I valued the feedback, and found it reflected the positive feelings I had taken away from my years at the center. I hoped to continue to have such a positive influence in future volunteer work with children.

Of course, my last morning volunteering at the center, when it was time for my interactions and "data-gathering" to end, I was wistful. One of my final journal entries captures my feelings:

On this last day of my final "regular" morning at the center, all sorts of little routine things struck me as valuable and perhaps becoming somewhat taken for granted. What really stand out for me are the verbal and nonverbal tokens of affection from the children and staff toward me and from me to them. These years of volunteering here taught me that love, attention, and affection are so basic to all of our human agendas living here under the sun, even when we get distracted by conflicts (often over the same needs), material goods, or routine rules and procedures. Children are refreshing in that they are more forthright about love, affection, and attention being on their agenda; as children grow up they learn to hide or disguise these needs, although all people still have them. It is a paradox of our society that as we grow old enough to learn and understand our needs for love, affection, and attention, we live more and more of our lives in places and relationships where such needs are not expected to be met; and indeed are at times viewed as unnecessary. I think one of the elements of the organizational culture of many child-care centers that attracts me is the forthright value placed on love, attention, and affection in such places. When the staff loves the children, their love expands to include one another (with exceptions, of course). This can make a child-development center with these values a wonderfully supportive place to work. However, if love, affection, and attention are not valued (as in so *many* typical workplace cultures), a child-care center can become as rigid, cold, conflict ridden, and stressful as any other workplace; and what is worse, the children learn and absorb these same humanity-stifling values, as well. As Ms. Stacey today put it to me, "If they have love put inside them before age seven, they'll always have love inside them. If they have hate put inside them by then, they'll *always* have hate inside them."

I found my time with the children to be among the most wonderful times of my life. The experiences were worth the effort of managing such new, strong, and at times conflicting emotions. I liked the emotion management sought by the child-care center's culture; needing to show emotions of nurturing, support, and compassion forced one to overcome life's irritations and focus on the children for a while. I took it as a personal challenge to take those emotional lessons and apply them to my own personal relationships in family and organizations. I feel enriched indeed by the experience.

15

Findings and Implications: Child Interactions and Child-Care Cultures

Though we were all children ourselves once, many adults seem to view children almost as aliens. Adults have much uncertainty over how to initiate or respond to communication with children. Should children be treated "just like adults"? Should their communication be taken only in a nonserious or humorous way? Or, should their messages be ignored and handled by those adults who are "in charge" of them? When adults unfamiliar with child interactions entered the child-development center, these three communicative "disconnects" were quite common and a source of humor for those of us used to communicating with children. However, when I myself encountered children in unfamiliar contexts, I would become uncertain as well. Trying alternative, fresh perspectives was often the best approach an uncertain adult could take when communicating with a child. We must be willing to put aside our standard communication expectations, and see the world as exciting, new, and different—the way a child does. Then both the child and adult are willing to experiment with communication styles until one is found mutually effective. This is difficult for adults who try standard messages on children and get an unexpected result; then they may give up and view the children as uncommunicative or worse. For some children, an adult's standard greeting may be entirely new and intimidating, and so they are uncertain how to respond.

One result of this mutual uncertainty I noted quite often. When a child found a pleasing communication pattern that resulted in rewarding, focused interaction with an adult, the child would seek to repeat that pattern at every meeting. Most often, this was in the form of a specific game he or she wanted to play; sometimes it would be in the form of a standard greeting. For instance, a three-year-old girl said, "There is a crab here, going to get you!" each time she saw me for several weeks after we played a game involving a pretend crab. As the children and I adapted to the pattern the other was trying to en-act, we created shared meaning between us (Denzin 1977) and reduced un-certainty in preparation for further interaction (Berger and Bradac 1982). Sym-bols could be built on already familiar symbols until we had developed a comfortable, shared, social reality (Mead 1934). Many times, adults feel sure of social reality and seek only to impose their view of reality on a child, thus stunting or ending communication between them. When children realized that I was open to understanding their reality, and would readily accept their mes-sages, they responded with a growing closeness of relationship that could be surprising, moving, and even scary at times.

The culture and communication climate of the child-development center of-fered children and adults multiple and reinforced chances to relate to one an-other as people. Our interactions transcended instrumental purposes for being there, even as the children pursued relationships for primarily instrumental rea-sons. Often a boy or girl ceased to be simply "a child" to me as we entered "the world of relation" (Buber 1958, 6). Each child was an important person to me in my life, and I had evidence that, for a time at least, I was an important adult individual for many of them. Though all of us adults and children related to oth-ers to a greater or lesser extent, our personhood and individuality depended on and emerged from our interactions with others. Even when close relationship stances did not occur, the potential was there, in our context and interactions at the center. The human longing for connection with others had a chance of enactment with each new relationship with another (Buber 1958). Fulfilling such longing seemed more sought after and more likely in the emotionally ex-pressive culture of the child-development center. The recency of the children's infantile longing for attachment likely added urgency to their continuing hunt for relationships (Solomon and George 1999). While work in organizations becomes, as we get older, increasingly about using and organizing people and materials, the emotional and spiritual fulfillment humans derive from such work depends on our relationships with others (Buber 1958). Experiencing life at the child-development center drove the point home to me—most of our lives are centered on relating to others and how we fit into the relationships we develop. Giving and receiving emotional and meaningful symbols are key to anyone's happiness. Ideal child-care center cultures would promote and preserve such relating among children as they grow, but also among staff members and parents—perhaps even influencing our "instrumental" economic and organiza-tional relating in the wider social world. A dash of relating can open our eyes to others and bring much personal fulfillment.

The open, up-front communication agendas of young children were refreshing and fun to observe. Preschool children have a natural honesty that could shock someone with adult face-management sensibilities. Adults have learned to facilitate interaction and respect social reality by muting strong ex-pressions of feelings, especially criticisms. The children I observed were more ruled by their feelings, seldom could hide them, and struggled to communicate them appropriately. If they were angry or did not like someone, they would make that crystal clear with both verbal and nonverbal messages. Along with this abruptness, however, was an almost overwhelming readiness to show liking and affection, and to try all sorts of ways to get another to spend time with them. There was a pervasive sense of freshness and hope when communicating with children. Expressions of dislike were almost always temporary—one never knew what difference even a few minutes would make in a child's feelings, communication style, and strategies used. Each interaction thus gained an extra edge of excitement, as the children viewed the world with newness and wonder; and their communication reflected this state of change and excitement.

The children's natural honesty did not preclude their use of a wide variety of communication strategies and even manipulations. As children gained more and more verbal skills, the staff members at the child-development center where I observed encouraged the children to try them out. Clearly, the children were acquiring through interaction the skills they needed for influencing other children, as well as adults (Delia, Kline, and Burleson 1979; Keyton 1994; Parker 1986). Children's primary goals in a desirable relationship were invoked in the ranked order of control, inclusion, and affection. Most children did have one or two friends who would be given more of their time or attention over several weeks or months. All were concerned with managing relationships with adults, as well. Crucial communication skills were enacted as children made statements about friendship, but key behaviors for managing friendships were nonverbal as well, involving being present in proximity and using acceptable varieties of touch.

CHILD-CARE COMMUNICATION GUIDELINES

A variety of strategic options were available to children for relationship management. While young children's vocalizations have been categorized into five groups (questions, commands, narratives, songs or rhymes, and sound play—Ochs and Schieffelin 1983), strategies for growing, maintaining, and ending relationships have been found to encompass ten categories: statements about friendship, proximity, touch, listening, expressing feelings, engaging in conflict, joking or teasing attempts to use humor, commanding or controlling others, invoking rules, and taking on play roles with mutual expectations (Meyer and Driskill 1997). These strategies have been illustrated throughout earlier chapters, but what are the implications for child-care centers and those involved or interested in creating them? Eleven guidelines were suggested by my observations at the child-development center.

VIEW FRIENDSHIP, TOUCH, AND PROXIMITY AS KEY, TAKEN-FOR-GRANTED RELATIONSHIP COMMODITIES

Touch, proximity, and open negotiations about friendship were hallmarks of preschool children's relationships. Adults must recognize the seriousness of such symbols for children, while understanding that children so young do not attach long-term, abstract, socially contextual connotations to the notions of touching another, sitting next to another, or saying "I'm not your friend." While preschool children must learn restraints about the use of touch and proximity, they also crave affectionate touch, and thus it is part of any strong relationships with them. Adults should prepare for and guide extensive touching behaviors without becoming too "rejecting."

Children viewed friendship as valuable and desirable, but also saw it as a limited commodity that could be traded for other desirable goods or actions. Only so much friendship was available for each person, in their perception, so threats of reducing or further dividing friendship were taken very seriously. Friendship was also viewed as temporary and changeable; a pleasant friendship was one to be guarded, because it might end if the other party moved away to play somewhere else or began to talk with another person. Children would check with one another often, asking "Are you my friend?" and "Are you still my friend?" Statements of the type "If you'll play with me I'll be your friend" were very common relationship-management tools, as were the negative versions: "I won't be your friend if you do that!" Providing friendship was directly invoked as a compliance-gaining technique, and children learned very young to apply the notion of reciprocity in friendship— "what I do for you, so you should do for me" (as explored in Haslett and Samter 1997). Children would trade favors for friendship—"If you let me play with that toy I'll be your friend" and "If you're not my friend you can't come to my birthday party" were two common trades. Children related friendship to practical acts like playing together, sharing a desired toy, or giving something to another.

The idea that friendship could transcend doing something together in the present was just beginning to be grasped by some of the five-year-old children. Many would reconfirm their friendships often: "Are you my friend?" If they got a positive answer, but did not immediately play with the other, they were learning that friendship could be ongoing without any immediate "payoff" in direct contact with the other. Immediate physical proximity or object exchanges could gradually be supplanted by more abstract, ongoing "friendship state" exchanges. The ability to reciprocate and meet the other's expectations was crucial for building relationships. When a child did not receive much or enough in return for what was given, the relationship would gradually end.

Nonverbal indicators of friendship also remained crucially important to preschool children. One of the strongest ways for them to communicate about relationships was through the use of proximity. Being near or next to someone for any length of time symbolized a strong or growing relationship for them. Children who were "friends" wanted to sit next to one another, and one child angry at another would quickly move away or exclaim, "No! I don't want to sit next to you!" The physical closeness they displayed, at ages four and five, was directly related to the relational closeness they perceived.

Expressing affection, especially through touch, was also highly important to children. This norm is "grown out of" by most people in our society, especially when interacting in groups or organizations outside the family. Yet one who interacts with young children on a regular basis must prepare to receive and give affection much more often than in a "typical" organization. Proximity and touch were among the strongest relational symbols for young children; an emotionally close relationship without physical closeness or affectionate touches seemed inconceivable to most of them. Children would want to hold hands with, hug, get picked up by, or sit in the lap of trusted adults. Since touching others is greatly restricted in most organizations in Western culture, all children within it, as they grow into adults, are caught in a communicative bind. Humans need to touch and be touched, but yet may shrink from it since so much touch can be inappropriate, abusive, or violent. The staff at the center where I observed were prohibited from ever touching for punishment, but they would seldom hesitate to hug or pick up the children, especially to comfort them, but also just for fun. As a participant in the center with the children, I had to get used to being touched much more often than at most other times in my life. I also had to encounter negative touching—hitting, kicking, and even biting—that to me was horrible, but to the children could express passing anger, frustration, or even playful affection.

The norms adults follow restricting touch were not yet fully understood by four- and five-year-old children. They touched and sought touch quite often and expected it as an indicator of an ongoing relationship with both adults and peers. As an adult interacting with them, I had to learn to tolerate and even grew to like such affection. Yet, I could not let "clingy" hugging or holding distract from other organizational purposes, especially learning (theirs as well as my own) and promoting child choice and independence. Appropriate times and methods must be found to allow children to express and receive affection if a healthy communication climate is to be maintained. One artifact of the crucial nature of the issue of touch was one of the most commonly invoked classroom rules, posted on the wall: "Keep your hands to yourself." Children who overused positive or negative forms of touching required extra guidance by teachers and sparked more discussions about responses. Children needed to learn to regulate their touching and especially their hitting, but they were determined and at times desperate to enact touch as symbolizing closer or damaged relationships.

PROVIDE FOR FREE PLAY INVOLVING ROLE TAKING

Free time for play gave preschoolers their greatest chance to practice strategies for relationship management, as taking roles in creative, ever-changing games led them to develop themselves as individuals and form social orders among peers. Free play should constitute an important part of any child-care center's daily schedule. The most common strategy for initiating and strengthening relationships among four-year-old children was proposing or taking roles in the games that occupied most of their time each day. Creativity in play fostered creativity in relationship management. Through cooperation in play, shared meaning and trust would develop among the children. Roles taken in play could become very serious and spark real conflict. Persistence paid off in relationships—often a child who continued to stay and play in proximity to others would overcome their initial refusal to play with him or her. The level of trust felt among those in the group deciding whether to accept a newcomer, based on recent interactions, affected whether one child's bid to join in play would be accepted or rejected. As children learned to trust me and noted that I would play along with some games, they would attempt to take roles and get me to take a role. One little girl would often say to me, "Pretend you're my daddy. OK?" Then, she would tell me some innocuous things, but would have a comfortable "play role" within which she could interact with me. Many of the children, especially boys, would initiate a relationship with me by getting me to chase them or play hide-and-go-seek with them. This certainly fit the children's common pattern of creating closer relationships by role-playing or joining in games together.

Even "romantic," boy-girl relationships were enacted by four-year-olds, as children would say they were "married," or say "she's my girlfriend." Like most other relationships the children had, they took these quite seriously and could be hurt or angered by rejection; yet such relationships would only last a few hours, usually. Once in a while one would last for several days.

Clearly, all the children wanted to maintain a sense of control over their activities and relationships. The children who almost always sought control by the same means, especially if through teasing or violence, were pegged as undesired friends and not allowed control. Those who could accept that relationships would change over what for them was the long term (several days) seemed more willing to communicate flexibly to develop more relationships. Children who tried different strategies and were willing to yield control at intervals were more popular with and had more influence over other children— a finding consistent with previous research with children (Haslett and Samter 1997; Howes, Hamilton, and Matheson 1994; Rubin and Ross 1982). Once in a while, a child would rebel and refuse to comply with one of these more popular children, causing the more popular child to try other means of control.

Communicating flexibly in relationships was a valuable skill learned at varied paces by the children. Those who were very limited to one or two friends over a long time period, or who focused primarily on relationships with adults, were noticeably deficient in their communication skills; the lack of flexibility in relationships was a key indicator of limited communication development. Reasons for those limits were often uncertain; children mature and master any cognitive activity at varied rates, but two included their home life and communication models the children were exposed to prior to coming to the center. Those limited children, however, clearly lacked power in relationships, as they found themselves more dependent on the few relationships they did have, and would often focus more on relating to teachers or other adults present.

COMMUNICATE ADULT SUPPORT TO CHILDREN

Adults must balance support for dependent preschool children with promoting their independence, one of the basic dialectical tensions in a relationship (Baxter 1988). What makes this dialectic more poignant for young children is their natural dependence on trusted adults and their often strong emotional response to any disruption of such a secure relationship. While strong attachment-seeking behaviors by children can seem stifling or "clingy" to adults, they also allow more chances to relate and for adults to model a close, comfortable, balanced relationship that provides for more independence of both parties. Such relationships are enhanced (and may be made possible) by allowing the child some extra closeness.

Children would use a variety of strategies to form relationships with adults, the extent of which depended on their need for adult support (their goal) and their view of the appropriateness of certain actions (their assessment of the situation). Children would seek to repeat rituals that led to closeness and reinforced certainty in their relationship with adults. Even simple adult acts like giving a child a little drawing could communicate a great relational message to him or her. I also noted competition among the children for adult attention; this was a commodity to be prized and led to conflict on multiple occasions. Several children developed what could be called "love-hate" relationships with me as an adult. At times, they would be loving and want my attention, other times they would be inexplicably angry or say, "Get out of here" or "Leave me alone." My attributed explanation for these angry incidents was, at first, that I had done something to anger them—perhaps shown attention to other children and moved away from them. Later it became clear that they were reflecting their current relationships with other adults, especially their father or another male figure, onto me. Sometimes, this would lead to ambivalence for a child over whether to approach a relationship with me or avoid one.

The children who alternated between friendly and unfriendly responses were often trying to build a close relationship with me, but were frustrated when things would not always go their way or they found that they always had to "share me" with other children. I never wanted to be drawn in too much by one child, as I felt that would distract me from my observations of all the children. Being shown such strong signs of love, at times, I thought how easily I could be "wrapped around the little finger" of a child whose priority was developing a relationship with me. I gradually learned the art of balancing children's bids for time and attention, moving from one child to another without seeming to suddenly abandon a child I was currently interacting with.

A chasing game was the most common way children initiated or joined in a relationship with me outside. The mock hunt, with me grabbing them or letting them get away, seemed to allow the children a way to build a basic friendly relationship with me. Getting a push on the swings was another move to get adult attention; even long after the children could pump their own legs to keep themselves going they would ask, "Push me!" Once they found a pattern of interaction with clear roles for each party to take, the children would repeat it relentlessly to reinitiate and build relationships. Gradually, once the children were comfortable with our initial play or interaction ritual, most would gain more confidence to try additional forms of interaction.

ADJUST TO VARIABLE PHASES OF GROWING RELATIONSHIPS WITH CHILDREN

Relationships continually balance and adjust the contrasting interests of self and other. Children must practice maintaining such balances through unstructured communication with one another. Adults should expect lightning-fast relationship development at times, while also patiently handling a slow progress through relationship phases. As children invoke symbols through communicating, they establish and reinforce a social order. They also adapt to whatever social order is laid down by the power of adults in charge and alter their communication strategies to fit at varying rates. As I tried to make sense of how my relationships with children developed, I noted my recurring surprise when they would suddenly hug me, get in my lap, or greet me seeking affection. "When did this happen?" I would ask myself. As time passed, I realized that I was more surprised the sooner in the relationship with a child such affection happened, but I did note patterns that led up to that evidence of a developed relationship. Each step closer in a relationship would be preceded by a lull, or a distancing, or a settled phase marked by a drop in affection. Conville (1991) noted four phases of relationships, one involving stability of closeness (security), one involving stability of distance (alienation). The other two phases involve moving closer or further apart in a relationship (the resynthesis and disintegration phases). I experienced evidence of these relationship phases during my interactions with children. In a cyclical pattern, our relationships would grow closer, and then stabilize, grow a little more distant, then stabilize again, and then grow even closer than before. This suggested an ongoing development following a helical pattern like that Conville (1991) outlined.

As I observed patterns in my relationships with children, I could distinguish unique, specific phases marked by expected actions by both parties. A typical relationship between a child and myself as an adult passed through six potential phases, though not always moving through all six, and moving at varied rates of speed. Some children moved through the first two or three phases, and our relationship stabilized there. Others very quickly passed through all six, and were very close to me until they no longer attended the center. One artifact of my situation was usually lacking a set of distancing or closure phases as our relationships ended. A child simply no longer attended the center, and our relationship was over. Once in a while, I would know when a child's last day would be, and I would make an effort to say goodbye while making it sound like an exciting event and not a sad one. Some children who had grown very close to me would tell me they were leaving and say goodbye in their own way, often becoming very affectionate in their last days at the center. These instances were moving yet atypical, and thus I accumulated rich evidence of how my relationships grew with children, but very seldom could document a relationship "falling apart."

The first phase of a growing relationship involved a child becoming comfortable enough interacting with other children or teachers in my presence, but not directly with me. This seemed to be the basic "safety" phase. The child would not hold back, or act extra quiet and reticent, when I was nearby. In this first phase I was accepted, but not welcomed, by a child. I was clearly still seen as a stranger or distant adult, but there was no fear of me shown by the child.

Then, in the second phase, a child would show appreciation for my interaction with him or her, but would not initiate interaction with me. This was like a "welcome" phase, in that a child would feel rewarded for interacting with me, and would nonverbally show this through a smile, or a look, or simply by remaining nearby. The child liked my interaction with him or her, but did not feel comfortable initiating interaction with me yet.

Third, a child would initiate interaction with me regularly. These were "practical interactions" most of the time, like asking me to help put on a jacket or tie a shoe. Such children might ask me to join a game they were already playing. Another common way for children in this stage to involve me would be with a demanding, "Push me!" as they sat on a swing. During these interactions the children and I had time to learn about each other and see how comfortable and how fun our further interaction would be. Usually, children in this stage would not initiate greetings with me, but once my interactions with children and other teachers in the classroom began, they would feel comfortable talking to me.

During the fourth phase, a child would regularly greet me warmly when I came into the classroom or was first seen. This was an "affectionate greetings" phase. The child would gain my attention quickly, and what followed would be a familiar pattern of interaction for both of us, whether a game, or activity, or typical statements. In these third and fourth phases, repeated patterns became very noticeable in our relationship and were often reinitiated by the child.

The fifth phase could be labeled the "touching" phase. The child would seek to confirm our relationship through touch, whether holding hands, giving a hug, sitting on my lap, or getting a back ride. This was the phase that would dramatically bring the relationship to the center of my attention. When this phase was reached within days of my meeting a child, I was very surprised, even when it happened three years running with different children. Such children demanded that I be willing to touch or hold them and considered this natural in a loving relationship, which, in their eyes, we had. As an adult in my researcher role, I had to struggle at times to remember why I was there, as the relationships grew in importance to me as well. I cared about and loved these children even as I sought to study their communication, and there was no question that I would lose some "objectivity" as I was drawn into these ever-closer relationship phases.

The impact a researcher can have on relationships in organizations was most vividly demonstrated by the children who reached the sixth and closest phase. At this point, the child would run over for a hug on seeing me, giving me some kind of effusive greeting, and would expect me to spend a lot of time with him or her. This could be called the "special love" phase, as I could not help reciprocating the feelings of children who so clearly wanted me in their life. I would hear from center staff members that such children would ask about me on days I was not present, or parents would tell me their child missed me if I was gone for a few days. These children had made their relationship with me a priority at the center, and some would not always understand that I had to give attention to other children as well, or stay in the background during some lessons or classroom activities. Many children reached phase three in relating to me, but over the years, more and more would reach phase four or five. One or two each semester might reach phase six. This pattern of phases, repeated by a wide variety of preschool children of both genders and varied cultural backgrounds, illustrated how children work to improve communication and develop relationships with adults. The relationship patterns also served as a primer for understanding how all people use communication to develop and manage relationships.

EXPECT A HIGHER INTENSITY OF EMOTIONS EXPERIENCED

Working with children forced me as an adult to more clearly label and effectively channel my own emotions. We expected this of the children, and

I had to practice it myself—an enlightening and extended experience of handling some negative but many positive emotions. I became more involved with the children than simply as a researcher or observer. As relationships grew, developed, and ended, I had emotional responses to each event. My relating to children took the form of an emotional cycle of gratifying relational growth, followed by some kind of overreaching or frustration, leading to my backing away from close relations; this would spark growth once again. The overall emotional direction was positive. While children could express emotions more strongly than was always comfortable, those emotions were genuine. I learned, loved, and grew from the experience of interacting with children in the child-development center setting. I sought to take the emotional lessons and fulfillment I received and apply them to my own family and organizational relationships.

HELP CHILDREN MANAGE EMOTIONS

Emotions should be controlled and expressed in socially accepted ways, but child-care center staff had to help children acknowledge, label, and talk about their emotions with some freedom of expression for growth and learning purposes. Joking in a friendly way served to unite staff members and children, as well as to reframe perceptions to overcome stressful or sad events. A major challenge faced by children at ages four and five was learning how to control their feelings and appropriately express them. The children at the center struggled to move from yelling, screaming, crying, or hitting to verbalizing feelings. Teachers were often reminding children to "use words" to express what they felt or wanted, along with the common "keep your hands [or feet] to yourself." One could fairly easily read what children that age felt, but their peers as well as adults could be put off by a loud or abrupt display of feelings. One who was a "crybaby" (as labeled by peers) or was always "telling on" someone was not trusted by the other children. Children who had the hardest time were those who had learned that crying or screaming were effective at getting them desired attention at home or in other contexts. At the center, these behaviors were outside the norm, and they alienated children and adults when overused. Several times I observed staff members allow children to cry or throw a temper tantrum, while making clear that activities would proceed and that one could not always get one's way, especially by crying or screaming. Children who expressed their feelings in the opposite way, by growing quiet and withdrawn, were naturally easier to overlook. Indeed, it was difficult to tell what such children really felt or why they were quiet. For the most part, though, children's feelings were quite clear, and their main challenge was how to appropriately communicate them to others.

MOLD AND ENACT CONSISTENT VALUES AND RITUALS

Any time one is immersed in the organizational culture of a place, the temptation is to seek keys to how communication serves to preserve it. As I participated in communication at the child-development center, I was struck by how fulfilling communication was there; the culture rewarded and enhanced communication among staff members and children. I sought some key cultural bases for the open, enjoyable communication climate in the center. Since the center or classroom rules form the crucial context for preschool children communicating, adults must establish simple rules clearly and follow and enforce them consistently. Lack of discipline and, conversely, too much adult control both inhibit comfortable, flexible communication among children.

My observations elicited two key elements for promoting communication in child-development centers. Both the adult attitudes toward communication and the environment created for children's communication determine children's ability to learn about communication and practice it. First, how do the adults feel about communication? Do they enjoy it, and use many different strategies, or are they primarily communicating for command or management purposes? If communication is valued, children respond by trying out a variety of communication strategies and feel supported in doing so. If communication is subordinated to power relationships, which can very easily happen even in the best of child-care centers, children learn to communicate using a much narrower set of strategies, following restrictions about what they perceive is expected or tolerated. Second, what kind of activities do the children engage in? Are they allowed to play and talk with one another a lot during the day? Are conflicts immediately suppressed by adults, or can the children handle conflicts themselves even when emotions get bruised? (Of course, adults must intervene when physical safety is threatened.) Play goes a long way toward allowing learning through experimentation with different communication styles. Yet adults, with their greater level of power, must set the tone. How much creative play is allowed? How many restrictions are there on types of play, and are these restrictions constant or in tandem with a schedule of expected activities?

If adults use humor and other varied tones and compliance-gaining techniques, children follow with their own attempts at communication variety. If adults are rigid in requiring that children use only certain kinds of talk or refrain from talking entirely, the climate of communication becomes more restricted, or closed. Who speaks the most becomes much less varied and much more dependent on who holds the power in the classroom. Thus, the lead teacher serves as the key communicator in any child-care classroom, overriding even center directors in importance. Certainly, the director sets the communication tone for the teaching staff, but individual staff members transfer that communication climate to the children.

Adults had the most impact on the formation of the child-care culture at the center where I observed, consistent with earlier research (Anderson 1989; Haskins 1985). Adults planned the schedule and modeled the types of messages expected at the center. The children had great leeway with topics and content, but the form of their messages and their relationships would be consistent with adult staff behavior at the center. The children differed most from the adults in their willingness to air negative feelings openly. While adults at the center would never call names or openly question another's character, the children would do so and would much more readily engage in open conflict. A child's conflict with adults was dangerous and pointless, as a child would never "win" and would consistently suffer negative consequences. However, a child could enforce norms on other willing children and thus participate in creating the organization's culture—though with a smaller influence than adults. The power differences were so clear that no one questioned them. The director was in charge, the lead teacher had similar powers in each classroom, and all adults asserted power over children. Within this hierarchy, however, communication was comfortable and free flowing.

EXPECT AND RESPOND TO
REPEATED PATTERNS IN COMMUNICATION

Every culture derives shared meaning through repeated rituals. Adults planned the daily schedule of activities that the children learned and expected to repeat at the child-development center. A routine served as a stable background on which all, adults and children both, were comfortable relating to one another. Yet, adult-planned schedules were far from the sole venue for repeated communications. Even spontaneous interactions or games that turned out to be fun were commonly taken up by the children with a determined repetitiveness. The repetition provided a familiarity or sense of safety, it seemed, reducing uncertainty and reinforcing an ongoing and rewarding relationship (Berger and Bradac 1982; Denzin 1977). Such repeating patterns became short-lived "traditions" that structured the children's interactions and served as a foundation for relationships (Nervius 1989). Children participating in such communication rituals clearly felt a sense of inclusion. Adults often initiated or repeated such events, but the children were so pervasively repetitive at times they could wear out the patience of most adults. A tolerance for repetition (and a structured set of activities during a typical day) reinforces children's comfort with relationships and provides a basis of stability on which children can experiment with relationship management strategies.

Children could internalize consistent, clear, and simple rules and invoke them to influence others. Adult agreement on and reinforcement of these rules provided for a supportive climate overall (Palmerus and Hagglund 1991). The rules were a comfortable backdrop to all interaction, and adults and children could consistently and confidently invoke them. All parties acknowledged the rules and accepted the social order they maintained, even if children forgot to follow them at times. When they did not follow the rules, there was no mystery as to why they got in trouble with an adult or received objections from their peers.

Listening was a key value at the center, as adults sought to teach and remain in control. Children, too, internalized listening as a key indicator of positive communication, as those who listened to them were rewarded with friendship and further interaction. Children who showed they were listening by altering their actions or messages found that their relationship with the person speaking would grow closer. Adults who showed children they were listening to them would become more in demand by the children. Some children would tell adults about other children who were mean to them or events at home, not even expecting an action in response, but simply grateful to be listened to. Conversely, ignoring someone meant that interaction or a relationship was not desired at that moment. I would observe children ignoring other children and even adults at times when I knew they could hear the message, but simply did not want to receive it. "Please listen" and "You're not listening" were the most common reminder comments given to children at the center. The most skilled communicators among the children had found a balance between listening well and being listened to regularly. Listening was basic to any relationship and began to meet children's control, inclusion, and affection needs. Control was achieved by having another child or adult pause and give attention; inclusion came from perceiving one's input as welcome; and affection could result from gratitude over being listened to. The power of listening as the basic communication activity needed for relationship formation was demonstrated time and again at the child-development center.

Growth in the relationships of children at the center clearly matched a reduction of uncertainty. Thus, when communicating with children, adults, rather than insisting on a predetermined pattern of communication they may want to impose, should let the child initiate and run through an interaction that he or she may be used to. Adults can also initiate a pattern, and if the child finds it pleasing, that pattern may be used to reinitiate communication with that child for many interactions to come. Rejecting the familiar pattern may be perceived as rejecting the relationship, unless some kind of compensating pattern is substituted. In large part to reduce uncertainty, humans are creatures of habit, and this was evident in the communication of three-, four-, and five-year-olds.

Once rituals were established, creating a sense of comfort and shared meaning, all parties at the child-development center expected communicative creativity. When children or adults were new to the center, much hesitancy and uncertainty were evident. Once that person recognized the basic expectations, however, he or she grew more comfortable engaging in different communication styles, whether assertive, playful, humorous, or even visibly upset. Children especially would gradually blossom this way. Familiar symbols and routines reinforced belonging within the culture, but from there engaging in a wide variety of communication strategies was most effective for children, consistent with earlier findings (Foot, Chapman, and Smith 1995).

BALANCE ADULT POWER WITH CHILD CREATIVITY

Adults should remember that children communicate in a world where large persons apparently always are in control and may, arbitrarily, change the goals of the "communication game." A gesture of support or greeting from an adult can have major positive effects, even when a child may be uncertain about how to respond. As a child learns a comfortable pattern, and develops his or her own sense of control, new and more open strategies are tried. Power always impacts how adults enact roles in relationships with children, as well as how children relate to one another and to adults. At the center, a hierarchy always seemed evident, headed by the lead teacher in the absence of the parent, followed by assistant teachers, then "extra adults" in the classroom like myself, and then influential child peers. The center director was also invoked at times as having even more power than the lead teachers, though she was not often directly involved. The lead teachers were stable for the most part during my years at the center, and their long experience and decisiveness gave them high levels of power over all in the classroom, adults as well as children. Assistant teachers saw more turnover, as college students and parents came to work for a semester or two and then would move on. I noted that each teacher team had to develop an understood hierarchy to know who would make final decisions when the lead teacher was not present. This hierarchy was negotiated informally through interaction and experience over days and weeks, but then was reinforced through ongoing communication patterns (Mumby 1993). The children could definitely tell over time who had the most power, as that adult would be the one they would approach most often with problems or to get something changed.

Leaders would develop among the children, too. Several other children usually wanted to play with these leaders, who would decide what the group would play. These child hierarchies were more flexible than the adult ones, yet showed fairly strong stability over the course of a semester or school year. A question always affecting my own interaction was "How much power should I expect or be expected to wield over the children?" Semester after semester, children realized that I was an adult, with some resulting power, but I was relatively powerless on major issues of discipline and class activity, as well as more willing to play "on their level." I was not on the staff but gradually came to be treated as such; I became more experienced at the center than the newer assistant teachers were. I was careful to give advice only if I was asked or it was clearly needed, and to state that I was a volunteer; I would follow the lead of the staff members, who were formally empowered to make decisions like what activities would be done or when we would go in- or outside. Almost every semester, renegotiation would take place as the assistant teachers and I once again became comfortable with our roles in the hierarchy. My level of control eventually settled into that of a friendly assistant teacher.

The children were mindful of adults' power, approaching me to play a game or for help settling an argument, approaching an assistant teacher to get a drink of water or report bad behavior by a peer (though I received many of these messages as well). The lead teacher was viewed by the children as having the final word on activities or knowledge. Talking to a lead teacher about an issue was seen as a "big deal," and I observed many children shrink from such interaction, especially if they thought they might be in the wrong. Chances to interact with or play with lead teachers were especially prized, and lead teachers clearly had the most influence on the children.

As children got older, the power distance between them and adults actually increased. Three- and four-year-olds, even with their limited communication skills, would often quickly involve me in their play, ask to be read to, or show affection. School-aged children, though much more skilled at communication, would spend several days or weeks around me before they would freely interact with me, or, in some cases, even say "hello"! As the children became more aware of the social hierarchy and the expectations of each level, they were much more likely to follow social norms and avoid the risk of straying away from expected hierarchical relationships. Even younger children, however, were clearly aware of adult-child power differences. Sometimes, a child would have to repeat an adult's name several times before being acknowledged, and children would pretend not to hear an adult at times when I knew they could hear. People at the same level more often quickly acknowledged and understood what was being communicated, as there was little or no power difference to overcome.

While adults sought control to keep all safe and accomplish teaching and living tasks with the class, children would get more commanding as they became more familiar with adults. Reminders of polite, respectful communication had to be given to the children at such times. When individual children pushed the limits of standard forms of control, time-outs were used in response, though this was the least-preferred control strategy of the adults at the center. Children given the opportunity to make a variety of choices during their day showed a greater sense of control and confidence in communicating. Adults, however, felt the need to retain control and restrict choice making for reasons of safety, schedule, and classroom order. Outside and inside play were kept distinct, and the children's play was acknowledged and supported even when adult control was asserted. For instance, if children were getting loud and overactive indoors pretending to be animals, one of the teachers might say, "I want all animals to go to a table. We do that outside." To get control over the children, statements and persuasion would be tried first, and only then would coercion or some form of force be attempted. Outrageous or violent behavior resulted in removal from the classroom. Consistency and presence led to adult control much more than threats or coercion. The lead teachers were often the least overtly controlling adults, but they wielded the most power simply due to their establishing expectations and sticking to them. Children would not test the lead teacher the way they might test other adults, to see how much control they would insist on.

Positive discipline techniques have become a strongly reinforced norm at accredited child-care centers like the one where I observed, with the goal "Tell kids what to do; not what not to do." A child may not know what to do in place of an undesired act. At the child-development center, I observed positive statements tried first. "Keep your hands to yourself," a child might be told. If problems continued, redirection was the most common response. "Move away," or "Move to another area," an uncooperative child would be told. A further violation would often result in the child being taken aside for a talk about why an action was a poor choice. If misbehavior persisted, time-out was used as a last resort for children age three and older. This was an "ultimate" threat; others included expulsion to a different classroom or the director's office, or a talk with or note to the child's parents. Almost always, as teachers moved up this slope of serious sanctions, one was effective. Actually, redirection was usually effective in itself, though time-out was fairly common, being used almost daily in each classroom.

Key classroom rules were kept clear and simple, and were posted on a wall in big letters in most classrooms. From time to time, during a group or circle time, the teacher would remind children of the rules, especially if several children had lately been having trouble following them. These sessions were also good for part-time staff, as they reinforced acceptable behavior and helped all adult workers be on the same page when it came to expectations for the children. Frequent, regular meetings among staff members were also crucial for discussing discipline problems and insuring consistency in adult response. When teacher aides were unsure of a rule or the appropriate response to an infraction, contradictory and confusing messages could be sent to the children.

As long as a desired task or activity was the focus, control by the teacher was secondary and needed only to get the task done. When teacher control became the focus, more and more time was taken to assert that control and to counter children resisting it. Often, simply proceeding with the activity

would reinforce teacher control more effectively than forcing total compliance before proceeding. Usually, the teachers realized this and would avoid
diverting too much time to uncooperative children, first continuing the
activity to see if a child would refocus. If the child did not refocus, one
teacher or aide would take that child aside or sit him or her out. The center
was quite successful at maintaining discipline and order without using sanctions like time-out or removal from the classroom very often; those events
stood out when they happened. Such an approach provided for an enviable
combination of love and support along with control and order.

REFRAIN FROM STIFLING
CONFLICTS OR ENDING THEM ABRUPTLY

Four- and five-year-old children were able to manage a wide variety of
conflicts on their own, without adult interference. They learned the effectiveness of varied conflict styles along the way. Adults may effectively refrain
from interfering in child conflicts unless a major disruption or violation of the
rules (such as violence) seems imminent. Children then have more flexibility and creativity in managing their own conflicts and relationships. Adults
may need to promote discussion and sharing, however, overcoming a natural competitive style adopted by many children.

Children would reflect and be affected by the adult attitudes toward communication and conflict at the child-development center. If adults regularly
and outwardly confronted conflict through discussion, children more likely
would, too. If adults kept conflict hidden, children felt the pressure to do so
as well, but conflicts then emerged between them in more violent or sudden
ways. At times, the pressure to avoid expressing anger or disagreement in
front of children may shut down communication and make the climate more
defensive. The difficulty at a child-care center is accepting that there will be
some conflict among staff members, and having in place an open attitude
toward communicating about conflict and dealing with it. Hiding it, I found,
did not work, as unspoken feelings could build up into uncomfortable
silences and closed communication. Every center (as every organization)
must seek a balance between open communication that can handle conflict
and keeping communication friendly and civil.

Children were expected to handle their own problems unless a conflict
clearly endangered other children or the overall peace of the classroom or
playground. Then adults would intervene by saying, "Both of you move
away"; taking a disputed toy away; or, in very serious incidents, having both
children sit in time-out. The natural inclination of teachers and staff is to find
a way to stop a conflict as soon as possible, but that act prevents the children
from learning to manage conflict; it then becomes something to be avoided
or disguised. Allowing children to manage their conflicts allowed them to

practice key communication skills, since accounting for, adjusting to, and being kind to another person have been found to be crucial for developing effective peer relationships as well as popularity (Burleson 1994; Foot, Chapman, and Smith 1995; Sypher and Applegate 1984). Telling a teacher was recommended if a child was being hit or hurt but telling a teacher too often made a child a tattletale, something no one approved of, not even the teachers. Still, if talking to the other child would not work, then telling the teachers was recommended over violence or screaming. While competitive conflict styles were most common among the children, growing sophistication in communication strategies would lead children to try accommodation, compromise, or problem solving. A child's frequent use of violence would lead to a lack of trust on the part of peers, and even adults, in the classroom. Developing friendships thus became much harder for such children.

One mitigator of conflict was humor, which helped staff members get along even in stressful situations. While for adults humor served as a social facilitator, for children such was not always the case. Children more likely invoked the crucial distinction between laughing "with" others and laughing "at" others (Meyer 2000). Laughing together was an indicator that a relationship was "safe" and growing closer (Graham 1995; Socha and Kelly 1994). Being laughed "at" was a declaration of a social division and viewed by children as a verbal attack. I noticed that laughter from peers was viewed as hurtful much more often than was laughter from an adult. Being able to laugh together was a key indicator of a positive communication climate, among both children and adults.

SEEK TO ESTABLISH A STRONG CHILD-CARE CULTURE

The adult attitudes toward communication and the environment created for children's communication activities led, in this observed case, to a strong and nurturing child-development center culture. Communication was viewed as positive and necessary, and children were encouraged to try a variety of message strategies, even in conflicts. Staff members were fairly open in their communication with one another, and friendly and supportive. Some conflicts were suppressed, which continued the perceived calm and supportive climate but let the conflicts needlessly get worse before they were, in the end, discussed and managed in spite of hurt feelings. A real strength for the center was consistency in rules and discipline, providing a stable background of communication routines the children could rely on. Staff members conferred in regular meetings, but did so more often in informal chats about rules, expectations, child behavior, and adult responses. Also pivotal was a willingness to experiment, be creative, and have fun with communication. Staff members and children would laugh with one another almost daily; the times when this was not the case were more authoritarian or conflict ridden, leading to more defensiveness and uncertainty in everyone's communication. Most of the time, communication was a key source of the learning and fun at the center, making it a rich "communication laboratory" for growing children, teachers, and interested researchers alike. I hope the knowledge and experiences preserved in these pages add some enrichment and understanding to all those whose lives include relating to children.

References

Allen, R. R., and K. L. Brown. 1976. *Developing communication competence in children.* Skokie, Ill.: National Textbook Company.

Anderson, B. 1989. Effects of public day care: A longitudinal study. *Child Development* 60:857–66.

Anderson, E. S. 1986. The acquisition of register variation by Anglo-American children. In *Language socialization across cultures,* ed. B. B. Schieffelin and E. Ochs, 153–61. New York: Cambridge University Press.

Baxter, L. A. 1988. A dialectical perspective on communication strategies in relationship development. In *Handbook of personal relationships,* ed. S. Duck. New York: Wiley.

Berger, C. R., and J. J. Bradac. 1982. *Language and social knowledge: Uncertainty in interpersonal relations.* London: Arnold.

Bigelow, B. J., G. Tesson, and J. H. Lewko. 1996. *Learning the rules: The anatomy of children's relationships.* New York: Guilford.

Black, J. B., and H. Bern. 1981. Causal coherence and memory for events in narratives. *Journal of Verbal Learning and Verbal Behavior* 20:267–75.

Bochner, A. P., and C. Ellis. 1992. Personal narrative as a social approach to interpersonal communication. *Communication Theory* 2:165–72.

Bradbard, M., R. Endsley, and J. Mize. 1992. The ecology of parent-child communications about daily experiences in preschool and day care. *Journal of Research in Childhood Education* 6(2):13–23.

Browning, L. D. 1992. Lists and stories as organizational communication. *Communication Theory* 2:281–302.

Buber, M. 1958. *I and thou.* 2nd ed. New York: Charles Scribner's Sons.

Burleson, B. R. 1982. The development of comforting communication skills in childhood and adolescence. *Child Development* 53:1578–88.

——— 1994. Comforting messages: Significance, approaches, and effects. In *Communication of social support: Messages, interactions, relationships, and community,* ed. B. R. Burleson, T. L. Albrecht, and I. G. Sarason, 3–28. Thousand Oaks, Calif.: Sage.

Burleson, B. R., and P. A. Waltman. 1987. Popular, rejected, and supportive preadolescents: Social cognitive and communicative characteristics. In *Communication Yearbook* 10, ed. M. L. McLaughlin, 533–52. Newbury Park, Calif.: Sage.

Cahn, D. D. 1987. *Letting go: A practical theory of relationship disengagement and reengagement.* Albany: State University of New York Press.

Carlson, H. L., and M. Larson. 1991. Helping children resolve conflict peacefully: A professional development model. *Early Child Development and Care* 68:159–70.

Carr, J. B. 1988. *Crisis in intimacy: When expectations don't meet reality.* Pacific Grove, Calif.: Brooks/Cole/Wadsworth.

Caruso, D. 1989. Quality of day care and home reared infants' interaction patterns with mothers and day care providers. *Child and Youth Care Quarterly* 18:177–91.

Cazden, C. B. 1972. *Child language and education.* New York: Holt, Rinehart & Winston.

Ceglowski, D. 2000. Research as relationship. *Qualitative Inquiry* 6:88–103.

Cheney, G. 1991. *Rhetoric in an organizational society: Managing multiple identities.* Columbia: University of South Carolina.

Cicourel, A. V. 1974. *Cognitive sociology: Language and meaning in social interaction.* New York: Free Press.

Clarke, S., and K. Alison. 1986. Family day care: A home away from home? *Children's Environment Quarterly* 3:34–46.

Conville, R. L. 1991. *Relational transitions: The evolution of personal relationships.* New York: Praeger.

——— 1997. Between spearheads: *Bricolage* and relationships. *Journal of Social and Personal Relationships* 14(3):373–86.

Corsaro, W. A. 1985. *Friendship and peer culture in the early years.* Norwood, N.J.: Ablex.

Crawford, L. 1996. Personal ethnography. *Communication Monographs* 63:158–70.

Cupach, W. R., and S. Metts. 1994. *Facework.* Thousand Oaks, Calif.: Sage.

Delia, J. G., S. L. Kline, and B. R. Burleson. 1979. The development of persuasive communication strategies in kindergarteners through twelfth-graders. *Communication Monographs* 46:241–56.

Delia, J. G., and B. J. O'Keefe. 1979. Constructivism: The development of communication in children. In *Children communicating: Media and the development of thought, speech, understanding,* ed. E. Wartella, 157–85. Beverly Hills, Calif.: Sage.

Denham, S. A. 1998. *Emotional development in young children.* New York: Guilford.

Denzin, N. K. 1977. *Childhood socialization.* San Francisco: Jossey-Bass.

Ervin-Tripp, S., and C. Mitchell-Kernan. 1977. *Child discourse.* New York: Academic Press.

Fine, G. A. 1987. *With the boys: Little league baseball and preadolescent culture.* Chicago: University of Chicago Press.

Fine, G. A., and K. L. Sandstrom. 1988. *Knowing children: Participant observation with minors.* Newbury Park, Calif.: Sage.

Fisher, W. R. 1987. *Human communication as narration: Toward a philosophy of reason, value, and action.* Columbia: University of South Carolina Press.

Foot, H. C., A. J. Chapman, and J. R. Smith. 1995. *Friendship and social relations in children.* New Brunswick, N.J.: Transaction.

Giddens, A. 1979. *Central problems in social theory.* Cambridge: Cambridge University Press.

Goodall, H. L. 1990. A theater of motives and the "meaningful orders of persons and things." In *Communication Yearbook* 13, ed. J. A. Anderson, 69–94. Newbury Park, Calif.: Sage.

Goodall, H. L. 1994. *Casing a promised land: The autobiography of an organizational detective as cultural ethnographer,* expanded ed. Carbondale: Southern Illinois University Press.

Goodwin, M. H. 1990. *He-said-she-said: Talk as social organization among black children.* Bloomington: Indiana University Press.

Graham, E. E. 1995. The involvement of sense of humor in the development of social relationships. *Communication Reports* 8:158–70.

Graue, M. E., and D. J. Walsh. 1998. *Studying children in context: Theories, methods, and ethics.* Thousand Oaks, Calif.: Sage.

Greig, A., and J. Taylor. 1999. *Doing research with children.* London: Sage.

Hall, E. T. 1959. *The silent language.* Garden City, N.Y.: Doubleday.

Hartup, W. W. 1989. Social relationships and their developmental significance. *American Psychologist* 44:120–26.

Haskins, R. 1985. Aggression among children with varying day care experience. *Child Development* 56:689–703.

Haslett, B. B., and W. Samter. 1997. *Children communicating: The first five years.* Mahwah, N.J.: Erlbaum.

Hazen, N. L., and B. Black. 1989. Preschool peer communication skills: The role of social status and interaction context. *Child Development* 60:867–76.

Heath, S. B. 1983. *Ways with words: Language, life, and work in communities and classrooms.* Cambridge: Cambridge University Press.

Heslin, R., and M. Patterson. 1982. *Nonverbal behavior and social psychology.* New York: Plenum.

Holmes, R. M. 1998. *Fieldwork with children.* Thousand Oaks, Calif.: Sage.

Howes, C. 1987. Social competency with peers: Contributions from child care. *Early Childhood Research Quarterly* 2:155–67.

Howes, C., C. E. Hamilton, and C. C. Matheson. 1994. Children's relationships with peers: Differential associations with aspects of the teacher-child relationship. *Child Development* 65:253–63.

Katriel, T. 1991. *Communal webs: Communication and culture in contemporary Israel.* Albany: State University of New York Press.

Keyton, J. 1994. Going forward in group communication research may mean going back: Studying the groups of children. *Communication Studies* 45:40–51.

Knapp, M. L., and A. L. Vangelisti. 1992. *Interpersonal communication and human relationships.* 2nd ed. Boston: Allyn and Bacon.

Kuehne, V. 1988. Younger friends/older friends: A study of intergenerational interactions. *Journal of Classroom Interaction* 24:14–21.

Lamb, M., C. Hwang, A. Broger, and F. Booksten. 1988. The effects of out-of-home care in the development of social competence in Sweden: A longitudinal study. *Early Childhood Research Quarterly* 3:379–402.

Leavitt, R., and M. Power. 1989. Emotional socialization in the postmodern era: Children in day care. *Social Psychology Quarterly* 52:35–43.

Lincoln, Y. S., and E. G. Guba. 1985. *Naturalistic inquiry.* Beverly Hills, Calif.: Sage.

Mannarino, A. P. 1995. The development of children's friendships. In *Friendship and social relations in children,* ed. H. C. Foot, A. J. Chapman, and J. R. Smith, 45–63. New Brunswick, N.J.: Transaction.

McLaughlin, S. 1998. *Introduction to language development.* San Diego: Singular.

Mead, G. H. 1934. *Mind, self, and society.* Chicago: University of Chicago Press.

Meyer, J. 2000. Humor as a double-edged sword: Four functions of humor in communication. *Communication Theory* 10:310–31.

Meyer, J., and G. Driskill. 1997. Children and relationship development: Communication strategies in a day care center. *Communication Reports* 10:75–85.

Miles, M. B., and A. M. Huberman. 1984. *Qualitative data analysis: A sourcebook of new methods.* Beverly Hills, Calif.: Sage.

Mumby, D. K. 1993. *Narrative and social control: Critical perspectives.* Newbury Park, Calif.: Sage.

Nervius, N. 1989. Relations between young Mexican American children and play paradigms. *Journal of Genetic Psychology* 150:441–43.

Ochs, E., and B. B. Schieffelin. 1983. *Acquiring conversational competence.* London: Routledge and Kegan Paul.

Pacanowsky, M. E., and N. O'Donnell-Trujillo. 1982. Communication and organizational cultures. *Western Journal of Speech Communication* 46:115–30.

———— 1983. Organizational communication as cultural performance. *Communication Monographs* 50:126–47.

Palmerus, K., and S. Hagglund. 1991. The impact of children/caregiver relations on activities and social interaction in six day care centre groups. *Early Child Development and Care* 67:29–38.

Parker, J. 1986. Becoming friends: Conversational skills for friendship formation in young children. In *Conversations of friends: Speculations on affective development: Studies in emotion and social interaction,* ed. J. M. Gottman and J. G. Parker, 103–38. Cambridge: Cambridge University Press.

Parker, J. G., and S. R. Asher. 1993. Friendship and friendship quality in middle childhood: Links with peer group acceptance and feelings of loneliness and social dissatisfaction. *Developmental Psychology* 29:611–21.

Philippot, P., R. S. Feldman, and G. McGee. 1992. Nonverbal behavioral skills in an educational context: Typical and atypical populations. In *Applications of nonverbal behavioral theories and research,* ed. Feldman, 191–213. Hillsdale, N.J.: Erlbaum.

Piaget, J. 1971. *The language and thought of the child.* New York: World.

Pilotta, J. J., Widman, T., and Jasko, S. A. 1988. Meaning and action in the organizational setting: An interpretive approach. In *Communication yearbook* 11, ed. J. Anderson, 310–34. Newbury Park, Calif.: Sage.

Rawlins, W. K. 1992. *Friendship matters: Communication dialectics and the life course.* New York: Aldine de Gruyter.

Rubin, K. H., and H. S. Ross. 1982. *Peer relationships and social skills in childhood.* New York: Springer-Verlag.

Saarni, C., and H. Weber. 1999. Emotional displays and dissemblance in childhood: Implications for self-presentation. In *The social context of nonverbal behavior,* ed.

P. Philippot, R. S. Feldman, and E. J. Coats, 71–105. New York: Cambridge University Press.

Schein, E. H. 1985. *Organizational culture and leadership.* San Francisco: Jossey-Bass.

Schwartzman, H. B. 1993. *Ethnography in organizations.* Newbury Park, Calif.: Sage.

Selman, R. L. 1980. *The growth of interpersonal understanding: Developmental and clinical analyses.* New York: Academic Press.

Smircich, L. 1983. Concepts of culture and organizational analysis. *Administrative Science Quarterly* 28:339–58.

Socha, T. J., and B. Kelly. 1994. Children making "fun": Humorous communication, impression management, and moral development. *Child Study Journal* 24:237–53.

Solomon, J., and C. George. 1999. *Attachment disorganization.* New York: Guilford.

Stafford, L., and C. L. Bayer. 1993. *Interaction between parents and children.* Newbury Park, Calif.: Sage.

Sypher, H. E., and J. L. Applegate. 1984. *Communication by children and adults: Social cognitive and strategic processes.* Beverly Hills, Calif.: Sage.

Sypher, H. E., and B. D. Sypher. 1988. Affect and message generation. In *Communication, social cognition, and affect,* ed. L. Donohew, H. E. Sypher, and E. T. Higgins. Hillsdale, N.J.: Erlbaum.

Van-Crombrugge, H., and L. Vandemeulebroecke. 1991. Family and center day care under three: The child's experience. *Community Alternatives International Journal of Family Care,* 3(2):35–58.

Vanlear, A. 1991. Testing a cyclical model of communicative openness in relationship development: Two longitudinal studies. *Communication Monographs* 58:337–61.

Vargas, M. F. 1986. *Louder than words: An introduction to nonverbal communication.* Ames: Iowa State University Press.

Wanzer, M. B., M. Booth-Butterfield, and S. Booth-Butterfield. 1996. Are funny people popular? An examination of humor orientation, loneliness, and social attraction. *Communication Quarterly* 44:42–52.

Werner, O., and G. M. Schoepfle. 1987. *Systematic fieldwork: Ethnographic analysis and data management.* Newbury Park, Calif.: Sage.

Wilmot, W. W., and J. L. Hocker. 1998. *Interpersonal conflict.* 5th ed. Boston: McGraw-Hill.

Wood, B. S. 1976. *Children and communication: Verbal and nonverbal language development.* Englewood Cliffs, N.J.: Prentice-Hall.

Zigler, E. F., and E. Gilman. 1996. Not just any care: Shaping a coherent child care policy. In *Children, families, and government: Preparing for the twenty-first century,* ed. E. F. Zigler, S. L. Kagan, and N. W. Hall, 94–116. New York: Cambridge University Press.

Index

accommodating/yielding conflict style, 185–86

adults: attempts to enforce rules on, 72–73; children arguing with, 107–8; children's interpretation of laughter from, 141–43; children's trust of, 26–27, 65, 100; comfort by, 45, 127; communicating support to children, 231–32; competition for attention from, 231; consistency on discipline, 88–89; indications of need for attention from, 117; intervention in friendship, 45–47; intervention of, 113; jealousy of time spent with, 120–21, 171, 182; mimicking of, 146, 148; modeling of problem-solving behavior from, 189; need to alter communication style, 225–26; relationship ambivalence with, 121–23; rule reinforcement from, 69–70, 73; simple acts from, 119–20; uncertainty as to how to interact with children, 225; use of humor by, 141, 236; view of touching, 229. *See also* conflict, among adults; uncertain relationships

affection, 163–74; altered affection norms, 173–74; balanced responses to, 172–73; from children who haven't seen for a while, 222–23; conflict concerning, 201–12; direct statements of, 166–67, 173–74, 220–21; getting through play, 167–70; importance of in child-care centers, 223–24; overview, 163–64; strong displays of, 217–18; sudden affection, 164–67. *See also* feelings; physical contact

"affectionate greetings" phase of relationship, 234

alienation phase of relationship, 6

Allen, R. R.,, 9

alliances, changing, 30–31

anger: between children, 87; countering, 213–16; toward adults, 121–23, 130, 136–37; violent tantrums, 135–36, 180, 235. *See also* fighting

anxiety: seeking adult attention because of, 118; separation anxiety, 126–28

apologizing, examples of, 74, 106, 193, 215

approach/avoidance pattern, 118

arguing with adults, 107–8

assistant teachers, 239

attention-seeking behaviors, 63–64, 125–26, 160, 180–81

authority, of researcher (author), 18
avoiding conflicts, 187–88, 201

back rides, 25–27; conflict over, 205–7;
    withholding for bad behavior, 81–82
back rubs, 22, 104
bad behavior, 63–64; disobedience,
    134–35, 138; screaming, 235. *See also*
    discipline; fighting
ball games, 87, 100, 109
Berger, C. R., 4
Bigelow, B. J.,, 13
biting. *See* fighting
bombing (Oklahoma City), 219–20
bossiness: effect of familiarity on, 96–97.
    See also control
boyfriend-girlfriend-like relationships.
    See romantic relationships
boys, interaction initiation from, 8
Bradac, J. J., 4
brothers, interaction between, 92
Brown, K. L., 9–10

carrying and holding. *See* picking up
    children
Ceglowski, D., 18
chase games, 21–23, 30–31, 123, 172
checking relationships, 38, 53–54
child-care centers: description of one
    chosen for research, 15–16; versus
    home care, 10; number of students
    per classroom, 12; organizational
    culture, 11–12; reason for choosing
    for research, 1
Christmas time, 218–19
classroom, number of students per, 12
classroom patterns, 20–21
classroom rules: and discipline, 83–84;
    invoking for own benefit, 95;
    reinforced by children, 112–13
cliques. *See* alliances
closeness, friendship through, 58–62
clowning, 145–46. *See also* humor use
comforting children, 45, 127
commands: from children to other
    children, 32; from children to
    teachers, 96–97; in classrooms, 20–21

commonality, as reason for friendship,
    54, 92–93
communication: adult versus child
    communication methods, 2; child-
    care communication guidelines, 227;
    deficiency in communication skills,
    231; development of communication
    skills, 6–9; effect of adults view of,
    236; effect of discipline on, 236;
    effect of family on, 9; effect of
    feelings on, 7; gender differences in
    initiating interaction, 8; initiation of,
    113; listening, 137–41, 238; need for
    adults to alter style of, 225–26;
    nonverbal indicators of friendship,
    229. *See also* repeated interaction
    patterns; role-playing
competition: for adult attention, 231;
    instigated by children, 108–9
competitive conflicts, 176–85; example
    of territorial violation, 176–77; in
    games, 152, 157, 182–83; journal
    entry about, 184–85; over perceived
    scarce resources, 179–90; over
    possession of toys, 178; overview,
    176; posing negative consequence
    for, 190–91; short duration of,
    177–78, 178–79; stemming from
    desire for attention/friendship,
    180–81
compliance-gaining tool, friendship as,
    54–55
compromise conflict style, 188–94
conflict, 175–94; accommodating/
    yielding conflict style, 185–86;
    avoiding style, 187–88; compromise
    or problem-solving conflict style,
    188–94; overview, 175–76; refraining
    from stifling or ending abruptly,
    242–43. *See also* competition
conflict, among adults, 195–212;
    avoiding conflicts, 201; confrontation
    and shock, 205–12; example of,
    199–200; holding as an initial point
    of conflict, 198–200; overview,
    195
contact. *See* physical contact

control, 89–115; by adults, balancing, 239–42; children's control strategies, 90–97; in classrooms, 20–21; deciding appropriate level of, 87–88, 111–15; experimentation with different methods of, 230–31; failed control strategies, 98–100; within friendship, testing, 32–37; in games, 90–91; hierarchical power differences, 106–7, 108–9, 111–12, 236; issues between adults, 111; of lead teacher vs. other teachers, 102–3; maintaining, 100–105; overcoming power differences, 123–25; over-exercise of, 105; overview, 89–90; power differences, 106–11; of self, 97; and social rules, 72–75; through alliances, 56–58; uncertain power difference, 118–21. *See also* discipline; friendship, as commodity; hierarchies of relationships

Conville, Richard, 5

Conville's helical model of relationships, 48

creativity of children, 239–42

crying, 19, 134, 137, 235

cultural education, rule disruption as, 75–76

culture of child-care centers, 11–12

day-care centers. *See* child-care centers

Denzin, N. K., 14

discipline, 77–88, 134–35; adult consistency on, 88–89; balance in, 79; effect on communication, 236; explaining reasons for, 101–2; in loving manner, 83; and older children, 85–87; overview, 77–78; professed apathy toward, 73; and shared classroom rules, 83–84; testing, 84–85; time-out, 78–80; for violent behavior, 241; from volunteer, 81–82; by walking away/refusing to play, 81–82

disintegration phase of relationship, 5–6

dislike, expressions of, 84

disobedience, 134–35, 138

disrespect, 107, 114

distancing: as phase in relationship development, 232–33; of self from children, 127, 216

distractions, as means of avoiding conflict, 187

duration of relationships, 29–30

emotional impact of working with children, 213–24; atmosphere of emotional whirlpool, 216–18; countering negativity, 213–16; emotional closings, 223–24; emotional markers, 218–23; overview, 213

emotions; experienced by adults interacting with children, 234–35. *See also* feelings

equality, conflict over, 206–8

ethnic diversity of child-care center, 16

expressing feelings. *See* feelings

expressions of dislike, 84

expressiveness in relationships, 48

familiarity, effect on politeness and bossiness, 96–97

family; children's concerns about, 122–23; role in child development, 9. *See also* separation anxiety

feelings, 133–49, 235; acknowledging, 128; children's freeness of expression, 226–27; effect on communication, 7; importance of listening, 137–41; managing feeling expression, 134–37; overview, 133; stress on using words, 235. *See also* affection; humor use; negativity, countering

field trips, maintaining order during, 102–3

fighting: discipline for, 83, 183; episodes of, 30–31, 32, 33, 36, 43–44, 46, 63–64, 81; instigated by media, 183; over ball games, 87; short duration of, 178–79

films, viewing in school, 87

Fine, G. A., 14
friendship: adult intervention in, 45–47; among opposites, 32; as commodity, 38–40, 52–53, 95–96, 228–30; commonality as reason for, 54, 92–93; competitive conflicts as result of trying to develop, 180–81; as a compliance-gaining tool, 54–55; long-term, 31–32; nonverbal indicators of, 229; as ongoing relationship, 53–54; as power through alliances, 56–58; rejecting based on conduct of other party, 79; testing control within, 32–37; through closeness, 58–62; through proximity, 58–62; verbal confirmation of, 59–60; weakening of, 33–34. *See also* initiating and strengthening relationships; relationships; uncertain relationships
future, planning of, 41–42

games, 21–23; ball games, 87, 100, 109; chase games, 123, 172; competitive conflicts in, 182–83; control in, 90–91; desire to enact real activities instead of, 168–69; getting affection through, 167–70; participation by older and younger children, 92; playing house, 167–68. *See also* role-playing
gender differences, in initiating interaction, 8
gifts, 169
gingerbread cookie game, 23–25
girlfriend-boyfriend-like relationships. *See* romantic relationships
girls, interaction initiation from, 8
giving, 6
Graue, M. E., 12–13
greetings, 30, 234; adult initiative in, 119; pattern of, 21, 22–23
Greig, A., 13
grudges, 36–37

health, and physical contact, 62
Heath, S. B., 16

helical model of relationships, 48
hide-and-go-seek, 24–25
hierarchies of relationships: among children, 31–32, 40, 56, 239–40; among children and teachers, 236–37; among teachers, 239
hitting. *See* fighting
holding and carrying. *See* picking up children
holiday time, 218–19
hollering, 134
hugging, 66, 165–66
humor use, 5, 141–49, 243; from adults, 147–48; children's interpretation of laughter from adults versus peers, 141–43; clowning, 145–46; effect of adult use of humor, 236; effect on relationships, 149; jokes, 143–44; mimicking adults, 146, 148; playing tricks, 146

ignoring others, 139, 140, 238
initiating and strengthening relationships, 151–61; ambivalent role-taking, 158–61; choosing roles, 157–58; overview, 151–52; role-taking failures, 154–57; seriousness of role-playing games, 160; taking and assigning roles, 152–54
interaction initiation, 8
interaction patterns, repeated. *See* repeated interaction patterns
intervention of adults, 113
intimacy, 6

jealousy in relationships: attention-seeking behaviors, 126–28; between children, 37–42, 97; between children and adults, 120–21, 171, 182. *See also* separation anxiety
jokes, 143–44. *See also* humor use

Katriel, T., 14
kicking. *See* fighting
kissing, 166
Knapp, M. L., 4

language, how children learn, 14
lap sitting. *See* sitting on lap
laughing. *See* humor use
lead teachers, 239, 240
Leavitt, R.,, 12
Lewko, J. H., 13
listening, 137–41, 238
long-term friendships, 31–32
love. *See* affection
love-hate relationships, 37, 122, 231

male figures, boys' relationships with, 49
marriage, children talking about, 41–42, 153–54
media, influence on children, 183
mimicking adults, 146, 148
mothers, effect on child's conduct, 117
movies, viewing in school, 87

naptime, 104
nap time, 202–3
narratives, benefits of, 13–14
negative speech, avoiding, 77–78, 84
negativity, countering, 213–16
noise, 86
noninclusion, 84
nonverbal indicators of friendship, 229

Oklahoma City bombing, 219–20
older children: and discipline, 85–87; interaction with younger children, 92
ongoing relationships, 53–54
opposites, friendship among, 32
order, maintaining, 20–21, 100–105
organizational culture of child-care centers, 11–12

parents, role in child development, 9–10
passivity, 75–76
patterns. *See* repeated interaction patterns
personal space, 58
PG-rated movies, 87
phases of relationships, 232–34
physical contact, 49–50, 62–66; adult view of, 229; back rubs, 22, 104;

balance in, 229–30; children's needs for, 163; and health, 62; hugging, 66; picking up children, 27, 65, 171–73; as relationship commodity, 228–30; "touching" phase of relationship, 234. *See also* affection; back rides; feelings; fighting; sitting on lap
Piaget, J., 13
picking up children, 27, 65, 171–73
piggyback rides, 25–27
play: age when begins, 11; getting affection through, 167–70. *See also* games; role-playing
politeness, 96–97, 240
popularity, 8, 11
positive discipline, 77–78, 84
possessiveness in relationships. *See* jealousy in relationships
power. *See* control
Power, M., 12
"Power Ranger" play, 183
pretending. *See* games; role-playing
problem-solving conflict style, 188–94
protection, of children by other children, 30
proximity: friendship through, 58–62; as relationship commodity, 229–30
punishment for bad behavior. *See* discipline

quiet children, 9, 136, 235
quiet time, 85–86

reading to children, 124–25
reciprocity, 53
recording events/thoughts, 16
recurring routines. *See* repeated interaction patterns
rejection, conflict over, 206–8
Relational Transitions, 5
relationships, 29–50; adjusting to variable phases of, 232–34; adult intervention in, 45–47; with adults, 47–50; categories of strategies for, 227; changing alliances, 30–31; checking, 38, 53–54; Conville's helical model of, 48; duration of,

29–30; effect of laughter on, 149; friendship as commodity, 38–40; growing, 47–50; hierarchies of, 31, 40, 56; importance of listening, 137–41; key interactional tensions to manage in, 4–5; lack of flexibility in, 230–31; long-term friendships, 31–32; love-hate relationships, 37, 122, 231; management strategies, 12; motivation to establish and stay in, 4; ongoing, 53–54; overview, 29–30; phases of, 5–6, 232–34; romantic, 40–45, 86, 105, 153–54, 230; spatial symbolism of, 58–62; with teachers, 30; testing control within friendship, 32–37; trying out romantic relationships, 40–45. *See also* fighting; friendship; initiating and strengthening relationships; jealousy in relationships; uncertain relationships

repeated interaction patterns, 2, 19–28, 237–39; back rubs, 22, 104; chase games, 21–23, 30–31, 123, 160, 172; classroom patterns, 20–21; getting close through, 27–28; individual repeated patterns, 21–23; molding and enacting consistent rituals, 236–37; overview, 19–20. *See also* back rides; games; greetings

research methods, 14–17

response to adults, 107

resynthesis phase of relationship, 6

rituals. *See* repeated interaction patterns

role of researcher (author), 17–18

role-playing: ambivalent, 158–61; choosing, 157–58; failures in, 154–57; importance of, 230–31; seriousness of, 160; taking and assigning roles, 152–54; teaching children via, 189

romantic relationships, 40–45, 86, 105, 153–54, 230

routines. *See* repeated interaction patterns

rules. *See* social rules

"safety" phase of relationship, 233

school. *See* classroom patterns; teachers

screaming, 235

security phase of relationship, 5

self-control, 97

self-image, 2, 106

separation anxiety, 126–28

shared meanings, 11

sharing, 107–8, 107–8, 218–19

show-and-tell, 94–95

siblings, interaction between, 92

similarities, as reason for friendship, 54, 92–93

sitting on lap: competition over, 124–25; disagreements about, 198–99, 201–2, 203, 207–8; early in relationship, 164–65

sitting together, 59–60

social reality, 2

social rules, 67–76; and absence of teacher, 69; attempts to enforce on adults, 72–73; overview, 67–68; and power structure, 72–75; rule disruption as cultural education, 75–76; rule reinforcement from adults, 69–70, 73; simple, 68–70; use of to manage relationships, 70–71.

social structure: development of, 31–32, 40; how children learn about, 14

space, personal, 58

spatial symbolism of relationships. *See* proximity

"special love" phase of relationship, 234

spitting, 180–81

stability, 237

staff members. *See* teachers

status symbols, 54

story-telling, 139

symbol use, 1–2, 6

tantrums, 135–36, 180, 235

Taylor, J., 13

teacher aides, 196

teachers: assistant teachers, 239; authority of, 74, 102–3; children imitating, 90–91; children's view of relationships with, 30; and classroom

patterns, 20–21; following rules during absence of, 69; hierarchy of power, 239; lead teachers, 239, 240; mimicking of, 148
television, influence on children, 183
telling on others, 138, 243
temper tantrums, 135–36, 180, 235
territorial violation, 176–77
territory, personal, 58
terrorist bombing (Oklahoma City), 219–20
Tesson, G., 13
testing discipline, 84–85
threats, 34
time, spending with children, 62
time-out, 78–80, 241
timidness, 119
touching. *See* physical contact
"touching" phase of relationship, 234
toys from home, 94–95
trading, for conflict resolution, 191
transitions, adjusting to, 216–17
tricks, 146
trust, between children, 30, 32, 37, 100, 159
trust of adults: approach/avoidance pattern, 117–18; and back rides, 26–27; in games, 100; and laughter, 141–43, 149; from older versus younger children, 106; and politeness, 65
typecasting children, 181

uncertain relationships: and attention-seeking behaviors, 125–26; becoming a key adult, 128–31; overcoming power differences, 123–25; overview, 117–18; relationship ambivalence with adults, 121–23; uncertain power difference, 118–21; uncertainty and separation anxiety, 126–28

values, molding and enacting consistent, 236–37
Vangelisti, A. L., 4
verbal confirmation of friendship, 59–60
videos, viewing in school, 87
violence. *See* fighting
violent tantrums, 135–36, 180, 235

Walsh, D. J., 12–13
"welcome" phase of relationship, 233
withdrawal of friendship, 54–55
withdrawn children, 9, 136, 235

yelling, 235
younger children, interaction with older children, 92

About the Author

John Meyer is a professor of speech communication at the University of Southern Mississippi. He has worked with children for over fourteen years and published in several major communication journals, including *Communication Theory, Communication Studies, Communication Research*, and the *Southern Communication Journal*. Along with children's communication, Dr. Meyer's research interests include organizational communication and humor use in communication. He has taught a wide variety of communication courses, including communication and conflict, small-group communication, and business and professional speaking. He lives in Hattiesburg, Mississippi, with Louise, his wife of twelve years, and his son Matthew, age seven.